Breakthrough to Peace

"The splitting of the atom has changed everything save our modes of thinking, and thus we drift toward unparalleled catastrophe."

—ALBERT EINSTEIN

Breakthrough to Peace

Introduction by Thomas Merton

A New Directions Paperbook

Library of Congress Catalog Card Number: 62-17272

First published as ND Paperbook in 1962

ACKNOWLEDGMENTS

We wish to thank the publishers of the magazines and books listed below for kind permission to reprint material in this collection: *The Atlantic Monthly* for "The Morals of Extermination" by Lewis Mumford; *War/Peace Report* for "What Would It Really Be Like?" by Tom Stonier; *The Saturday Review* for "Shelters, Survival and Common Sense" by Norman Cousins; *Commentary* for "The Question of Civil Defense" by Erich Fromm & Michael Maccoby, Copyright 1962 by the American Jewish Committee; The Center for the Study of Democratic Institutions for "Man or Megaperson?" by Howard E. Gruber; *Psychiatry* for "Breaking the Thought Barrier" by Jerome D. Frank; Sheed & Ward, Inc. for "The Defense of the West" by Walter Stein from *Nuclear Weapons: A Catholic Response*, edited by Walter Stein, Copyright © 1961 by the Merlin Press, Ltd., and © Sheed & Ward, Inc., 1962; Harper & Row for "Human Nature and the Dominion of Fear" from *International Conflict in the Twentieth Century* by Herbert Butterfield, Copyright 1960 by Harper & Row, Publishers, Inc.; Channel Press for "Can War Be Cured?" from *That Difficult Peace*, by Joost A. M. Meerloo, Copyright 1961 by Joost A. M. Meerloo. "The Case for Christian Dissent" appears in different form in *German Catholics and Hitler's Wars*, published by Sheed & Ward, Inc. Excerpts from *On Thermonuclear War* by Herman Kahn are quoted by permission of the publishers, Princeton University Press, and from "Some Specific Suggestions for Achieving Early Non-Military Defense Capabilities and Initiating Long-Range Programs" (RM-2206-RC) by permission of The RAND Corporation.

Designed by Gilda Kuhlman

Manufactured in the United States of America.

New Directions Books are published by James Laughlin at Norfolk, Connecticut. New York Office: 333 Sixth Avenue (14).

Contents

Thomas Merton | Introduction

The nineteenth century can be called an age of peace and comfort, though if we reflect a little we will remember the war in Crimea, the Indian Mutiny, the Opium War in China, the Franco-Prussian War and the bloody and utterly savage war between the northern and southern United States. In spite of these conflicts our grandfathers believed that war was gradually getting to be a thing of the past. They did not know that these were all preludes to the gigantic struggle which has continued to rend and batter the world of the twentieth century. But now in 1962 we are beginning to realize that our age has been practically nothing but one big fire of war dying down only to flame up in greater fury, growing in its appetite for violent destruction, and gradually threatening the very survival of civilized man.

The First World War, we are told, was not fully intended by anyone; but political and military strategists moved one step too far and could not turn back. The war was confidently and savagely fought with the expectation that it would end all wars and make the world finally and imperturbably safe for the free and comfortable life.

The very treaty which attempted to restore order to Europe and to guarantee that there would be no further conflict made another and greater war inevitable. And yet during the twenties and thirties, there was a succession of peace conferences, a procession of peace movements, not to mention the non-violent revolution in India. Men studied, talked, agitated, prayed and suffered to bring about a permanent peace. Never had so much been said about peace, never had war been so thoroughly and universally execrated. Militarists remained, of course, but it cannot be denied that serious efforts at disarmament were made. So serious were these efforts that, when the Second World War broke out, the western nations, particularly America, were not ready. Before Pearl Harbor the majority of Americans strenuously and articulately opposed entrance into the war. France, meanwhile, relied with blind faith on the Maginot Line, a complex and expensive system which proved completely useless against deadly new weapons of attack. The allies cannot be said to have "wanted" war. But they wanted a political and economic situation that made war inevitable.

In the unexampled and criminal frightfulness of World War II, massive attacks on defenseless civilian centers came to be accepted as perfectly normal in spite of protests of the Pope and other spokesmen for traditional ethics. It was believed that systematic terrorism was essential to beat down all resistance of the "Fascist war criminals" and bring them to an unconditional surrender that would definitely end all war. Finally the atomic bomb was dropped on Hiroshima and Nagasaki—the climax of this ruthless policy.

Yet at the very moment when the bomb fell, the cold war between America and Russia was already on. The threat of this bomb, which ended the hot war with Japan, was to be the chief weapon of the cold war. Instead of producing peace, the atom bomb started the most fantastic arms race in history.

Nuclear deterrence has proved to be an illusion, for the bomb deters no one. It did not prevent war in Korea, Indochina, Laos, the Congo. It did not prevent the Russian suppression of the Hungarian revolt. And now those who once relied on deterrence, on the threat of massive retaliation, are insensibly moving toward a policy that assumes a *first strike capacity*. This policy is dictated by the very weapons themselves. The missile armed with a nuclear warhead is the perfect weapon of offense, so perfect that no defense against it has yet been devised. An H-bomb is the cheapest of all mass engines of destruction. It costs only two hundred and fifty thousand dollars to make, and one can go all the way up the megaton scale without prohibitively increasing either the expense or the engineering difficulty. It has been said that the H-bomb "gives more destructive power for the dollar" than any other weapon in existence. Knowing man's love for a good bargain, this atrocious estimate should certainly give us food for thought.

There has been relatively little agitation for peace since World War II. One feels that public opinion has been embittered and disillusioned by the futility of the peace movements after the First World War. This disillusionment is of course compounded by the fact that the biggest "peace movement" in the world today is simply part of the Soviet propaganda front, and is another powerful psychological weapon in the cold war, cynically exploiting the deepest desires of modern man and his most pathetic need in what is frankly a war effort, leading inevitably to hot war or to revolution. In this grim situation, with the U.N. too weak and unsubstantial to offer any hope of a higher authority to restrain the lawless and truculent aspirations of national powers, we seem to be drifting helplessly toward another disaster which will make all previous wars look like rumbles in a back alley. As long as each nation remains the sole judge of its own case, and decides for itself what is right and wrong without further appeal except to the power of the bomb, it would seem that war must be inevitable. The question that now seems to preoccupy leaders and policy-makers is not whether war can be avoided, but whether war can be kept within "safe" limits.

In this situation, where the issues are too enormous for the mind of the average man to grasp, when the threat is too appalling for his political habits and instincts to instruct him adequately, the tendency is to take refuge in fanaticism or in passive desperation.

Fanatics yield to the pressures of inner resentment and frustration, and seek a show-down because they cannot bear the intolerable burden of waiting and uncertainty. The passive and the despairing accept the absurdity of life with a shrug and seek forgetfulness in an automatic, drugged existence which renounces all effort and all hope. In both cases people become more and more resigned to their destruction and to the destruction of the civilized world. Indeed, one gets the feeling that they are almost eager to see the whole thing blow up, and get it over with.

This precisely is the great danger. This is what the open mind, the humanist and Christian mind, the mind which desires the survival of reason and of life, must now confront most decisively. No one of us can say for sure what the future will bring, but we are not responsible for what is beyond our control. We are responsible for the present and for those present actions and attitudes of ours from which future events will develop. It is therefore supremely important that we get a grip on ourselves and determine that we will not relinquish either our reason or our humanity; that we will not despair of ourselves, or of man, or of our capacity to solve our problems; that we will make use of the faculties and resources we still have in abundance, and use them for positive and constructive action in so far as we can. We will resist the fatal inclination to passivity and despair as well as the fatuous temptation to false optimism and insouciance which condition us equally well to accept disaster. In a word we will behave as men, and, if Christians, then as members of Christ.

Our problem is a moral and spiritual problem. It is a problem of enormous and frightful complexity. We have no alternative but to face it, in all its ramifications, and do what we can about it. This is the duty which history itself has imposed on us, which our forefathers, in their mixture of wisdom and folly, have bequeathed to us. It will not do us any good to wish we were other than we actually are, or that we were in some other century, some other planet. We cannot escape present reality. We cannot all offer ourselves to be frozen up and comfortably hibernate through the critical years that are to come, in order to wake up painlessly in a new world.

But if we are to face the problem as it is, we must first of all admit its true nature. If it is a *moral* problem, then it implies the appropriate response of reason and of freedom. It implies choice, based on knowledge. It implies willingness to study, to reason, to communicate. It implies the capacity to judge.

It implies not only that judgment which the individual makes in the secrecy of his conscience, but also political expression and action.

We must judge and decide not only as individuals, preserving for ourselves the luxury of a clean conscience, but also as members of society taking up a common burden and responsibility. It is all too easy to retire into the ivory tower of private spirituality and let the world blow itself to pieces. Such a decision would be immoral, an admission of defeat. It would imply a secret complicity with the overt destructive fury of fanatics.

Moral decisions have to be based on adequate knowledge. The scientist must tell us something reliable about the behavior of bombs and missiles. The political commentator must keep us in touch with the developments of strategy and with the plans that are being made for our defense or for our destruction. He must tell us what underlies the fair assurances we read in the mass media or hear in the speeches of the statesman and publicist. We must be informed of what goes on in the rest of the world, what is hoped and feared by our opposite numbers in the land of "the enemy." We must try to remember that the enemy is as human as we are, and not an animal or a devil.

Finally, we must be reminded of the way we ourselves tend to operate, the significance of the secret forces that rise up within us and dictate fatal decisions. We must learn to distinguish the free voice of conscience from the irrational compulsions of prejudice and hate. We must be reminded of objective moral standards, and of the wisdom which goes into every judgment, every choice, every political act that deserves to be called civilized. We cannot think this way unless we shake off our passive irresponsibility, renounce our fatalistic submission to economic and social forces, and give up the unquestioning belief in machines and processes which characterizes the mass mind. History is ours to make: now above all we must try to recover our freedom, our moral autonomy, our capacity to control the forces that make for life and death in our society.

It is necessary to discuss the fateful problems of our time, and independent minds have not hesitated to do so, even though the trend of the masses is toward an ever more submissive and inert acceptance of meaningless slogans. No such slogans will be found in this book. Nor do these writers offer easy solutions. Indeed, they do not pretend to an infallibility which can promise anything beyond the austerity of a task that may turn out to be fruitless. But they seek to offer sincere and unprejudiced judgments of our predicament and their analysis is not without very significant hopes, if only we can be faithful to the reason and wisdom which we have not yet irrevocably lost.

The fact remains that we may lose both, through our own fault, and forfeit our heritage of civilization and of humanity to enter a post-historic world of technological animals. There is no guarantee even now that reason can still prevail. But we must do what we can, relying on the grace of God for the rest.

The essays in this book attempt to break through thought barriers and open up rational perspectives. Hence each one of the writers assumes, in his own way, that the questions he raises are not already closed forever by prejudice or by the informal dictatorship of "thought control." If we assume that the basic questions have already been answered, our doom is sealed. On the contrary, if we recognize that we still have the obligation and, we hope, the time to re-examine certain fundamental assumptions, we may perhaps be able to open the way for developments in policy that will help future generations work out a fully constructive and peaceful solution.

The moral or political principles on which our most critical decisions are to be made may, in themselves, be relatively simple, but the assumptions on which they are based are immensely complicated. It is not difficult to appeal to traditional norms of justice and law, and apply them to our present situation in such a way as to come up with logical and plausible conclusions. But the very plausibility of the conclusions tends to be the most dangerous thing about them, if we forget that they may be based on premises which we take to be axiomatic and which, in fact, have been invalidated by recent developments of weapons technology. Indeed, the technological data on which we are basing our moral or political decision may be profoundly influenced by certain assumptions which have been fed into the computers in the first place. There is a very serious danger that our most crucial decisions may turn out to be no decisions at all, but only the end of a vicious circle of conjectures and gratuitous assumptions in which we unconsciously make the argument come out in favor of our own theory, our own favorite policy.

The written and spoken statements of nuclear "realists" seem to give grounds for very grave concern in this regard. It would be a disaster if ethical and political thought were to take too seriously the claims of men who dismiss the noxious effects of fallout as altogether negligible, and who minimize the destructive power of the bomb whenever they consider the possible destruction of our own cities. Yet on the basis of such conjectures as these, a moralist or a publicist, exercising a really decisive effect on a huge segment of public opinion, might issue a declaration in favor of nuclear war, and this judgment might itself be the deciding factor in swinging the whole policy of the United States in the direction of preemptive attack. Even more serious than this, is the fact that the moral, or amoral preconceptions of the military mind, and particularly the oversimplified assessment of a political threat, implemented by a dogmatic and fanatical political creed, will certainly have grave influence upon military decisions at a high level.

It is therefore vitally important to create a general climate of rationality, and to preserve a broad, tolerant, watchful and humanist outlook on the whole of life, precisely in order that rash and absurd assumptions may not have too free a circulation in our society.

That is what these essays attempt to do. All of them, in their own way, approach the problems related to nuclear war with a freely questioning mind, in search of facts and principles which tend to upset the crude assumptions already too widely accepted by the majority, particularly in America. Hence these essays all share a common note of urgency and protest, and by that very fact alone they manifest their intention to continue fighting in defense of genuine democracy, freedom of thought, and freedom of political action.

One of the most absurd and dangerous of all prejudices is the popular assumption that anyone who doubts that the bomb is the only ultimate solution, proves himself by that very fact to be subversive. For those who believe this, these essays will prove disturbing. The present writers prescribe austere remedies. They demand thought, patience, the willingness to face risks, in order to enter new and unexplored territory of the mind. They refuse to be satisfied with negativism and destruction, or with the despair that masks as heroism and prepares for the apocalyptic explosion in which all the humanized, social and spiritual values that we know will go up in radioactive smoke.

The perspectives in this book are, then, humanistic in the deepest and most spiritual sense of the word. They look beyond the interests of any restricted group toward the deepest and most critical needs of man himself. In so doing, they are, at least implicitly, faithful to the Judaeo-Christian tradition on which our civilization was built. There is no hope for us if we lose sight of these perspectives. There is no other human way out.

Lewis Mumford | The Morals of Extermination

Since 1945, the American government has devoted the better part of our national energies to preparations for wholesale human extermination. This curious enterprise has been disguised as a scientifically sound method of ensuring world peace and national security, but it has obviously failed at every point on both counts. Our reckless experimental explosion of nuclear weapons is only a persuasive salesman's sample of what a nuclear war would produce, but even this has already done significant damage to the human race. With poetic justice, the earliest victims of our experiments toward genocide—sharing honors with the South Pacific islanders and the Japanese fishermen—have been our own children, and even more, our children's prospective children.

Almost from the beginning, our investment in nuclear weapons has been openly directed against a single country, Soviet Russia. In our government's concern with the self-imposed problem of containing Russia and restricting by force alone the area of Communist penetration, we have turned our back on more vital human objectives. Today the political and military strategy our leaders framed on the supposition that our country had a permanent superiority in nuclear power is bankrupt, so completely that the business probably cannot be liquidated without serious losses.

As things stand now, we are not able to conduct even a justifiable police action, as a representative of the United Nations, with the backing of a majority of the nations, without the permission of Russia and China. When they refuse permission, as they did in Korea, the limited war our strategists fancy is still open to us turns into an unlimited humiliation, as the painful truce that continues in Korea should remind us, for every original issue remains unsettled. But if we challenge that veto, our only recourse is to our absolute weapons, now as fatal to ourselves and the rest of mankind as they would be to Russia and China. The distinguished army combat generals who have publicly recognized this state of impotence have been forced out of the armed services.

This situation should give us pause. While every scientific advance in nuclear weapons and intercontinental missiles only widens to planetary dimensions the catastrophe we have been preparing, our leaders still concentrate the nation's efforts on hastening these advances. Why, then, do we still listen to those mistaken counsels that committed us to the Cold War, though our own military plans have wiped out the possibility of war itself and replaced it by total annihilation as the only foreseeable terminus of the tensions we have done our full share to produce? By what standard of prudence do we trust our lives to political, military, and scientific advisers who have staked our national existence on a single set of weapons and have already lost that shortsighted gamble, even if they become desperate enough to use these weapons or remain blind enough to believe that they can conceal that loss by not using them?

What was it that set in motion the chain reaction of errors, miscalculations, delusions, and compulsions that have pushed us into the impossible situation we now occupy? Every day that we delay in facing our national mistakes adds to both the cumulative dangers that threaten us and the difficulty of undoing them.

The first step toward framing a new policy is to trace our path back to the point where we adopted our fatal commitment to weapons of mass extermination. This moral debacle, it is important to remember, was not a response to any threat by Russia or by Communism; still less was it imposed by Russia's possession of similar weapons. Actually, the acceptance of extermination antedated the invention of the atom bomb.

The principles upon which the strategy of extermination was

based were first enunciated by fascist military theorists, notably General Douhet, who believed, like our own Major Seversky, that a small air force could take the place of a large army by confining its efforts to mass attacks on civilians and undermining the national will to resist. This reversion to the vicious Bronze Age practice of total war was a natural extension of fascism's readiness to reintroduce terrorism and torture as instruments of government. When these methods were first carried into action, by Mussolini in Abyssinia, by Hitler in Warsaw and Rotterdam, they awakened horror in our still morally sensitive breasts. The creed that could justify such actions was, we thought correctly, not merely antidemocratic but antihuman.

In the midst of World War II a moral reversal took place among the English-speaking Allies, such a transposition as happened by accident in the final duel in *Hamlet,* when Hamlet picks up the weapon Laertes had poisoned in advance in order to make sure of his enemy's death. The fascist powers became the victims of their own strategy, for both the United States and Britain adopted what was politely called "obliteration bombing," which had as its object the total destruction of great cities and the terrorization and massacre of their inhabitants.

By taking over this method as a cheap substitute for conventional warfare—cheap in soldiers' lives, costly in its expenditure of other human lives and in the irreplaceable historic accumulations of countless lifetimes—these democratic governments sanctioned the dehumanized techniques of fascism. This was Nazidom's firmest victory and democracy's most servile surrender. That moral reversal undermined the eventual military triumph of the democracies, and it has poisoned our political and military policies ever since.

Civilized warfare has always been an atrocity per se, even when practiced by gallant men fighting in a just cause. But in the course of five thousand years certain inhibitions and moral safeguards had been set up. Thus, poisoning the water supply and slaying the unarmed inhabitants of a city were no longer within the modern soldier's code, however gratifying they might once have been to an Ashurbanipal or a Genghis Khan, moral monsters whose names have become infamous in history. Overnight, as it were, our own countrymen became such moral monsters. In principle, the extermination camps where the Nazis incinerated over six million helpless Jews were no different from the urban crematoriums our air force improvised in its attacks by napalm bombs on Tokyo. By these means, in a single night, we roasted alive more people than were killed by atom bombs in either Hiroshima or Nagasaki. Our aims were different, but our methods were those of mankind's worst enemy.

Up to this point, war had been an operation conducted by military forces against military targets. By long-established convention, a token part, the army, stood for the greater whole, the nation. Even when an army was totally defeated and wiped out, the nation it represented lived to tell the tale; neither unarmed prisoners nor civilians were killed to seal a defeat or celebrate a victory. Even our air force, the chief shaper of our present policy, once prided itself on its pin-point bombing, done in daylight to ensure that only military targets would be hit.

As late as the spring of 1942, as I know by personal observation, a memorandum was circulated among military advisers in Washington propounding this dilemma: If by fighting the war against Japan by orthodox methods it might require five or ten years to conquer the enemy, while with incendiary air attacks on Japanese cities Japan's resistance might be broken in a year or two, would it be morally justifiable to use the second means? Now it is hard to say which is more astonishing, that the morality of total extermination was then seriously debated in military circles or that today its morality is taken for granted, as outside debate, even among a large part of the clergy.

More than any other event that has taken place in modern times this sudden radical change-over from war to collective extermination reversed the whole course of human history.

Plainly, the acceptance of mass extermination as a normal outcome of war undermined all the moral inhibitions that have kept man's murderous fantasies from active expression. War, however brutal and devastating, had a formal beginning and could come to an end by some formal process of compromise or surrender. But no one has the faintest notion how nuclear extermination, once begun, could be brought to an end. Still less can anyone guess what purpose would be accomplished by it, except a release by death from intolerable anxiety and fear. But this is to anticipate. What is important to bear in mind is that atomic weapons did not bring about this first decisive change; they merely gave our already de-moralized strategy a more effective means of expression.

Once extermination became acceptable, the confined tumor of war, itself an atavistic pseudo-organ, turned into a cancer that would invade the blood stream of civilization. Now the smallest sore of conflict or hostility might fatally spread through the whole organism, immune to all those protective moral and political restraints that a healthy body can mobilize for such occasions.

By the time the atom bomb was invented our authorities needed no special justification for using it. The humane pleas for withholding the weapon, made by the atomic scientists, suddenly awakened to a moral crisis they had not foreseen while working on the bomb, were automatically disposed of by well-established precedent, already three years in operation. Still, the dramatic nature of the explosions at Hiroshima and Nagasaki threw a white light of horror and doubt over the whole process; for a moment a sense of moral guilt counteracted our exorbitant pride. This reaction proved as short-lived as it was belated. Yet it prompted Henry L. Stimson, a public servant whose admirable personal conduct had never been open to question, to publish a magazine article defending the official decision to use the atom bomb.

The argument Mr. Stimson advanced in favor of atomic genocide—a name invented later but studiously reserved for the acts of our enemies—was that it shortened the war and saved perhaps more than a million precious American lives. There is no need here to debate that highly debatable point. But on those same practical, "humanitarian" grounds, systematic torture might be employed by an advancing army to deter guerrilla fighters and to blackmail the remaining population into accepting promptly the torturer's terms.

That only a handful of people ventured to make this criticism indicates the depth of moral apathy to which our countrymen had sunk in less than a dozen years. Those who used this illustration, however, were not surprised to find that the French, themselves the victims of Hitler's carefully devised plans of torture and mass extermination, would authorize the use of military torture in Algeria a decade later. Our own country had forecast that depravity by our national conduct. This conduct still remains without public examination or repentance, but, unfortunately, retribution may not lie far away. Should it come, Civil Defense estimates have established that it will at once wipe out forty million American lives for the one million we once supposedly saved.

Let us be clear about cause and effect. It was not our nuclear weapons that committed us to the strategy of extermination; it was rather our decision to concentrate on the methods of extermination that led to our one-sided, obsessive preoccupation with nuclear weapons. Even before Russia had achieved a single nuclear weapon, we had so dismantled our military establishment that we lacked sufficient equipment and munitions to fight successfully such a minor action as that in Korea.

The total nature of our moral breakdown, accurately predicted a half century ago—along with the atom bomb—by Henry Adams, can be gauged by a single fact: most Americans do not realize that this change has taken place or, worse, that it makes any difference. They have no consciousness of either the magnitude of their collective sin or the fact that, by their silence, they have individually condoned it. It is precisely as if the Secretary of Agriculture had licensed the sale of human flesh as a wartime emergency measure and people had taken to cannibalism when the war was over as a clever dodge for lowering the cost of living—a mere extension of everyday butchery. Many of our professed religious and moral leaders have steadily shrunk from touching this subject; or, if they have done so, they have naïvely equated mass extermination with war and have too often given their blessing to it, for reasons just as specious as those our government has used.

It is in relation to this gigantic moral collapse that our present devotion to nuclear weapons and their equally de-humanized bacterial and chemical counterparts must be gauged.

When we abandoned the basic moral restraints against random killing and mass extermination we enlarged the de-structive capacities of our nuclear weapons. What was almost as bad, our pride in this achievement expressed itself in an inverted fashion by our identifying our safety and welfare with the one-sided expansion of our weapons system. Thus we surrendered the initiative to our instruments, confusing physical power with rational human purpose, forgetting that machines and weapons have no values and no goals, above all, no limits and no restraints except those that human beings superimpose on them.

The one thing that might have rectified our government's premature exploitation of atomic power would have been a public assize of its manifold dangers, even for wider industrial and medical use. As early as the winter of 1945-1946 the Senate Atomic Energy Committee made the first full inquiry into these matters, and the physicists who appeared before this committee gave forecasts whose accuracy was fully con-firmed in the tardy hearings that were later held before a joint congressional committee. Almost with one voice, these scientists predicted that Soviet Russia would be able to pro-duce a nuclear bomb within five years, possibly within three. On that basis, the nations of the world had three "safe" years to create through the United Nations the necessary political and moral safeguards against the misuse of this new power.

There was no salvation, the more alert leaders of science wisely pointed out, on purely national terms. Naturally, Russia's totalitarian isolationism and suspicion made it difficult to arrive at a basis for rational agreement, but our own sense of holding all the trump cards did not lessen this difficulty. All too quickly, after the Russian rejection of our generous but politically unsound Baruch proposal, our country used

Russian hostility as an excuse for abandoning all further effort. Even before we had openly committed ourselves to the Cold War itself—a now obsolete pre-atomic military concept—our leaders preferred to build a threatening ring of air bases around Russia rather than to pursue with patient circumspection a course directed toward securing eventual understanding and cooperation. So the difficult became the impossible.

As late as 1947 this situation, though grave, was not disastrous. Our very mistakes in turning to mass extermination were capable, if openly and honestly faced, of leading both ourselves and the world back to the right path. Up to then, our totalitarian weapons system had not yet consolidated its position or threatened our free institutions; the organs of democratic society, invigorated rather than depressed by the war, had not yet been enfeebled by official secrecy, repression, suspicion, craven conformism, or the corruptions of absolute power, shielded from public criticism. Meanwhile, unfortunately, the strategy of mass extermination, which did not bear public discussion or open assessment, was rapidly taking shape.

For a brief moment, nevertheless, our leaders seized the political initiative, though they were handicapped by ambivalent intentions and contradictory goals. Our contribution to organizing the United Nations, though it had been originally proposed by the United States, was as cagey and inept as Russia's, for the frustrating Council veto was an American conception. Under a more imaginative leadership two other, admirable American proposals came forward, UNRRA and the Marshall Plan. Both these agencies had great potentialities, for at first we had the intelligence to offer their benefits even to Communist countries.

Had we followed these efforts through, they might have permanently increased the whole range of international cooperation. In wiser executive hands, these initiatives would not have been prematurely terminated. Rather, they would have been employed to reduce world tensions and to win general assent to a program for giving all nations the prefatory exercises in magnanimity and understanding essential to the re-establishment of moral order and the control of our de-moralizing weapons. But even in their brief, limited application these agencies did far more to fortify the assisted nations against oppressive Communist dictatorship than all the billions we poured into NATO and SEATO to build up futile armaments for wars neither we nor our allies were capable of fighting. Witness our long series of backdowns and letdowns: Czechoslovakia, Korea, Vietnam, Poland, East Germany, Hungary, Egypt.

In our commitment to the strategy of extermination, under a decision made when General Eisenhower was Chief of Staff, the United States rejected the timely warnings of the world's leading scientists and the common counsels of humanity. Instead of holding a series of world conferences in which the dangers of nuclear energy could be fully canvassed, not alone by physicists but by thinkers in every threatened field, our official agencies deliberately played down these dangers and used every available mode of censorship to restrict the circulation of the knowledge needed for such an appraisal. In this obstinate desire to exploit nuclear power solely for our national advantage, our government relied upon insistent publicity and indoctrination to build up a false sense of security. Instead of regaining our moral position by ceasing the reckless experiments whose mounting pollution justified a world-wide apprehension, we flatly denied the need for any such cessation and allowed Russia, after it had come abreast of us, to take the moral lead here. Even at a United Nations conference in 1959, which clearly demonstrated the dangers, our representatives helped vote down the Russian preamble to the conclusions of the conference, which called for a cessation of all further nuclear testing.

To explain this obstinate commitment to the infamous policy of mass extermination one must understand that its side reactions have proved as demoralizing as its central purpose. Within a bare decade, the United States has built up a huge vested interest in mass extermination—in the weapons themselves and in the highly profitable manufacture of electronic equipment, planes, and missiles designed to carry them to their destination. There are tens of thousands of individual scientists and technicians engaged in nuclear, bacteriological, and chemical research to increase the range and effectiveness of these lethal agents, though we boast we already have a stockpile of nuclear weapons capable of wiping out the entire planet. There are also corporate bodies—the Air Force, the Atomic Energy Commission, great industrial corporations, and extravagantly endowed centers of research—whose powers and presumptions have been constantly widened along with their profit and prestige. While the show lasts, their careers depend on our accepting the fallacious assumptions to which they have committed us.

All these agents now operate in secret totalitarian enclaves, perfecting their secret totalitarian weapons, functioning outside the processes of democratic government, immune to public challenge and criticism or to public correction. Whatever the scientific or technical competence of the men working in this field, their sedulous restriction of interest and the limited conditions under which they work and have contact with other human beings do not foster wisdom in the conduct of life. By vocational commitment they live in an underdimensioned and distorted world. The sum of their combined judgments is still an unbalanced judgment, for moral criteria have, from the start, been left out of their general directives.

Is it any wonder that even in the narrow segments of science where they claim mastery our nuclear officials have made error after error? They have again and again been forced to reduce their estimate of the "permissible" limit of exposure to radiation, and on the basis of knowledge already available they will have to reduce these estimates still further. Thus, too, they made an error that startled themselves, in their undercalculating the range and the lethal fall-out of the hydrogen bomb, and they sought to cover that error by concealment and calumny, at first denying the plight of the Japanese fishermen they had injured. Some have even used their authority as scientists to give pseudo-scientific assurances about biological changes that no one will be able to verify until half a century has passed. Furthermore, in matters falling within their province of exact knowledge, the judgment of these authorities has repeatedly proved erroneous and mischievous.

All this should not surprise us: neither science nor nuclear energy endows its users with superhuman powers. But what should surprise us is the fact that the American nation has entrusted its welfare, safety, and future existence to these imprudent, fallible men and to those who have sanctioned their de-moralized plans. Under the guise of a calculated risk, our nuclear strategists have prepared to bring on a calculated catastrophe. At some unpredictable moment their sick fantasies may become unspeakable realities.

Does anyone really think that, unless a miracle supervenes, there can be a more favorable outcome to the overall policy we have been pursuing? If this policy had a color of excuse before Russia had achieved her first nuclear weapon in 1949, it became thoroughly discredited in Korea in 1950 and became suicidal as soon as Russia's superiority in rocket missiles was established. The fact that Russia now has equal or better weapons of extermination and has joined us in these same insane preparations doubles our danger but does not halve our original guilt. Neither does it nullify our willful stupidity in now clinging to an obsolete, discredited strategy, based on a negation of morality and a defiance of common sense.

The only possible justification of our continued reliance upon weapons of total extermination would be that they do no present harm and would never be used by either side under any extremity of provocation. Can any mature mind comfort itself with either hope? Even our experimental explosion of nuclear bombs, at a rate of more than two for Russia's one, has poisoned our babies' milk, upset the delicate ecological balance of nature, and, still worse, defiled our genetic heritage. As for the possibility that nuclear weapons will never be used, our children in school know better than this every time they are put through the sadistic mummery of an air-raid drill and learn to "play disaster." Such baths of fear and hostility are gratuitous assaults against the young, whose psychological damage is already incalculable; their only service is to bar more tightly the exits that would permit a real escape.

There are people who would defend these plans on the grounds that it is better to die nobly, defending democracy and freedom, than to survive under Communist oppression. Such apologists perhaps exaggerate the differences that now exist between our two systems, but they err even more seriously in applying to mass extermination a moral standard that was defensible only as long as this death was a symbolic one confined to a restricted number of people on a small portion of the earth. Such a disaster, as in the bitter-end resistance of the Southern Confederacy, was still relatively minor and retrievable; if the original resolve to die were in fact an erroneous one, in a few generations it could be corrected. Nuclear damage, in contrast, is cumulative and irretrievable; it admits no belated confession of error, no repentance and absolution.

Under what canon of sanity, then, can any government, or any generation, with its limited perspectives, its fallible judgment, its obvious proneness to self-deception, delusion, and error, make a decision for all future ages about the very existence of even a single country? Still more, how can any one nation treat as a purely private right its decision on a matter that will affect the life and health and continued existence of the rest of mankind?

There are no words to describe the magnitude of such insolence in thought or the magnitude of criminality involved in carrying it out. Those who believe that any country has the right to make such a decision share the madness of Captain Ahab in *Moby Dick*. For them Russia is the White Whale that must be hunted down and grappled with. Like Ahab in that mad pursuit, they will listen to no reminders of love, home, family obligation; in order to kill the object of their fear and hate they are ready to throw away the sextant and compass that might give them back their moral direction, and in the end they will sink their own ship and drown their crew. To such unbalanced men, to such demoralized efforts, to such dehumanized purposes, our government has entrusted, in an easily conceivable extremity, our lives. Even an accident, these men have confessed, might produce the dire results they have planned, and more than once has almost done so. To accept their plans and ensuing decisions, we have deliberately anesthetized the normal feelings, emotions, anxieties, and hopes that could alone bring us to our senses.

No one can guess how a sufficiently wide recovery of moral responsibility and initiative might be brought about. Neither can one predict at what moment our nation will see that there is no permissible sacrifice of life, either in experimental preparation of these vile weapons or in a final conflict whose very method would nullify every rational end. Certainly it seems doubtful that popular pressure would bring about such a change in government policy, except under the emotion of a shattering crisis, when it might well be too late. But great leadership, exerted at the right moment, might clear the air and illuminate the territory ahead. Until we actually use our weapons of extermination, there is nothing that we have yet done that cannot be undone, except for the existing pollution of our food and our genetic heritage with strontium 90 and carbon 14. But we must make a moral about-face before we can command a political forward march.

Yet if once the American nation made such evaluation of the morality of extermination, new policies and appropriate decisions would quickly suggest themselves. This would do more to effect an immediate improvement in the relations between the two powers now committed to preparing for mutual extermination than endless parleys between their heads of government.

A moral about-face does not demand, as those whose minds are congealed by the Cold War suppose, either a surrender to Russian Communism or a series of futile appeasements; neither does it mean any increase in the dangers under which we now live: just the contrary. Those who see no other alternatives are still living in the pre-nuclear world; they do not understand that our greatest enemy is not Russia but our treacherous weapons, and that our commitment to these weapons is what has prevented us from conceiving and proposing the necessary means for extending the area of effective freedom and, above all, for safeguarding mankind from meaningless mutilation and massacre.

No dangers we might face once we abandoned the very possibility of using mass extermination would be as great as those under which we now live; yet this is not to say that a bold change of policy would be immediately successful, or that before it had time to register its full effects in other countries it might not tempt Russia to risk measures to extend over other areas its own monolithic system of minority single-party government. But need I emphasize that these possible penalties could hardly be worse than those our government meekly accepted in Czechoslovakia, Poland, and Korea, at a time when we still hugged the illusion of wielding absolute power through our monopoly of nuclear weapons? While sober judgment need not minimize these transitional difficulties and possible losses, one must not underestimate, either, the impact of a new policy, wholly concerned to re-establish the moral controls and political cooperations necessary to enable mankind to halt the threatening misuse of the extraordinary powers that it now commands.

Even in a purely military sense, this changed orientation might produce the greatest difficulties for those Communist governments who misunderstood its intention and sought to turn it to their private national advantage. Russia would no more be able to escape the impact of our humane plans and moralized proposals than it was able to avoid the impact and challenge of our nuclear weapons. If we rallied the forces of mercy, human-heartedness, and morality with the vigor with which we have marshaled the dehumanized forces of destruction, what government could stand against us and face its own people, however strong its cynical suspicions and misgivings?

This is not the place or the moment to spell out a new policy which would start with the complete renunciation of weapons of mass extermination and go on to build constructive measures addressed to all those tasks which the Cold War has caused us to leave in abeyance. Fortunately, George Kennan, the only official or ex-official who has yet had the courage to admit our earlier miscalculations, has already sketched in, with some boldness, the outlines of a better policy, and his proposals might be amplified and enlarged in many directions once we had overcome our official obsession with Russia and our fixation on mass extermination as an ultimate resource.

But the key to all practical proposals lies in a return to human feelings and sensitivities, to moral values, and to life-regarding procedures as controlling factors in the operation of intelligence. The problems our nation has tried to solve by mechanical weapons alone, operated by a detached and demoralized mechanical intelligence, have proved insoluble by those means. A great leader would know that the time has come to reinstate the missing human factor and bring forth generously imaginative proposals addressed to mankind's survival and working toward its further development.

Tom Stonier | What Would It Really Be Like?

An H-Bomb on New York City *

In flesh and blood terms, what would a thermonuclear explosion over a city mean—at the time of the blast, in the days,
weeks and months following, and to generations as yet
unborn?

Let us assume one 20-megaton thermonuclear device
(equivalent to 20 million tons of TNT) is exploded two miles
above Columbus Circle in midtown Manhattan.

As the bomb explodes, the sky fills with a bluish-white in-
candescence whose heat at the center approaches that of the
sun itself. It rapidly expands until it is four miles wide. To the
west it spans the Hudson River; to the east it reaches across
the East River to Queens. Times Square, Rockefeller Center,
big ocean liners, Central Park, the United Nations are instantly incinerated.

Material in the fireball begins to condense and spread out
as it reaches altitudes of five to 10 miles, thus forming the
mushroom cloud. About 25 miles up, it burns itself out.
Meanwhile, a huge pressure wave traveling initially at speeds
many times that of sound has spread out from the center of the
explosion, crushing everything in its path until it gradually
loses its force. Immediately behind this shock front comes the
wind at speeds initially exceeding a thousand miles per hour,
toppling whatever might still be standing. (Structures like

* This article is based on a paper, "The Anticipated Biological and
Environmental Effects of Detonating a 20-Megaton Weapon on Columbus Circle," prepared by Dr. Tom Stonier for the Scientists' Committee
for Radiation Information. The original paper was about 100 pages
long, highly technical and heavily documented. This adaptation was
made by the editors of War/Peace Report.

ical target"—the hurling of a man against a hard surface. perts have determined that for a 160-pound man serious ad and skeletal injuries occur if the velocity of the body ceeds 10 feet per second at the moment it collides with a rd surface. With a 20-megaton ground burst, a 160-pound an would achieve this critical velocity after having traveled nly one foot if he were 8.5 miles from the blast, or after ten eet if he were 15.6 miles distant.

For those who survived the immediate heat and blast, the next great problem would be the firestorm.

Firestorms would be an almost inevitable consequence of bombings in the megaton range on a large city, according to W. T. Ham in testimony before the Holifield Committee. "Just what measures can be adopted for survival during a firestorm are not readily apparent," he said. "Survivors of the initial effects of blast, thermal and ionizing radiation from a megaton burst must cope also with the incinerating heat of firestorms. Severe burn casualties from secondary fires will outnumber vastly flash burn casualties from the fireball."

One of the firestorms on which the most complete data is available occurred in Hamburg on July 27, 1943. In this raid 60,000 inhabitants of the city perished, almost as many as were killed in the atom bombing of Hiroshima. Wind velocity exceeded 150 miles per hour; burning gases rose to 15,000 feet; temperatures exceeded 1,400° F. In view of the current interest in shelters, it is noteworthy to observe the fate of people in air-raid shelters in the Hamburg firestorm.

Many persons were simply cooked to death as if they had been in an oven. In other shelters people were found in positions indicating they had died unaware of the imminent danger. Some of these evidently were victims of heat stroke. A much larger percentage, however, showed characteristics of carbon monoxide poisoning. Wood fires normally contain three per cent carbon monoxide; a concentration of .5 per cent in the air may cause death after one hour's exposure.

Others in Hamburg remained in their shelters too long before attempting to flee the firestorm; only those who escaped in the early stages had any hope of reaching safety.

telephone poles and radio towers which might resist the shock front are much more vulnerable to the winds that follow.)

The outward-rushing wind, which creates a giant vacuum in the central area, gradually loses its force as it moves into the suburbs, and the surrounding air rushes back into the city. These reverse winds, in turn, fan the fires that have been started by the bomb's heat and also as a result of blast effects (for example, broken gas mains, electrical short circuits and upset stoves). It is conservatively estimated that a 20-megaton detonation could start at least one million fires within the limits of New York City alone. Even if the fire department, which normally handles about 150 fires a day, somehow remained intact, it could not cope with the conflagration. But, like other New Yorkers, most of the 12,000-man force would be unable to respond. Moreover, their equipment would not be operative, and even if it were the lack of water pressure and the streets lined with rubble would make effective countermeasures impossible. So the unchecked fires would probably coalesce to form a firestorm which could cover a circular area from thirty to fifty miles across, or even more. Like a fire burning beneath a chimney, a firestorm sucks in air from around its edges, creating winds at its edges with up to hurricane force.

What would have happened to the people under and around the burst?

The study indicates that almost six million out of eight million New Yorkers would have died within the first few days, mostly from blast and heat. If the burst occurred on a weekday, when 900,000 commuters were in the city, the figure would be correspondingly higher. In the suburbs many more would die in the first few days from blast and heat.

Near the center, most people would be killed almost instantly from the heat. At distances of up to twenty-seven miles from ground zero an individual might receive third degree burns; second degree burns may be suffered by persons up to thirty-two miles away; first degree burns would occur at forty-five miles. Second and third degree burns received under such circumstances could well prove fatal.

The other great immediate cause of death and injuries would

be blast effects. However, very few would die as a direct result of the shock wave, for the human body can stand fairly high pressures. A person close to the burst would more likely be killed first either by heat or other blast effects. For the same reason, immediate nuclear radiation would not be an important cause of death.

The most dangerous blast effects result from falling buildings and their contents, and from people being picked up by winds and hurled against hard surfaces. For a forewarned population that took cover indoors, falling buildings would probably be responsible for more initial casualties than any other single factor. Blast damage to a building may happen in various ways. A building may be blown over, or its four walls may collapse inwards because of external pressure. An already weakened building may be damaged further by the violent outward wind following the shock front and then by the rush of air back in to fill the partial vaccum. In addition to all this, there is the ground shock, which, like an earthquake, may tumble a building.

The bomb could totally destroy ordinary unreinforced brick or wood-frame houses ten miles away; such homes twenty miles away would remain standing but would need major repairs. Some damage, such as broken windows, would be incurred by most structures fifty miles or more away. There would be many individual variations, depending on the peculiarities of construction and behavior of the shock front. The explosion of a mere 20-kiloton bomb (with one-thousandth the power of this one) has been known occasionally to break windows seventy-five to one hundred miles away.

If the 20-megaton burst were at ground level on Columbus Circle, it would blast a hole, in granite, half a mile wide and 240 feet deep, big enough to contain a 20-story building. This would penetrate all three subway systems. Since a blast wave traveling in a tunnel loses its energy much more slowly than when it is traveling in the open air, the death-dealing force could be expected to run through the entire underground-connected portion of the subway system.

The second major blast effect is "displacement of a bio-

Reprinted with permission from *The New York T*

If It Were 50 megatons . . .

The study on which this article is based was begun when 20-megaton weapon was considered the largest in nuclea arsenals. However, the Soviet Union has now detonated a 57-megaton device. The map shows what a 50-megaton bomb exploded over Wall Street would do to the New York metropolitan area: at 2.75 miles, all but the heaviest concrete buildings leveled; at 14 miles, blast sufficient to destroy or damage most homes; at 35 miles, fatal burns to those exposed, wooden homes burned; at 45 miles, fires in dried leaves, similar matter; at 49 miles, second degree burns to any exposed persons. Although some scientists state that even 500- and 1,000-megaton bombs are possible, it is generally agreed that more devastation can be caused by using more of the relatively smaller weapons.

Once the heat became unbearable, hundreds of persons were seen leaving shelters and running into the streets, where they slowly collapsed, as if from utter exhaustion. Many who died this way were found naked. Somehow the heat or fire burned their clothing, except for their shoes, yet only singed their skin.

It is thus apparent that the most serious threat to a population surrounding a target area may well be the firestorm. Obviously, this matter has the utmost significance in appraising any shelter program. The key question is the probable extent of the firestorm. In the case of the low air burst of the 20-megaton weapon, the firestorm might extend well beyond New York City limits, probably on the average at least eighteen miles from Columbus Circle.

In spite of the wide public discussion of the potential fallout threat, this hazard is at least as uncertain and perhaps much more difficult to predict in detail than any of the preceding hazards. Unfortunately, almost every assumption that needs to be made in this type of calculation is uncertain. The smooth contours set forth in theoretical calculations are produced by simplified wind structures, and these often do not exist. At several altitudes winds may show varying velocities and varying directions. Thus a five-megaton burst of the 1956 Redwing series in the Pacific produced a fallout pattern resembling a maple leaf. In that instance, one hour after the blast the radiation at hot spots 50 miles away was found to be two-and-a-half times as much as at the explosion site itself.

Many other assumptions on fallout must be questioned. One is that eighty per cent of the radioactive material produced will return to earth as local fallout. It could be much less. Another problem is that all information on local fallout has been obtained from kiloton bursts on silicate, or megaton bursts on coral sand. Fallout resulting from a surface burst in a city on granite might possess quite different properties from those studied so far. Large amounts of iron condensing early in the cloud would influence particle formation and rate of descent. It is also difficult to assess the contribution of radiation from such structural materials as steel, glass and concrete, containing sodium, silicon, iron, copper, zinc, manganese and cobalt.

Another question mark is weathering—what happens to fallout after it has settled. Not much is known, and what there is, is classified. As physicist Ralph E. Lapp has pointed out, there is an urgent need for reliable data on the physical and chemical behavior of fallout particles on soil surfaces, building materials and surfaced roads. One would also expect an effect on plant and animal life as they relate to soil surfaces.

It is clear from the foregoing that it is impossible to predict what the fallout situation would be in any specific New York locality in the event that a 20-megaton weapon were detonated on Columbus Circle. If the burst were at ground level, the fallout field might be expected to be about 4,000 square miles, with some hot spots where one could receive a fatal dose in two minutes, while in others it might require 40 minutes. If winds were as they were on October 17, 1958 (the day of the attack for the Holifield hearings)—west-southwest at an average of 40 miles per hour—Long Island would be inundated by fallout.

If, however, the burst were in the air, there would be relatively little local fallout. If the burst were above most of the atmosphere, 20 miles or more up, there would be no local fallout, less blast damage, but greater heat damage. In this case a person 40 miles away (or even more) looking directly at the fireball could be permanently blinded; permanent burns of the retina are possible at distances of more than 300 miles. Thus, fallout effect is maximized with a ground burst; blast effect with a low air burst; heat effect with a high air burst. If an enemy had ample bombs, he might explode several at various altitudes to achieve the various effects.

Like the physical considerations of fallout, the biological considerations are also uncertain. Human populations exposed to relatively high levels of fallout have been small. There was virtually no fallout in Japan since both detonations involved air rather than surface bursts. All radiation injuries resulted from the initial nuclear radiation. The best data comes from studies of Marshall Islanders, American service personnel and

Japanese fishermen accidentally injured following the detonation of a nuclear device in the Pacific in the spring of 1954.

While it is not possible to make a reasonable estimate of radiation deaths from the 20-megaton bomb, it is possible to give this rule of thumb as to the survivability of exposed persons: If vomiting occurs promptly within a few hours and continues and is followed in rapid succession by prostration, diarrhea and fever, death is almost certain to follow within a week. If vomiting occurs early and is of relatively short duration, and is followed by a period of well-being, there is a strong chance that symptoms of serious radiation sickness, which may or may not be fatal, will begin to develop within a few weeks. Persons who have been exposed but show no external symptoms of radiation sickness may still be significantly affected since even sublethal doses of radiation lower defenses against infection.

Assuming an individual in the New York area has survived heat, blast, firestorm and fallout, what will be his further problems in a post-attack world? First, what would it mean for New York City to have been destroyed? Consider what New York City was:

The city itself had a population of eight million, and another five million lived nearby. It was the financial capital of the non-Communist world, home of the U.N., corporate capital of the nation, center of American culture, the nation's No. 1 manufacturing city, the leading wholesale and retail market of the country, the transportation hub of the Northeast and the country's major communications center. The seventeen-county New York-Northeastern New Jersey Standard Metropolitan area contained ten per cent of the nation's total labor force, twelve per cent of its managers, fifteen per cent of its physicians, sixteen per cent of its accountants, auditors, architects, chemists and electrical engineers, twenty per cent of the nation's research laboratories. Thus in a single blow the U.S. was deprived of perhaps five to ten per cent of its economic capacity.

In considering the social and economic disruption following this detonation of twenty megatons over Columbus Circle, it would be unrealistic to assume that the rest of the country had not been hit. When Hiroshima and Nagasaki were bombed (with weapons only one-thousandth as potent as a 20-megaton bomb), the rest of Japan was able to render help to survivors. In this case it must be presumed that other, if not all, metropolitan areas, as well as many minor cities and other targets, have been destroyed. In a general way, some of the problems may be imagined.

Medical treatment is available to only a small minority of people. Most of New York's 50,000 hospital beds have been destroyed, and even if they haven't they can scarcely accommodate the millions of injured. Many doctors and nurses have been killed, drug and plasma supply sources have been mostly destroyed. Thus even those with minor injuries are likely to succumb; second- and third-degree burns almost always become infected. Malnutrition, sublethal doses of radiation, fatigue and emotional stress further aggravate minor ailments. Epidemics are highly probable. They could be made certain if the enemy introduced diseases such as typhus, influenza, cholera or plague through bacteriological warfare.

Sources of power have largely ceased to be available beginning at the time of attack, and what sources remain are rapidly running out. Electricity may be available for a while in some areas where the producing facilities are intact, but as coal stocks are exhausted they will have to shut down. There is no way to transport more coal to the plants. Many gas tanks and mains have exploded, disrupting that source of energy. Gasoline supplies are rapidly being exhausted and cannot be replaced, as transportation systems are too damaged to transport the gasoline. Thus most people, even if not immediately, will soon be deprived of the use of their radio, television, telephone, automobile, stove, refrigerator, sink, bathtub, toilet, furnace and electric lights.

Water supplies can be destroyed in two ways: by contamination of reservoirs with fallout and by destruction of parts of the water supply system, such as mains and water towers. Also, without power, pumps cannot operate to put water into the system. Aside from the supply problems, it would probably be from two to four days before the water in open reservoirs hit by fallout would reach a level of radioactivity low enough to be acceptable. (The reason water would be drinkable after so short a time, although it would not be considered "safe" by present standards, is that only a small part of fallout is soluble in water.) Since it will take considerable time to repair supply systems, survivors may have to go to the reservoirs on foot or dig their own wells.

Food supplies have been interrupted on many levels. Large areas of land have been made so radioactive that farmers cannot work them safely for weeks or months. In the 4,000 square miles presumed hit with fallout from a surface burst on Columbus Circle, farmers would have to wait two years before the radioactivity fell to the level now considered safe for workers in atomic industries. Crops hit by heavy fallout have been ruined by radioactivity. Many food warehouses and processing plants have been destroyed, and those that remain have no power to operate. Finally, all transportation systems —rail, air and highways—have been so disrupted that food can move only sporadically. The consumer himself has to walk (or ride a bicycle perhaps) to any possible sources of food supply.

Money has become virtually worthless. It is no longer possible to pay by check because the nation's banking system is totally disrupted. Washington, D.C., presumably has been destroyed in the attack, and along with it the Federal Reserve System. Where banks are still intact, they have been the victim of runs by panic-stricken survivors. Not having sufficient currency to cover their accounts (as no bank ever does), the banks have been forced to shut their doors. Insurance companies are out of business. Even what currency is available is of little value What trade there is, is carried on by barter.

Housing is an immense problem. In the case of New York City, even without a firestorm, it is highly probable that very few, if any, of the city's two-and-a-half million dwellings would provide adequate shelter. There is considerable blast and fire damage in the suburbs, and, as indicated previously, fallout would be distributed in an unpredictable manner over 4,000 square miles. In the Holifield hearings, which assumed a "modest" attack of about 1,500 megatons on the entire nation, C. K. Shafer stated that out of the nation's 46.1 million dwellings, 11.8 million would suffer severe damage from blast, 8.1 million moderate damage and 1.5 million slight damage. Of those not damaged by blast, 500,000 dwellings would be hit by an amount of fallout requiring them to be evacuated for a year; another 2.1 million would have to be abandoned for several months; another 10.4 million could be made available for living 60 days after the attack—but only after major decontamination had been carried out. Thus, of the 46.1 million total dwellings, only 11.7 million, or about one out of four, could be inhabited during the first sixty days following the attack. If the attack occurred during the winter it would be difficult to imagine the hardship of survivors, as they faced the lack of housing, heat, food and medical supplies.

Yet another post-attack problem is the breakdown of the social organization. Government and law enforcement, since communications have been largely destroyed, quickly revert to the local level. With problems of hunger, sickness and lack of housing, disputes are inevitable, and many of them are settled by violence. Marauding bands of desperate refugees could become a problem in areas that have suffered relatively less damage.

Despite this catalogue of horrors, there will probably be some long-term survivors of the attack, although perhaps not very many from the New York metropolitan area. What will the long-term effects of the attack be on these persons and their progeny? Here the information is really scant. Nevertheless, there are a few clues.

Studies of survivors of the Japanese bombings indicate that those exposed to radiation there have had a higher incidence than normal of leukemia and cancer of the lung, stomach, breast, ovary and uterine cervix. A higher death rate from all causes was also noted in the exposed Japanese population. It is established that radiation leads to formation of cataracts, with babies being particularly vulnerable.

Radiation can also cause sterility. The gonads are among the most radiation-sensitive organs of the body. Likewise, radiation damage to the ovaries in the female can cause profound atrophy of the organ resulting in temporary or permanent sterility, depending on the dose.

Studies of exposed Japanese children have shown that radiation has probably had the effect of retarding their skeletal development and growth in weight and height. Particularly deleterious is the effect of radiation on the embryo. A high percentage of Japanese women who were pregnant at the time of exposure had abnormal terminations of their pregnancies.

Radiation effects do not, of course, stop with the current generation. It has long been known that radiation can induce mutations in organisms, and that more than ninety-nine per cent of these mutations are harmful to the race. It is extremely difficult, however, to determine the precise amount of genetic damage that radiation could cause.

Radiation might induce two principal types of mutations— those caused by lethal genes and those caused by non-lethal genes. Lethal genes will cause offspring to die before, during or shortly after birth. According to one set of calculations, it may require twenty-two generations for lethal mutant genes to die out. Non-lethal mutant genes, two per cent of which might show up as obviously defective persons in any one generation, would probably be maintained for more than fifty generations.

In contrast to the many uncertainties regarding genetic damage, there is one certainty: Damage to the human gene pool scarcely begins with this generation. It will still be expressing itself when our current controversies are ancient history.

Norman Cousins | Shelters, Survival and Common Sense

I

In home after home throughout the country, the question of fallout shelters has become a profoundly important and perplexing issue. The danger of thermonuclear war has become real enough—indeed, it has been given a razor's edge by the Berlin crisis—so that people are compelled to think seriously about protecting themselves and their families in the event of atomic attack. However grisly shelters may be as a subject for home conversation, parents are earnestly discussing and exploring the matter in terms of their responsibility to their children.

The purpose of this editorial is not to argue against fallout shelters per se. No one can quarrel against a decision by a citizen to prepare today against possible dangers tomorrow. But at least he is entitled to full and factual information before making up his mind. Indeed, he has the right to be protected against dishonest assurances of complete protection when no such assurances are possible or morally justifiable. And we can certainly quarrel with the idea that the family fallout shelter is a fit subject for exploitation by fast-buck operators.

The key fact, the dominant fact, in modern warfare is that the civilian will be the prime target. Every bit of scientific ingenuity will be mobilized and directed against him—wherever he may turn. All the inventiveness that has found a way to kill a city with a single explosive and that has devised a vehicle to carry a cargo of death from one continent to another in fifteen minutes—this inventiveness will not retire because people are going to burrow into the earth. Modern war intends to hunt down the civilian wherever he is, suffocating him or paralyzing him or driving him out into the open. No ventilating system has as yet been made available that can guard against gases that produce heart sickness, or disease germs that spread cholera, anthrax, plague, diphtheria, tularemia, brucelosis, typhoid fever, influenza, dengue fever, smallpox, pneumonia, amoebic dysentery, malaria, Rocky Mountain fever, Q fever, undulant fever, typhus—all of which are now in the arsenals of the major powers and primed for instant use.

Consider first of all the problem of ventilation. When a hydrogen bomb goes off, it produces firestorms over a vast area. A ten-megaton thermonuclear explosion will set loose firestorms over an area of 5,000 square miles. Oxygen is consumed by firestorms. Shelters may be equipped to cool off the air but they can't bring in air if none exists. Unless manufactured oxygen is made available, shelters in the areas affected by firestorms will become suffocation chambers. The need for manufactured oxygen has of course been considered but the difficulties of providing it on a mass scale are regarded as insuperable. Moreover, its volatility under such circumstances makes it a serious risk in its own terms.

The next major factor to be considered has to do with location. The problem of shelters is different in a city from what it is likely to be in the outlying areas. The principal problem in the city will be getting into a shelter in the first place and getting out of it in the second place. It is by no means certain that an attack will be preceded by warning. In fact, the factor of surprise is a molecular part of the make-up of missile-cum-nuclear war. And, even if warning should precede rather than follow an attack, it would be in the order of minutes. Evacuating a city is beyond possibility. Even getting people into cellars is a questionable enterprise. The idea that people in office buildings could take cover by clustering together in the hallways or stairwells or cellars has no validity in a situation involving multiple use of megaton nuclear bombs. The purpose of a thermonuclear bomb is to pulverize a city and all the people in it; as many such bombs as are required to execute that purpose will be used.

For those city dwellers who are able, despite the limited warning time, to take refuge in deep city shelters, the principal problem will be getting out of them—because of the tons of spilled brick and rubble overhead. Testimony before Congressional committees has made it abundantly clear that thermonuclear attack on cities would leave few survivors. In fact, military calculations of 80,000,000 American casualties in event of nuclear attack are based largely on the virtual annihilation of metropolitan populations.

The danger in the suburban areas will be represented not so much by blast as by firestorms and radiation. It is undoubtedly true that some lives can be saved in suburban shelters, assuming ventilation and disease germs will not be critical factors. But it is most certainly untrue that the reduced radiation after only a few days will necessarily subside to safety levels. Most of the radioactive materials released by a thermonuclear explosion are short-lived, but a few, like radioactive strontium and radioactive cesium, retain their killing power over many months. Even more important is the fact that present nuclear stockpiles have high versatility. Some bombs are packed with long-lived radioactive bullets that are designed to stay close to the surface of the earth for a long time.

Most of the specific inadequacies of shelters in cities and suburbs do not apply to country shelters. The main danger in country areas is the generalized one; that is, everything depends on the number of and nature of the bombs used in general attack. If upwards of 25,000 megatons of nuclear explosives are used in a major war—and the United States alone possesses far more than this amount, according to Congressional testimony—the long-term risk to all life in the northern latitudes will be a critical one. Secretary of State Dean Rusk has said that far more nuclear power is available than the entire human race could sustain.

However, no one now knows exactly how much nuclear megatonage will be exploded in a major war. So long as there is even a small chance that the megatonage will fall far short

of maximum possibilities, a country dweller may feel justified
in taking the shelter gamble. But at least he will not be kid-
ding himself about his chances. For the urban dweller, whose
city is a nuclear target, however, the chances may be too
slight to warrant calculation, even though a fraction of the
megatonage available will be used. It doesn't take too many
hydrogen explosives to expunge the cities. And anyone who
lives within fifty miles of a major city is vulnerable to the
effects described above.

Basically, therefore, the entire question of shelters is a personal one. The individual must make up his own mind based
on his own best understanding of the range of probabilities in
a nuclear war and his own philosophy of life. But it is un-
conscionable and contemptible to kid him, or to lead him to
believe that 97 per cent of the people in shelters can be saved,
or that life inside shelters can somehow be made glamorous,
or that Mary Jane will be able to call her friends on the telephone, or that, after the attack, life will be resumed as usual.
Life will not be resumed as usual. Those who survive will
embark upon an ordeal unlike anything the human race as a
race has ever known. The supply of uncontaminated food will
run out; even the rain will be poisoned.

When the survivors crawl out of their holes they will not be
looking at the world they knew. The crust of the earth will be
burned and clotted; anything that stands, whether a tree or a
structure, will be charred and skeletonized. There will be no
communications, there will be no hospitals, there will be no
institutions to attend to the needs of human society. This is
what nuclear war is. No deodorizing can change the fact.

Not all the advocates of shelters believe that shelters will
provide the advertised protection. Their position is strategical
and political rather than scientific. That is, they believe that
it is important for the enemy to know—as in the case of the
present Berlin crisis—that the American people have the will
to fight a nuclear war. And a widespread shelter program may
be considered evidence of such. Moreover, they believe that,
if we can get enough people underground at the time of an
initial attack, we may be able to destroy the enemy utterly

before he has time to attempt a second strike. This may leave us with enough people to carry on the work of rebuilding a nation.

The trouble with this strategical approach is that it works both ways. An enemy, determined to destroy this country in a first strike, may respond to the mass shelter program by polishing even further his surprise-attack capabilities.

Finally, if the case for shelters has any logic, it should become a government function. The government should plan a national program in line with its Constitutional responsibility. Moreover, if we are to take the need for shelters seriously, all our plans should be tied to the absence of warning time. This means that *deep* (perhaps 400 feet or more) mass underground shelters should be built from one end of the country to the other. They should be capable of growing their own food. They should have practically everything underground we now have above ground. They should have communications systems, hospitals, libraries, cultural centers. Most important of all is the fact that we should move into them immediately, for there will not be enough time to get into them once the bombs fall.

In short, if we take nuclear war for granted and wish to protect ourselves against its effects, we have to be prepared very soon to abandon our natural environment. There is no assurance, however, that the various groups linked together by the underground system would not find some way of getting at one another to do murder, if one group has something that another wants.

The time to make a stand is now, not later. The answer to nuclear war is a genuine peace. The answer to drift is direction. The answer to insanity is sanity. If the energy, money, and resources now going into shelters were to be put to work in the making of a better world, we would do far more to safeguard the American future than all the underground holes that could be built in 1,000 years. And if we are serious about shelters, let us make the United Nations into a shelter broad enough and deep enough to sustain an enforced peace under law.

The war has not yet begun. Freedom, however abused, still exists. Perhaps we can use that freedom to rally enough peoples around the idea of a world under law. President Kennedy's talk before the United Nations stated the problem and pointed to a way out. If enough Americans are willing to commit themselves personally to the support of the President's proposals, it might make a difference, a very big difference.

II

In Las Vegas, the head of the local civil defense agency called for a militia of 5,000 men to protect residents in event of thermonuclear war. The men would be trained to crush an expected invasion—not from foreign shores but from Southern California. It is believed that Los Angeles, as a major city, would be under direct attack. Survivors, warned J. Carlton Adair, the Las Vegas civilian defense official, "would come into Nevada like a swarm of locusts." Obviously, they would have to be repulsed.

In a less organized way, other Americans are preparing to kill Americans. A Chicago suburbanite, according to *Time* magazine, intends to mount a machine gun at the entrance to his fallout shelter and blast away at shelterless neighbors who might try to get in out of the radioactivity. Countless other Americans may be making no open declarations about their intentions but they are calmly going about the business of equipping their shelters with guns or tear-gas devices, just in case desperate neighbors might want to poach on their preserves during or after an attack. Some are now preparing their children psychologically to accept the murder of their playmates. All this goes under the heading of civil defense.

In Hartford, Connecticut, at a private meeting of local residents who had come together to consider civil defense problems, one citizen advised his neighbors that firearms were standard equipment for shelters, along with stocks of food and medicines. People who are wounded or suffering from radiation will run around like madmen trying to find shelter, he warned. And, since there will be only so much water and food for one's own family, the intruders will have to be turned back even if it means shooting them. A woman who lived next door to the citizen who had just given this advice had a question.

"John," she said, "you and your family have been our closest friends for ten years. Do you mean to say that if this city was bombed and my baby and I were caught in the open, and we were hurt, and came to your shelter you would turn us away?"

John nodded in the affirmative. His neighbor pressed the point.

"But suppose we wouldn't turn away and begged to get in?"

"It would be too bad," John said. "You should have built a shelter of your own. I've got to look out for my own family."

"But suppose we had built a shelter of our own, yet were caught by surprise, being out in the open at the time of an attack, and we discovered that the entrance to our shelter was covered with rubble and we had no place to turn except to you. Would you still turn us back?"

The answer was still yes.

"But suppose I wouldn't go away and kept trying to get in. Would you shoot us?"

John said that if the only way he could keep his friend out would be by shooting her and her baby, he would have to do it.

In doing so, he could claim spiritual sanction. He referred to a recent issue of an important religious journal which presented a "code of ethics" of Christian morality designed to anticipate difficult questions that might arise in shelters. One point in the code advised the Christians to "think twice before they rashly give their family shelter space to friends and neighbors or to the passing stranger." Finally, the Hartford citizen could cite Civil Defense Coordinator Keith Dwyer's pronouncement that there is "nothing in the Christian ethic which denies one's right to protect oneself and one's family."

People speculate on the horrors that would be let loose by

nuclear war. It is not necessary to speculate on such horrors. Some of the worst horrors are already here. The transformation today of otherwise decent people into death-calculating machines; the psychological preconditioning for an age of cannibalism; the wholesale premeditation of murder and the acceptable conditions thereof; the moral insolence of those who presume to prescribe the circumstances under which it is spiritually permissible to kill one's neighbors; the desensitization of human response to pain; the acquiescence in the inevitability of disaster; the cheapening of human personality with its concomitant of irresponsible fatalism—all these are part of an already existing, fast-swelling chamber of horrors.

It will be said that shelters and everything that goes with them are basic facts of nuclear war that do not disappear because we find them unpleasant. But this assumes there is no alternative. It assumes that everything has been done to prevent the holocaust from occurring in the first place. It assumes that we have no obligation to anyone except ourselves. Not until the individual declares a moratorium on the inconsequential in his life and invests himself fully in the effort to achieve a just and enforceable peace; indeed, not until the nation itself commits its moral energy, intelligence, and resources to a massive attempt to bolster the United Nations and give it appropriate powers of world law, however rigorous the opposition—not until these basic things are done is there warrant for defeatism. And even if these things are not done, there is never a warrant, social or spiritual, for cannibalism.

If we are truly interested in safeguarding this nation and the human values that go with it, we will scrutinize and memorize the nuclear facts of life. As a nation, we didn't fully understand the implications of these facts when we dropped the bomb on Hiroshima; we don't understand them yet. We have never quite comprehended that the use of such weapons constitutes a form of race suicide. It is impossible for any nation to wage nuclear war against another nation without also waging war against the human race. The winds are the conveyor belt of mass death. The nuclear gun contains three barrels: one is pointed against the enemy; a second is pointed against people who are not enemies; a third bends back completely and is pointed squarely at the holder.

An American demonstrates his patriotism not by pressuring for nuclear showdowns or by fast-and-loose talk about dropping hydrogen bombs but by tapping and putting to work the deepest wisdom the history of man has to offer. A new kind of force must be created which, when fully used, can safeguard this nation and its freedom and make a contribution to world peace in general. Military power no longer can accomplish that purpose.

President Kennedy's speech before the United Nations has the initial elements of that new kind of force. He made it clear that there is no security for anyone in a spiraling arms race; he called for total disarmament under adequate safeguards; he connected the need for disarmament to the need for establishing the institutions of world law: in short, he summoned the American people to a peace race. The full potential force of these words will be converted into a working program when the American people respond with depth and vigor. Earnest discussions among neighbors about their part in giving vital support to these ideas today may offer far more realistic protection for their families than shotguns for shooting down neighbors on a dreadful tomorrow.

If the battle for sanity and against cannibalism is lost, it will not be because of the inexorability of history but because men became so fascinated with the face of death that they lost hold of the meaning of life and the power inherent in it to shape its destiny.

III

The principal objections to the previous two editorials on fallout shelters came from those who said we missed the main point. They did not quarrel with the facts we advanced about the possible inadequacy of shelters. Their argument was directed to an issue completely separate from shelters per se. This is what they said:

The question of shelters is related to the war of nerves with the Soviet Union. The United States can afford to retreat no longer. If we back down on Berlin, it would be only a matter of months before an even larger threat would confront us. Therefore we have to make credible to the Russians the fact that we are prepared to fight for Berlin. We must mean it. We must not let them think we are so terrified of nuclear war that we don't have the nerve to fight. The Russians are scrutinizing us carefully for softness. If they see that the President really means business and is prepared to fight a nuclear war, and if they see that the American people are taking the possibility of nuclear war seriously and are not afraid to face up to it, they may not want to push us too far on the assumption we are bluffing. And a nationwide shelter-building program is the best evidence we can give them· that the American people have the will to fight and endure a nuclear war.

This is the whole point about fallout shelters. The facts in *Saturday Review* about firestorms and craters and suffocation hazards and bacteriological warfare may be true but they are irrelevant. In fact, they are dangerous. They are dangerous because they may dissuade people from building shelters. If this happens, it weakens our posture in dealing with the Russians.

The foregoing is a literal statement of the "credibility" theory. It is held by certain officials on the state and national levels. There is the candid admission that fallout shelters might not provide the protection as advertised, but the efficacy of the shelters is secondary to a strategical purpose. If one asks why this strategical purpose is not made clear to the American people as an intrinsic part of the argument for shelters, the answer one receives is that the people might not find it persuasive. It is felt they are not sufficiently sophisticated in complex questions involving strategical purpose and that only the hard line about personal and family safety is likely to work.

In a dictatorship, this kind of manipulation of public action and opinion might have some standing. In a free society, it is grotesquely out of place, and its advocates should be made to debate their propositions. It represents a surrender to the cynical view that only the few know what the many must believe and what they should be made to do. In this philosophy people cease to be people. They become pawns on a grand strategical chessboard to be deployed or sacrificed at the chessplayer's discretion. The American people may or may not agree with the reasoning of those who want to convince the Russians the United States is willing to fight a nuclear war, but they will not accept the proposition that they must become pawns in such an enterprise. Nor can they be expected to concur in the notion that their possible opposition to the credibility theory means they are unsophisticated about the complex problems of national survival.

Two issues are alive here. One is the irresponsibility and arrogance involved in a deliberate program of deceit and manipulation seeking to accomplish purposes that are not fully and directly stated. The other issue concerns the nature of the basic objectives and the quality of the reasoning behind them. The first issue needs no further exposition. We therefore proceed to the second.

The trouble with the credibility theory is that it makes the wrong things credible. It succeeds in convincing an enemy only that he must improve his nuclear capability to whatever point is necessary in order to cancel out a counter-move or possible advantage. Would United States policy makers change their position on Berlin or any other vital issue if the Russians began to build underground shelters both to prove to us that they really meant business and to increase their chances that some fraction of the population might survive after a nuclear war? Certainly not. Far from backing down on Berlin or any other issue involving our vital interests, we would make counter-moves to block or frustrate the Russian strategy. Our military people would resolutely produce nuclear weapons with ground-hugging, long-lived radioactivity characteristics. They would step up the production of firestorm-making nuclear bombs for the purpose of consuming oxygen and driving people from the shelters into the radioactive open. In short, we would regard the Russian strategy as a feeble ploy and hold fast to our position. Yet we expect that the Russians will be deflected or influenced by strategy that would not move us.

The big need today is not to make credible to the Russians that we are only a feather's touch from nuclear war, but to make credible to the world's peoples that the United States has the wisdom to match its power. Any major war between nuclear nations is also a war against the human race. It is impossible to confine the lethal radiation to the war zones. Since all people are involved, it stands to reason that we need to make credible to them our awareness of their rights and our sense of total responsibility in the pursuit of our vital interests.

We will never achieve true security in anything we do with or to the Russians. True security cannot be bought or contrived with nuclear power or with threats to use it. True security will be achieved in direct proportion to the reduction and elimination of anarchy in the dealings among nations. A country that commits itself fully to this objective and that pursues it with all the imagination and vigor at its command will be fashioning the only real protection available to it in the modern world.

IV

Dr. Willard F. Libby, former Atomic Energy Commissioner, has written a series of newspaper articles on fallout shelters in which he makes the following statement:

"Ninety to ninety-five per cent of us [will] survive, with proper protection."

If this statement is true, the national debate over shelters ends right here. Any system that can assure protection for at least nine out of ten Americans in a nuclear war is beyond argument.

If on the other hand, the statement is not true, then it clearly represents a profound act of public irresponsibility.

Consider the statement. It stands by itself in the newspaper article. It is not qualified. It does not attempt to correlate the number of casualties with the size and locations of a nuclear attack. It does not make a distinction between an attack directed at military targets and a generalized massive attack directed against population centers. It says nothing about chemical or bacteriological or radiological weapons which, according to the American military, will almost certainly be used in a nuclear war.

It says nothing about firestorms, causing shelters to collapse or converting them into incinerators. It says nothing about oxygen depletion in shelters during a *sustained* firestorm. It says nothing about the time of day an attack might occur. It does not say what would happen if the first wave of an attack came at a time of peak family dispersion, with fathers at work, children at school, and mothers at home or in the shops. It does not deal with the problem of warning time. It does not make known the fact that an adequate alert system does not now exist, or that enough mistakes have already been made in radar detection to emphasize existing imperfections in the system. It does not make known the fact that a nuclear attack would probably involve the large-scale use of missile decoys, absorbing a substantial part of a counter-missile defense effort. It says nothing about the possibility, which the Atomic Energy Commission itself has cited, that megaton explosives could be detonated many miles off the East and West coasts, and in the large lakes, inundating cities with radioactive wash.

This is not to say that, under certain circumstances, Dr. Libby's prediction might not be reasonably correct. What are these circumstances?

If an enemy decided to spare the cities, directing his attack at missile sites or at other strategic military centers; if he would expend for such a limited purpose no more, say, than 1,000 megatons; and assuming a warning system that gives people time to take cover, then substantial protection against short-term fallout danger is by no means impossible.

But Dr. Libby cannot guarantee that less than 1,000 megatons will be used. He has no way of knowing whether an enemy may hold to limited objectives though he possesses unlimited power. He cannot assure Americans that they will not be involved in a general nuclear war, utilizing upwards of

5,000 megatons of fission. Nor can he certify that an enemy, whom he regards as unscrupulous enough to hit us with nuclear weapons, will be too decent to switch from military targets to general targets if he feels he is losing the war.

And what if the United States has no intention, for its own part, of responding to a limited attack with a limited nuclear counterattack? What if the United States does not know the location of the enemy's launching sites, and has no choice but to wage a general nuclear war? Will an enemy hold to limited objectives while his own cities are being pulverized?

Even if we accept Dr. Libby's assumptions, this would probably involve an exchange of 2,000 megatons on both sides, with a terrible long-term radioactive reckoning awaiting the survivors. The short-term dangers of radioactivity might be met through fallout shelters, but people are not going to stay in their holes forever. When they come out, they will have no way of washing the sky of continuing fallout of radioactive poisons—strontium 90, cesium 137, carbon 14. These poisons produce leukemia and bone cancer, among other diseases. They attack the genes. The bomb at Hiroshima had a twenty-kiloton rating, or one-thousandth the rating of a twenty-megaton bomb. If the power of the Hiroshima bomb were to be represented on a scale as two feet, the fifty-megaton bomb would occupy one mile. Despite its relatively small size, the atomic bomb over Hiroshima produced a significant increase in the leukemia rate. Even now, sixteen years after the bombing, new leukemia cases traceable to the bomb are being reported every week in Hiroshima. What kind of toll will be exacted year after year following the explosion of 2,000 megatons of fission in a "limited" nuclear war?

Dr. Libby, as a former member of the U. S. Atomic Energy Commission, is familiar with the estimates of responsible scientists and military experts who contend that a general nuclear attack involving more than 7,500 megatons could convert the U. S. into a radioactive wasteland, with or without shelters.

Does a potential enemy have more than 7,500 megatons of fission at his disposal? He does. So does the United States. The total nuclear power available to all nuclear countries has been estimated to be well in excess of 60,000 megatons and is growing week by week.

What kind of weapons are part of this arsenal? What happens if they are used?

A twenty-megaton bomb, exploded fairly close to the surface of a large city such as New York, would produce a crater more than a half-mile wide and about 300 feet deep, causing the skyscrapers to disappear as though they had never existed.

It would be a mistake to assume that only one thermonuclear weapon would be used on a large city, although a large thermonuclear bomb could knock out any large city. In a general nuclear attack, several such bombs would be used. The average city basement or shelter would be meaningless. It would be like using a pneumatic drill against an anthill.

If a generalized nuclear attack made use of underwater explosives, these are the expectations envisioned by the U. S. Atomic Energy Commission:

A fifty-megaton burst at a depth of 2,700 feet in deep water would generate wave heights up to fifty feet against a shoreline 100 miles away.

A 100-megaton burst at about 4,000 feet in deep water would generate wave heights up to seventy feet against a shoreline 100 miles away.

The U. S. Atomic Energy Commission is also authority for the statement that a fifty-megaton burst in the lower atmosphere on a clear day would produce burns on the human retina up to 250 miles away.

It is, we repeat, an act of prime irresponsibility to lead the American people to believe that ninety-five per cent of them can be saved in their shelters. By the same token, neither can anyone say for certain that the full nuclear capability of an enemy will be used against the United States, destroying all life.

All that can or should be said is that there is a wide range of possibility in a nuclear war and that, lacking precise knowledge of the number and power of bombs that may be dropped, or where they will be dropped, or what chemical and radiological weapons may be employed in a varied attack, no assurances about a high or low level of safety in shelters can be made.

At the very least, some hard new thinking by government on the total shelter problem is indicated. In sounding the alarm that produced the stampede for shelters, it did not face up to madness that would ensue, nor the obvious injustices it would foster. Why should the size of a man's bank account have anything to do with his right to shelter protection? Moreover, if the danger of nuclear war is strong enough to dictate building home shelters, then that same danger should dictate that the cities be evacuated immediately, for there is no way of protecting them against a general nuclear attack. Similarly, the government ought to put a stop to the prodigious building of new glass skyscrapers in the large cities.

Finally, if a shelter program has any validity at all, the government cannot dodge its central place in the picture. The idea that each citizen should be individually responsible for his own shelter is as absurd and unworkable as expecting him to be responsible for his own electric supply or his own roads. Safety from attack is a government function. If it is not a government function, then nothing is.

Dr. Libby, however, insists that the individual be put on his own. He told a California audience the other day that he is resolutely opposed to the use of public funds for shelters. "If I were President," he was quoted as saying, "I would declare martial law and force everyone to prepare his own shelter."

Meanwhile, however, Dr. Libby is not President and martial law has not yet been declared. It is still permissible to ask questions, or even to raise the roof with public officials, present or retired, when what they say or do adds up to dangerous nonsense.

Also, it is still possible to consider fully the most important question of all: Where can we best put our energy, intelligence, and money to work in the cause of the national security, and, not to be unsentimental about it, in the cause of a world made safe for people?

The issue is not whether the American people should or should not protect themselves against possible disaster. Of course they should. The issue is whether the American people are entitled to full, honest information about the nature of the anticipated disaster and the problems involved in adequate protection. The issue, also, is whether it is too late to avoid a nuclear war without sacrifice of security or freedom.

We believe it is not too late, although it has never been later. The fact of Russia is a dominant fact, but it is not the predominant fact. The predominant fact is that peace cannot be found if we look for it in the wrong place. The wrong place is the arena of anarchy, filled with jostling and volatile national sovereignties. The right place is the arena of world law in which a structured peace can be built. The mere attempt to build such a peace is no assurance that it can be done. But the sheer fact of the attempt itself creates a rallying ground that may provide the best interim shelter available.

Erich Fromm & Michael Maccoby | The Question of Civil Defense
A Reply to Herman Kahn

Up until 1961 few Americans took the possibility of nuclear war very seriously. Many were convinced that such a war would never occur because it would be too destructive; others did not think about it at all. The change which took place in 1961 was brought about in the first instance by the acute Berlin crisis and President Kennedy's speech of July 25. The President told the nation after his Vienna meeting with Khrushchev that the Soviet leader had threatened to execute his Berlin plans within six months at the most, and since we were resolved not to accept such an ultimatum, the inference was that a thermonuclear war was a definite possibility before the end of the year. The President added in this context that he would announce the steps a citizen could "take without delay to protect his family in the case of an attack," and proposed a new $207-million shelter program.

The President's speech might not have been so effective had the soil not been prepared by the most vocal and most influential spokesman for civil defense, Herman Kahn, and a number of his colleagues, especially from the RAND Corporation. Mr. Kahn's basic approach can be described as being close to psychoanalysis. Not so much because he makes many statements about psychological matters (such as the quality and duration of grief, the discipline of people during and after a nuclear attack, the capacity to be happy in the post-attack world, etc.), but primarily because his central thesis is that, out of fear, people repress the awareness that thermonuclear war may come, and consequently they ignore the possibilities of defense. Hence in order to enable them to prepare adequately, the thing to do is to make them aware that a thermonuclear war can occur. No psychoanalyst could quarrel with this principle. The question is only whether an awareness that thermonuclear war is actually possible leads to an increased sense of realism or whether, as we believe, old illusions are replaced by even more dangerous ones. Kahn, whose good will and great ability we do not doubt, has on the whole given the opinion leaders and the political leaders of this country the impression that nuclear war need by no means be catastrophic—that, provided we take the proper steps, the country can recover, and that after ten or twenty years people can once again lead happy and prosperous lives. He has, indeed, qualified this general thesis by many "ifs," but it is the general thesis that has taken hold, while the qualifications have become the fine print which is forgotten.

There are two conceptions of the role of civil defense and, specifically, of a shelter program. The first—stressed in Kahn's testimony last August before the Holifield Committee [1] and also in President Kennedy's speech of May 25—sees the shelter program as "life insurance," and argues for it on the ground that it would save many millions of lives. At present the assumption is made that fallout shelters might save not only lives in rural areas, but also in the cities—since it is calculated that the Soviets are not likely to attack our cities. As we shall try to show later, this calculation is quite unwarranted, and the probability is that our urban population would be wiped out in a thermonuclear war. However, since millions of people living in rural areas away from population centers and military installations might be saved by fallout shelters, and since nuclear war is possible or even likely to occur, who would dare to dissuade a family or a community from constructing fallout shelters? We certainly would not.

Quite different from the "insurance" idea is the conception of civil defense as part of our *national strategy*. Many spokes-

[1] "Hearings Before a Sub-Committee of the Committee of Government Operations," House of Representatives, August 1961. All quotations in this article, unless otherwise designated, are from the record of these hearings.

men for civil defense contend that it will greatly improve our strategic position, that it may help to avert war. We shall try to show: (1) that there are severe limitations to the effectiveness of civil defense; (2) that is it more likely to provoke war than to deter it; (3) that even if it were optimally successful in war, it would not prevent the replacement of our democratic system by a totalitarian one. If we are right on these points, then even the justification of civil defense as "insurance" may have to be reconsidered. The true situation may be analogous to one in which a man takes out life insurance under conditions that considerably increase the likelihood of his death. In such a case, one might still not try to dissuade him if he wished to buy insurance, but certainly he and his friends would be right to have severe doubts about its usefulness.

The first and most fundamental limitation of any shelter program is that it could not save our urban population in the event of an attack against our cities. Rather than frankly accepting this fact, Kahn and other advocates of civil defense argue that if the Russians strike first they will try to destroy our missile and SAC bases, *not* our cities. Given such a strike, the greatest danger to those city dwellers fortunate enough to be living well away from strategic centers would be from delayed fallout, and thus fallout shelters might lower the immediate death toll from fifty to ten million people.[2]

On what grounds do strategists suppose that the Russians would not direct a first strike against our population centers? Kahn, in his book *On Thermonuclear War,* gives several reasons: (1) they have so few missiles that they would have to choose between attacking our military installations *or* our cities, and therefore in order to neutralize our striking power they would choose to hit our military installations; (2) they would not wish to attack our cities first, in order to hold them as hostages against our retaliatory strike; (3) "almost nobody

[2] This calculation assumes a strike with a yield no larger than 3,000 megatons, in spite of the fact that we have the power to launch over 40,000 megatons, and there is no proof that the Russians are behind us.

wants to go down in history as the first man to kill 100,000,000 people."

The weakness of Kahn's first point lies in its shortsightedness. Since it will take no less than a year for even a minimal civil defense program to bear fruit, calculations ought to be made not on the basis of present Russian missile strength, but on the number of missiles the Soviets may have a year or two from now. In addition, even if they did decide to make our military installations their main target, the Soviets might kill an additional 50 million people by diverting only a fraction of their missile strength to our ten largest population centers. (This is the kind of attack Kahn calls "counterforce plus bonus.") Further, we have so increased our strength in the past year that a successful attack against our bases would no longer cripple our retaliatory power. The Russians would thus be foolish to limit their attack to our military installations, knowing that their own cities would remain as hostages.

As to the second point—that they would avoid hitting our cities in order to hold them as hostages—Kahn imagines that after having destroyed our military bases, they would command us not to strike their cities on pain of having our own cities destroyed in retaliation. But is it realistic to assume that after the destruction of our military installations and the death of ten to fifteen million people, the Russians would expect our government to wait and listen to their demands rather than to use all its strength immediately in a mood of fury and revenge against the Russian cities?

And finally, as for the reluctance of a political leader to go down in history as the first man to kill 100,000,000 people, such considerations did not interfere with the decision to saturate cities with bombs during the Second World War; nor did they restrain the dropping of atomic bombs on Hiroshima and Nagasaki. Why then should we expect the force of moral considerations to be greater now when the survival of entire nations is at stake?

All this, it should be added, applies only to a first strike by the Russians. *If we were to initiate a first strike*—in retaliation for, say, a Soviet invasion of West Berlin—the Russians would not hit back at our empty bases; clearly, they would attack our cities.

Assuming, then, that our cities were attacked, what chance of survival would the urban population have? Almost none, given the effects of the megaton weapons. A 20-megaton groundburst leaves a crater 300 feet deep and a half mile in radius, destroying all underground shelters. Within a four-mile radius, the most heavily reinforced concrete structures are leveled. At eleven miles, the blast pressure destroys all conventional frame or brick buildings, and buries most basement fallout shelters, while winds of 160 miles per hour turn hurtling debris and human bodies into deadly missiles.

But blast is the least of the killers in thermonuclear war; fire, instant radiation, and delayed fallout would claim many more lives. Within at least a twenty-five-mile radius of a 20-megaton blast—an area of about 2,000 square miles—any exposed person would die of burns, and raging fires would soon begin to consume the air in fallout and blast shelters.[3] As long as there was fuel for these fires, they would burn on, unchecked. Even more widespread in its potential effect is the danger of blindness to those above ground at the moment of blast; anyone who glimpsed the explosion would be blinded, for it would emit a light pulse at less than 0.015 second (the time needed for a saving eye-blink).

While in the city itself almost nobody could survive, people living in the suburbs—even if they escaped instantaneous effects of blast, flying debris, heat, blindness, and radiation—would still be threatened by delayed fallout. At twenty-five miles from a 20-megaton explosion one might expect doses of 3,000 roentgens per hour arriving after about twenty minutes —enough to kill a person within two minutes, unless he were in a specially constructed fallout shelter. If he could succeed in reaching a shelter with a large shielding factor within twenty-two minutes after the blast, and if he could avoid

[3] In the fire-bombing of Hamburg during World War II, the firestorm caused a ground temperature of 1,400 degrees Fahrenheit in which all exposed humans were incinerated, while those in shelters were asphyxiated or burned.

glimpsing the fireball, a hard fight for survival would then have only begun.

What about saving the urban population by *evacuation?* While many reject the idea of evacuation, others (including Kahn) consider it a serious possibility. It is hard to see why. If we were to evacuate our cities for every political crisis, we would probably have to leave them empty for several months practically every year. Even if this were feasible (which it is not), after one or two such evacuations no one would leave, for the warning signal would come to be considered a repeated cry of "wolf." Further, every time we evacuated, we would give the Russians a reason for supposing that we were planning a first strike, and hence the chances of a preemptive attack would increase. As to evacuating cities *after* a warning, fifteen minutes would obviously not be enough time if the Russians struck first. If, on the other hand, *we* wanted to strike first, it would require many hours at the very least to evacuate all our major cities, and since such a move would be impossible to conceal from the Russians, they would obviously not wait for our attack, but would hasten to hit us first. At best we might secretly evacuate our leaders before striking, but how many of them would be willing to leave for safety knowing that their wives and children would soon be killed?

Finally, let us consider the possibility of protecting our urban population by vast underground shelters (which have also been proposed by certain enthusiasts of civil defense). In the case of a surprise attack it would take more than fifteen minutes to get people down to the streets from big offices and apartment buildings. The panic, and the struggle for elevators, doors, and the like could only result in the same kind of situation that arises in a theater when fire breaks out. Even if there were a shelter entrance not further than five minutes' brisk walk from any point in the city, it takes little imagination to visualize how many people would be trampled to death before reaching the shelter, and how few—even of the strongest and most brutal—would be saved.

If everyone in the city and its suburbs is likely to be killed, what are the chances for survival beyond the twenty-five-mile range? Here fallout would be the greatest menace. In some areas—say fifty miles from the blast—it would probably be necessary to remain in a fallout shelter for at least two weeks, and afterward it would be possible to leave it for only a few hours each week. How many people would find themselves in this situation depends on the magnitude of the attack, and on the amount of fallout generated by megaton bombs—something the experts have still not agreed upon. A problem in making any calculation is the lack of studies which outline exact fallout danger at different distances from the blast, or in accordance with various possible attacks. Neither are there sufficient data on the effects of other radioactive particles—for instance strontium 90, which might make farming impossible anywhere in the country. There are experts who think that many farmlands might require forty replantings before becoming safe again, and no one has disproved this estimate. Norman A. Hanunian of the RAND Corporation, who prepared the statistics on heavy attacks used by Kahn in his book, concludes his testimony to the Holifield Committee by stating that "the outcomes of future attacks are anything but precisely predictable. Fallout could create overwhelming disaster, but it might not. Whether it would depends to some extent on factors we have not examined today—on wind, for example. But it depends most importantly on the kind of war that the potential combatants may be prepared to fight." What kind of war can we expect? Ralph E. Lapp has written that present Soviet stockpiles are more than adequate for a 10,000- or 20,000-megaton attack, enough to saturate the whole nation with fallout.

Hanunian considers attacks of from 300 to 30,000 megatons, but the latter, as we have just seen, seems closer to Russian capability. In such an attack, with five-sixths of the bombs directed against military targets, Hanunian estimates that even a total fallout shelter system would be unable to prevent from 54 to 85 million people from being killed. What the experts have so far not studied are the *long-range effects* of 30,000-megaton bombings, which might so contaminate the countryside as to leave crops inedible, unstored water undrinkable, and food-giving animals dead from radioactivity. If a 30,000-megaton attack were to take place—as indeed is possible—what would become of Kahn's optimistic idea of the "B country" (the rural areas and the small towns) rebuilding the "A country" (the fifty-three major metropolitan areas)?

In summing up our discussion of the limitations of civil defense, let us take a brief look at the possible types of shelter program and try to determine how effective each is likely to be in the event of the kind of war we consider most probable —a war involving attacks on our cities, either directly or as "bonus."

The effectiveness of the current minimal program of marking and stocking shelter space mainly in urban areas would be most limited—except in the unlikely case that the enemy were to decide against attacking even the ten largest cities.

The next possible program—proposed by Walmar Strope of the Naval Radiological Defense Laboratories—is the $10- to $30-billion network of well-stocked communal fallout shelters built to house everyone in both rural and urban areas. In our opinion, these shelters could not protect the population of the cities. Perhaps in suburban areas twenty miles or more away from the explosions, some people could be saved (provided, of course, that they were well-organized, disciplined, and able to weather severe stress and disease). However, it does seem to be true that, depending on the type of attack, the time of day, and many other unpredictable circumstances, this program could save a large proportion of the rural population.

A final possibility is the science-fiction program that Kahn has suggested, which would cost $200 billion. This envisages underground space for factories and urban blast protection that could—as Kahn puts it in On Thermonuclear War—"probably take direct hits of 'small' bombs (say less than five MT) and [might] even take 'near' misses of 'large' bombs." Yet even after spending so much we would still have no security: since it is infinitely cheaper to increase striking power than it is to raise the level of protection, even the most hardened shelter cannot guarantee safety. If there were a possibility of adequate shelter, it would be found only in underground cities where we would have to live permanently. Is this troglodytic life the fulfillment of the American Dream?

Assuming, with all the qualifications introduced above, that a complete and thorough shelter program could save millions of people *in rural areas*, what would post-attack life be like for the survivors—psychologically, morally, economically, and politically? The situation in the shelters, of course, would vary with the different types of shelter and the amount of fallout in the particular locale. Privately owned luxury shelters would be comfortable, provided they were defended successfully and would-be intruders did not retaliate by blocking the air vents. In the public shelters, the danger of overcrowding would exist, especially if the program were not completed before the attack came. Moreover, we should expect that in many communal shelters disease and meager rations would exact a psychological toll.[4] People might have radios, which would boost their morale (provided transmitting stations were not destroyed), but this might also be offset by hearing that all big cities had been leveled, and that there was widespread disease. Further, unless the attack were to have occurred at night, many families would have been separated, with people not knowing whether their wives, husbands, or children had found protection. Given all these conditions, what would be the state of mind of those in the shelters, immediately after the attack and for some time to come?

Kahn's answer to this question is very optimistic.

> It is my personal belief, *he told the Holifield Committe,* speaking less as an expert than as a man who has read widely, that these problems [social, psychological, political, and moral questions] have been grossly exaggerated. Most people will not be psychologically deranged. One is not, for example, going to break up family

[4] This expectation runs contrary to the experiment of the Naval Radiological Defense Laboratories showing "positive" reactions and "considerable satisfaction in the communal experience" after two weeks. But the NRDL's study has limited applicability; the subjects were volunteer prison convicts who could leave at any time, and are therefore not comparable to survivors, fearful of surfacing to death, chaos, and despair, yet stifling in cramped quarters while they remain sheltered.

relations by a war. The family relation is a very stable one. . . . One is not even going to obliterate the fact that people are Americans. By and large, they will be about as honest, hard-working, reliable, and responsible as they are today. While everybody's life and thoughts will be affected by the war the character structure of the survivors is unlikely to be changed in any startling fashion.

In his testimony Kahn also speaks about "post-attack grief" and argues against the notion many people have that "because of the enormous number of casualties, all of the pleasure, all of the taste will permanently go out of life for almost everybody." "As far as I know," he says, "that just hasn't happened in anything that has occurred before, and one would not expect it to happen even as a result of a large thermonuclear war." One reason for believing that it would not happen is that "in a sense, grief is family-sized. If one loses a close relative or close friend, one will grieve. If one loses one's family, one will grieve even more. But, in some sense, that is about as far as one can go. Most people would not mourn for a million people much more than they would mourn for their family." Kahn also claims (in *On Thermonuclear War*) that a shock spaced over a few days "is good, not bad" so far as its psychological effects are concerned, because "the habits of a lifetime cannot be changed for most people in a few days." And here, finally, is how he summarizes his conclusions as to the psychological effect of a thermonuclear war in his book: "Despite a widespread belief to the contrary, objective studies indicate that even though the amount of human tragedy would be greatly increased in the postwar world, the increase would not preclude normal and happy lives for the majority of the survivors and their descendants."

Bearing in mind that Kahn himself states explicitly that he does not speak as an expert on such matters, and that he also says that the disaster studies which have been made are not sufficient to establish his case on solid scientific grounds, let us now consider the picture he paints of the post-attack psychological situation.

To begin with, the problem of post-attack psychic shock is

not one of families breaking up. The problem is how those families that would not be broken up would react to the break-up of the whole world around them. Kahn believes that the character structure of the survivors would probably not be "changed in any startling fashion," but he fails to say why he believes so, and his patriotic appeal to the fact that "people are Americans" is not an adequate substitute for good reasoning. Indeed, one might more plausibly assume that non-Americans accustomed to totalitarian discipline would, if anything, be less radically affected than the average American. Moreover, the notion that sudden shock is less far-reaching in its effects than prolonged suffering is totally indefensible. Vast psychiatric experience and a huge body of literature are there to show that traumatic neuroses are produced both in peace and war by sudden fright and by tension of an intensity which transcends the amount our nervous system can tolerate. Such neuroses can result in severe depression, suicidal tendencies, self-accusations, amnesia and disorientation, and states of anxiety—all of which may persist for many years. To be sure, long-lasting states of despair can also produce severe psychic damage, but to ignore (as Kahn does) the effect of sudden shocks of great intensity is only to make the picture rosier than it really is.

The experts testifying last August at the Holifield Committee hearings on civil defense tell us that no disaster study yet made reports the psychological consequences of devastation as wide and as great as would result from a thermonuclear war. We, however, would like to recommend to Kahn and his colleagues that they look into one disaster which *has* been studied, and which *is* comparable to a thermonuclear war in terms of loss of life and disruption of society: the Black Death of 1348–1349. As the distinguished historian William L. Langer writes, the Black Death was "the greatest single disaster that has ever befallen European mankind. In most localities a third or even half of the population was lost within the space of a few months. . . ." [5] Particularly relevant in the

[5] "The Next Assignment," *The American Historical Review*, January 1958.

context of the present discussion is the fact that the cities were the hardest hit by the Black Death. Professor Langer notes that with the Black Death the phenomenal economic progress of the 13th century came to a halt, followed by a prolonged depression, but he also feels that in some sense the economic effects were secondary to the long-range psychological consequences of those mass deaths. He writes that "the horror and confusion in many places brought general demoralization and social breakdown. Criminal elements were quick to take over, looting the deserted houses and even murdering the sick to rob them of their jewels." The period after the crisis was marked "by a mood of misery, depression, and anxiety, and by a general sense of impending doom," so much so that it has been suggested that people hesitated to marry and raise a family. (According to reports, this has also been true of the survivors of Hiroshima.) Langer's summation seems to us remarkably applicable to the most likely outcome of a thermonuclear war:

> It is perfectly clear that disaster and death threatening an entire community will bring on a mass emotional disturbance, based on a feeling of helpless exposure, disorientation, and common guilt. Furthermore, it seems altogether plausible to suppose that children, having experienced the terror of their parents and the panic of the community will react to succeeding crises in a similar but even more intense manner. In other words, the anxiety and fear are transmitted from one generation to another, constantly aggravated.

Which brings us to Kahn's idea that grief is "family-sized." The trouble with this idea is that grief is not the only problem when a thermonuclear war is in question. We must remember that the survivors would witness a sudden tearing apart of the whole fabric of society. For most people, the sense of stability, and even of their own identity, rests on the meaning society gives to their lives. What then might we expect would happen to men if everything that seemed to be certain became completely unstable within a matter of hours? Previous wars supply no precedent for such a situation. The soldier was of course exposed to great stresses, but life remained stable for him precisely because he knew that his family and the rest of society were still relatively unchanged. In thermonuclear war, however, no part of the social fabric would remain stable. Half of the population killed; most of the leaders gone; no transportation; unburied corpses; epidemics; no communications, electricity, or water supply; divided families; many months necessary to create the minimum conditions for renewing a semblance of life as it was previously known—and for what? What sense would life make? What hope would there be? How much fury would be generated in those who had fared worse than others? How many would blame themselves for being alive when others were dead? What would be the reaction of those who were just managing to get by when refugees turned up to be fed? How much rage would there be against the leaders or scapegoats who would be held responsible for having brought the war on? No, for the majority of people the problem would not only be grief, but the destruction of a way of life which had given meaning to their efforts, which had produced a sense of identity, as well as a sense of hope for the future.

If these would be the psychological effects of thermonuclear war, what shall we say about the *moral* consequences of such a war? Keeping in mind the fact that morality, like psychology, is in large part socially conditioned—that individual morality existing without support from the community is rare—let us try to imagine what the postwar moral atmosphere would look like. Let us imagine a situation in which millions of innocent people have been horribly killed; in which we may have defended our own safety by letting our neighbors die; in which we may have to fight for our minimum standards of living against thousands who come into our area to be fed and sheltered; in which we are envious of those who protected themselves better than we did; in which we are frightened and resentful of those who made thermonuclear war seem palatable and possible. What sort of ethics would develop in such a situation—something similar to a belief in God, in brotherly love, and in freedom, or the ethics of the jungle and the concentration camp? The question very nearly answers itself. Is it not indicative that even now people speak of the duty to defend their shelters with guns against those who have been less "provident" (or affluent), and that at least one "man of God" has said that such actions do not contradict Christian teaching? Yet not only do they contradict Christian teaching, they even contradict the ethics of military behavior which command the individual soldier to risk his own life in order to save his fellow-soldiers. In the light of all this, it seems quite obvious—and even the experts sometimes vaguely hint at it—that post-attack life would be possible only under a military dictatorship which used force to uphold even a minimum of social responsibility. Not morality but martial law would be the basis for whatever vestige of civilized behavior might survive a nuclear war.

In talking about recuperation, Kahn occasionally draws on the experience of the last two wars. Millions of people were killed, he points out, and billions were destroyed in property value, yet only a few years later things had more or less returned to normal, and most of the survivors were again leading "happy" and moral lives. This is simply not the case. The history of man since the First World War, though still to be written, would show an increasing brutalization; it would demonstrate that brutalization, approved by society, leads to further brutalization. The slaughter of the First World War was senseless; in contrast to the belief that this was the war to end all wars and to establish democracy, it was in fact fought for territorial aggrandizement and the ambitions of the contending political leaders. In that war, for the first time in modern history, a recognized moral principle—that unarmed civilians must not be attacked—was violated by the aerial bombardment of cities on both sides. Then came the state-approved massacres of Stalin and of Hitler, which were allowed to take place with astonishingly little moral protest, except for the kind motivated by political considerations. Finally—let us at any rate hope that it is the final development —came the indiscriminate slaughter of civilians in the Second World War, first by the Nazis, then by the Allies in the mass bombing of German and Japanese cities. What we see here—to use a favorite term of the atomic strategists—is the "escalation" of brutality from 1914 to 1945; if it were not for this escalation, these same strategists would not be able to write about forty or sixty million dead being "acceptable," nor would anyone be able to take such reasoning as "normal." The very fact that a balance sheet of death can today be calmly drawn up is the result of the brutalizing influence of two world wars and the systems of terror that have operated in our time. Many experts are unaware of the degree to which this brutalization is contained in the very discussion of the "acceptability" of killing fifty million people on each side, and they are equally unaware of the further brutalization which a thermonuclear war would produce. Moral development, indeed, is always the moral development of a society, and when a society commands mass murder and mass suicide, only very few will be able to hold fast to Judeo-Christian or humanist ethics.

Let us next consider how a thermonuclear war would affect the *economic* situation of the country. Kahn's estimates here, as in the psychological realm, are quite cheering. It is his thesis in *On Thermonuclear War* that "if proper preparations have been made, it would be possible for us or the Soviets to cope with all the effects of a thermonuclear war, in the sense of saving most people and restoring something close to the prewar standard of living in a relatively short time. But there is no reason to believe this will be true unless both nations investigate the problem more thoroughly than has been done so far, and then take the necessary preparations." S. G. Winter, an economist of the RAND Corporation, in his testimony before the August hearings of the Holifield Committee, is equally optimistic. If his assumptions are valid, he says, "it turns out that capacity is back to the 470 million level in just over a decade."

But what are the premises on which these estimates rest? In Kahn's case, the premise (as expressed in his book) is that we succeed in holding damage down to the equivalent of something like 53 metropolitan areas destroyed, and that "seven optimistic assumptions" materialize: "1—Favorable political environment. 2—Immediate survival and patch-up. 3—Maintenance of economic momentum. 4—Specific bottlenecks alleviated. 5—'Bourgeois' virtues survive. 6—Workable postwar standards adopted. 7—Neglected effects unimportant." Why these optimal conditions should all be fulfilled, neither Kahn nor Winter makes clear.

Winter arrives at his hopeful diagnosis by thus qualifying all his conclusions: "The issues are too complex to be fully understood, and consequently there is no possibility of providing answers that are beyond reasonable challenge." "No amount of research," he continues, "is likely to alter the fact that decisions will finally have to be based on a large measure of faith in, or skepticism about, the basic strength or resilience of the people and institutions of our Nation." However, he goes on to admit in discussing the research concerning economic recovery: "A good deal of competent and important work has been done, *but it does not really scratch the surface of this vast problem* and there is in particular, a definite need for a systematic and comprehensive re-examination of the whole problem." [Our italics.]

Such, then, is the scientific basis for the bright outlook of Kahn and Winter.

The picture grows even darker when we study the conditions Winter specifies for avoiding "complete failure in the recovery effort." Such failure would occur if "the effectiveness of the federal government and many state governments is greatly diminished, the banking system disrupted, most surviving firms are bankrupt, electric power and water supply systems are severely damaged, and the transportation network broken in many places, and where few survivors have the responsibility, authority, and plans to do anything about it." Is it not likely that this is precisely what would occur, even with a vast civil defense program? Another condition for recovery is a release from the necessity of spending money on rearmament; that is, the war must "produce a substantial or fairly permanent reduction in the external threat." How could this be expected to happen? If we were to have destroyed

Russian military power, China and other nations probably would still have escaped the worst of the war, and might by then have acquired nuclear weapons. Or are we to assume that after a war we would get universal disarmament, which now appears impossible?

There is yet a further condition which Winter believes important for a rapid recovery and the avoiding of bottlenecks: the willingness and ability of foreign nations to trade with us, and even to provide assistance for our reconstruction. This assumes, apparently, that the European countries and Japan would not have been involved in the war, for what other nations would trade with us or give us assistance? The Soviet Union? China? Australia and New Zealand? Or Latin America, which needs our assistance now? Eventually, Winter adds another condition to his prognosis for recovery: that all analysis of the economic problems hinges on relatively optimistic answers to the psychological problems that would arise in the post-attack situation. If this is the case, then it seems to us that the whole prognosis rests on a house of cards, many of which are themselves shaky, being made up as they are of questionable or improbable premises.

Apart from all this, both Kahn and Winter take insufficient account of the *interaction* of the various disasters that would result from a thermonuclear attack. To mention only a few such interactions: people would need instruction by radio, but most transmitters might be destroyed; people would need hospitals, but most would probably be demolished; certain injuries would have to be treated by extensive washing, but not enough water would be available; the dead would have to be buried in heavy fallout areas, but no one would be able to leave the shelter without getting lethal doses of radiation himself, while the bulldozers which, according to Kahn, might be necessary for mass burials would not be available. Our whole mechanized agriculture depends on gasoline, but the refineries situated near population centers (which make up two-thirds of all refineries in this country) might be destroyed; how could the remaining one-third be made sufficient to supply all agricultural and other needs? Winter, in answering questions after his testimony, was forced to admit that his optimistic calculations are based on the premise of an uninterrupted national transportation system. What value has an analysis of economic recovery that depends on such unrealistic assumptions?

If we bring some of the factors neglected by Kahn and Winter into the picture, what would the economic situation after a thermonuclear war look like? Let us assume that all urban centers, more than half (at the least) of the "survival industry," and two-thirds of the heavy industries are bankrupt. Many of their stockholders, who had lived in cities, are dead. Their stocks and bonds have been burned. Under such circumstances how many would be able to prove property rights? What about money in banks whose books had been destroyed by fire? Winter tells us that "a number of financial institutions are microfilming their vital records . . . but this is not by any means universal." Others, according to the same testimony, would be able to microfilm and store records in a safe place "if they had a day or two of warning." But what about the records of small firms and of individual wills, all of which would be destroyed in the population centers? We must expect that a disappearance of paper from our highly complex economy would wreak havoc with private property.

But even if it turned out to be possible to find records of ownership, another and much more serious threat to the free enterprise system would arise. Some parts of the country would be less devastated than others and would have to help those in worse condition. This could be done only if the state took over the economy and divided goods according to need. Even accepting Winter's optimistic estimate of recovery on the basis of a twenty-five per cent rate of growth in order to build up destroyed industries, the state would have to control capital investment, and manufacturing would have to be centrally directed in order to secure the production of the most vital necessities. Even if half the population and half the industrial plant were not destroyed, much of our capitalist economy would have to be replaced by a state-directed, centrally managed industrial system. Whether this system would be managed by a small group of industrialists or by the state, and whether individuals would to some extent retain nominal ownership while the state took over ownership of a large chunk of the national wealth, of one thing we can be sure: even the most favorable possible outcome of a thermonuclear war would lead to a centrally controlled managerialism. We have to consider, in addition, that the severe sacrifices and discipline necessary to recovery would make it imperative to introduce a system of total control not only of production, but of the population. To be sure, such a system might be imposed in the name of freedom rather than by martial law, but it would be totalitarianism all the same. The fact is, then, that even a "successful" thermonuclear war would leave the survivors with a political and economic system not too different from the one we are supposed to be fighting. The alternative, in other words, would not be "better dead than red" but "better red than 'red.'"

If no civil defense program can save our cities or the fabric of our society from the ravages of a thermonuclear war, can an extensive system of shelters nevertheless serve as a deterrent to the enemy? There are two very different forms of deterrence: deterrence *against attack,* and deterrence against *political provocation* (Deterrence I and II in Kahn's terminology). No one claims that shelters would deter an enemy from attacking us first, and President Kennedy has stated explicitly that civil defense "cannot deter a nuclear attack"; according to most experts, the only *attack deterrence* is a powerful second-strike (or retaliatory) capability. But what about *political deterrence*, the attempt to restrain the enemy from political provocations by threatening to strike him first?

According to Kahn and others, civil defense makes it more credible to the enemy that we might strike first; if we cannot protect ourselves against a retaliatory strike, the enemy might call our bluff, discounting the possibility that we would risk our population merely to defend, for example, access routes to Berlin.

Though—as we have seen—civil defense would not save our

cities and would even in the "best" case leave us with 50 to 70 million dead, it can be admitted that a shelter program does increase our first-strike credibility and thus improves our political deterrence. However, the enemy must still become convinced of our willingness to make such a sacrifice, and we are therefore forced to gamble on whether *he* would believe that a particular political aim was important enough for us to accept destruction of these dimensions. (As Kahn himself points out, most of our leaders would not start a war if they expected to lose more than 60 million American lives.)

But in addition to this, civil defense tends to provoke war precisely *because* it improves our political deterrence. The more credible we make our resolve to strike first, the more the Russians will expect us to attack during a crisis, and hence the more they will be likely to launch a preemptive strike. (Kahn himself writes in his book: "The one circumstance under which almost all Soviet experts agree the Russians might strike is the one in which they anticipate a strike from us.") Our own fear of Russian preemption will in turn make us more prone to strike first, and so on up the spiral. Thus, to the extent that our first-strike capacity becomes more credible, Russian preemption becomes more likely; in balance-sheet language, what we gain in political deterrence we pay for in an increased probability of war.

Aside from the war-provoking aspect of first-strike credibility, a large civil defense program tends to indicate that we are getting ready for war, and this might start a vicious circle of preparations, counter weapons, and counter preparations—which would have the combined effect of hastening the onset of war. Even if we could build a system of civil defense so perfect that it would reduce fatalities to the 3–5 million range—a prospect that at the moment seems no more than a dream—is it likely that the Russians would sit back while we were making ourselves invulnerable enough to force them into any concessions we chose? Notwithstanding our second-strike capability, they might attack before we had gotten very far in building our fortress. For, as Kahn points out, they tend to view strategy more in terms of chess than poker—and in chess

one exchanges queens in order to maintain a tactical position
that will otherwise deteriorate.[6]

Another way in which even a national fallout shelter program could increase the chances of war is by lulling the nation
into a false sense of security. We are even now being led to
believe the claims of *Life* magazine or Dr. Edward Teller, that
with some fallout protection most people could survive a
thermonuclear war, while the probable fate of our cities is
hardly publicized. To support this illusion of safety, all the
tricks of modern advertising are being drawn upon: gay pictures of teen-agers chatting in shelters, survival statistics based
on minimal attacks against military installations, claims of
overwhelming military superiority on our side, and even appeals to individuality and the spirit of the old frontier, as
though winning a thermonuclear war were a matter of showing manly courage. Thus Kahn says that "We are in a position
much like the pioneer. He had to carry a gun because the
Indians might attack him." (This analogy makes sense only
if one substitutes "neighbors" for "Indians.") Under the spell
of this false sense of security the American people may become more willing to support an adventurist military policy
rather than more fervent in demanding disarmament negotiations, just as our leaders may become less hesitant about
pushing their terrible buttons.

The belief that thermonuclear war need not be catastrophic
increases the possibilities of thermonuclear war. As Walter
Millis wrote in reviewing *On Thermonuclear War*, "Unless
thermonuclear war can be re-established in the official mind
as something which it is possible both to fight and to survive,
it is unlikely that there will be a thermonuclear war." We
share with Millis the opinion that thermonuclear war has been
avoided until now because neither side believed that it was
possible to survive such a war. Once it is accepted that thermonuclear war is essentially no more catastrophic than past

[6] Kahn himself comprehends the war-provoking aspect of a large civil
defense program, and suggests that even a nationwide program of
community fallout shelters should be constructed slowly, so as not to
"seriously perturb our own people, our allies, and the Rusisans."

"conventional" wars, a major restraint will be gone. It is precisely for this reason that we consider it so dangerous to underemphasize the fantastic damage that a thermonuclear war would surely bring about.

Suppose, however, that we are mistaken in our arguments and that Kahn's most optimistic estimates are right. What would the future look like in that case? We would have a totally effective civil defense program, and so—it must be assumed—would the Russians. The stabilized deterrent would work and war would be avoided for the next ten years, or, if a war came, only 3 to 5 per cent of the population of each side would be killed. But where are we then? Each new generation of weapons becomes more destructive; people get more frightened; the protection that shelters may give today will be useless against the much more destructive weapons of 1970. The shelter idea, adopted, may logically lead to building our cities underground, or—as has been seriously suggested—to selecting small numbers of people to live in such deeply buried shelters that they would be sure to survive; thus a new nation might be built up from a few thousand survivors. Against even this last hope for survival, Kahn admits that ten years from now we, or another nation, might develop a "doomsday machine" which could literally wipe out all life on this globe. What use, then, is even a good shelter program now if it will not halt the march toward doomsday? Or are we to believe that after a thermonuclear war in which only 3 per cent of the population has been killed, the leaders will gain enough wisdom to decide on complete disarmament?

To sum up: in debating the position of Kahn and other experts on civil defense we have been forced to accept their data on technical problems, even though we suspect that their data are themselves not free from the bias which quite naturally comes from their intention to prove that thermonuclear war is not only possible but also "acceptable." Not being physicists ourselves, and not having the facilities of big research organizations at our disposal, we can at least examine the logic and mode of thought on which the studies of Kahn and the others are based. Our main criticism is that their approach to the question of the survival of our nation, and even of civilization, is the approach of a gamble. That is, they tend to accept the idea that thermonuclear war need not be catastrophic on the basis of (1) complete uncertainty in many important areas of investigation; (2) an optimistic slant which leans more heavily on estimates of better rather than worse conditions; (3) unproven or definitely wrong assumptions; (4) neglect of various important factors as well as the interactions between factors.

At best, what these experts are giving the American public is a piece of optimistic guesswork governed by the logic of a gamble. With the life of a nation and perhaps of all mankind as the stake, it is neither wise nor sane to gamble. Herman Kahn's arguments leave us convinced that there is only one moral and rational way out of the grim predicament we are in: universal disarmament, combined with a political settlement in which neither side tries to upset the other's present position.

Howard E. Gruber | Man or Megaperson?

Talk of the psychopathology of war may conjure up images of frankly psychotic individuals, themselves lost to the world, suddenly possessed of the means to destroy it. We should not entirely dismiss this possibility, for although the governments of the major powers do not now suffer as much as they did a few years ago from the problem of senile psychosis, for example, the history of political power—from Nero to Hitler—has never been free of the suspicion of outright individual insanity.

But that is hardly the main problem. A greater threat is a form of collective insanity in which we prepare to kill tens or hundreds of millions of people in other countries with no hope of gaining anything from it, except, supposedly, a slightly lower casualty rate in our own country.

Sober estimates of the number of deaths occurring in the first two months after one or two days of thermonuclear war run from twenty-five per cent to seventy-five per cent of our population, the higher estimates being the more plausible. The political system that would emerge from the shelters with the survivors would be determined not so much by our political heritage as by the emergency conditions of life they would face for many years. Life might be distinguished from death, but victory would be indistinguishable from defeat.

Faced with such prospects, it is totally irrational to contemplate thermonuclear war as a defense of our present way of life or as a solution of present political problems.

The peculiar thing about this collectivity of death is that the individuals preparing it are, for the most part, individually sane and intelligent. The scientists on both sides are sound, the military men are sound, the statesmen likewise. (I repeat, for the most part.) The individuals are sound, but the combination is sick.

What is the essence of this pathology?

Its essence is the failure of civilized man to evolve appropriate new social institutions to manage a powerful new technology. Society changes fairly slowly. Technology changes rapidly.

This unbalanced growth is especially true today, when vast sums are spent on research to find new ways of changing technology, but those in charge of spending these funds, the political leaders of each country, have no desire to provoke important changes in the societies they enjoy governing.

In the process of biological evolution the conditions favoring the extinction of a species are extreme evolution along some lines of development, coupled with loss of capacity for change along other lines. The world inhabited by any species is always changing: only those species that can continue to change to meet new conditions can be expected to survive.

Similarly, in the process of social evolution, a society that becomes overcommitted to adaptations suitable for a single historical situation may lose that capacity for change which is essential to survival.

A great deal of our thinking about international affairs is dominated by the notion that the world is divided into two great social orders, *We* and *They,* one of which will prevail. But considering their short and troubled histories, it is foolish to behave as though either of the major contending systems—*We* or *They*—can lay any settled claim to the future. Just as historians today describe the decline of feudalism and the evolution of mercantile capitalism, historians a few hundred years from now—if there are any—will describe the evolution of new social orders out of today's struggles. We cannot avoid social evolution, but we can have some effect on its course. In particular, by means of thermonuclear war, we can arrange matters so that future civilizations have little or no historical connection with *Ours*—or *Theirs*—which will have perished, leaving only remnants that no one will wish to preserve. Or, we can recognize that *We* and *They* are both but transitory phases in the social evolution of man, thus enabling ourselves to take a more detached and flexible look at the problem of international conflict. There are more alternatives than *We*—or —*They*, and we need to set about looking for them.

Social scientists spend relatively little effort thinking about the future of social evolution. Much of the discussion of acculturation is overly static, in that it presupposes culture change from primitive beginnings to a fixed endpoint: the way *We* live *Now*. Or, of course, the way *They* live *Now*. Instead, we ought to allow ourselves to think through alternative models of social evolution which combine the emergence of totally new social inventions with existing ones appropriately gathered from the totality of contemporary society. What will the area we now call the United States be like when it has a billion inhabitants, universal higher education, a twenty-hour work week, and an average longevity of one hundred years?

The study of the future is not much more speculative than the study of the past, and it might free our thinking so that we can escape from the dangerous crisis mentality in which the world is divided into two unchanging orders, *We* and *They*.

George Bernard Shaw once wrote that a fanatic is a person who, having lost sight of his objectives, redoubles his efforts. I take it that our prime objectives are the preservation of human life and of the opportunity for man to evolve from where he is now to some unknown but enjoyable future. If a complex chain of thought leads to the conclusion that the wholesale destruction of human life and the reversion of human existence to the ugly aftermath of thermonuclear war is, under certain specified conditions, an acceptable solution to our problems—then there is something wrong with that chain of thought.

One difficulty in rejecting such arguments, however, is the intimidating way in which they are invested with the trappings of science: theoretical models, statistical assumptions, and computer technology. But theoretical models almost always contain errors, statistical assumptions are at best approximations, and computers very often go wrong. In scientific work, these errors are part of the game, but they are not fatal. We check and re-check our work, we test the same idea in a variety of ways, and we examine its plausibility in the light of larger conceptions.

Imagine, if you will, an electronic computer printing out the conclusion that the earth was blown up yesterday. We would automatically decide, on the basis of larger considerations, that something had gone wrong with the computer. Now if a computer tells us that we should blow up the world, or a large part of it, tomorrow, we have an equal need for a larger set of conceptions that tell us the computer is wrong.

In this sense, moral codes—such as the prohibition of genocide—are not mere emotionalism. They are rational checks on the correctness of intellectual operations. Our belief in the value of every human life is not mere liberal softness: it is the theoretical framework that tells us whether or not a strategic conclusion is within the bounds of reason.

Now, as I have said, the individuals engaged in strategic thinking are—as individuals—sane and moral men. This may suggest to you that they would not accept conclusions violating the extremely simple morality in question.

But the moral problem is not so simple. One of the great social discoveries of man is the need to struggle for what we believe, sometimes even at the cost of life itself. In the thermonuclear age, the morality of human survival confronts most sharply the morality of struggle for principle. Now, in defending a principle with your own life, the presumption is made that you preserve the principle for other men to enjoy. If, however, your struggle takes a form that kills other men by the millions and creates conditions that make the principle meaningless, your death is worthless. Therefore, forms of struggle must be found that defend the principle without destroying life itself. The failure to recognize and resolve this dilemma has led to the pathologically one-sided morality which sees thermonuclear war as a potential solution to political problems.

There is a kind of Gresham's Law about moral behavior.

The number of casualties acceptable in war is determined as much by the going moral standards as by military capability. Remember, when we prepare ourselves militarily to inflict 20-40-60 million casualties upon another country, we prepare them morally to inflict a like number on ourselves.

Perhaps you will have noticed that in the early part of this discussion I permitted myself to accept an important change in fundamental moral assumptions. I spoke of the danger that our *civilization* might perish even though some individuals would survive. This is a profound change in the unit of strategic analysis. Those who have learned to think in terms of megaton bombs have also learned to think of survival and death in terms of megapersons. Although I like to think of myself as a modern man, I have not come that far. For me, an individual life is not a small fraction of a megaperson, it is an individual life. If we abandon that fundamental unit of moral analysis it is only to provide ourselves with a rationalization, an intellectual facade, because when all is said and done, no matter how tough we are, we have not yet learned to look squarely at the human horror of thermonuclear war.

In his book, *The Uncertain Trumpet,* General Maxwell Taylor has described the confused and shifting strategic thinking of our own security establishments—the National Security Council and the Joint Chiefs of Staff. It is probably safe to assume that the same moral and strategic confusion prevails in other countries as well. The military mind examines seriously only a very narrow range of alternatives, from limited war to unlimited war. We can help them to broaden this perspective by injecting into the public discussion a much wider range of possibilities.

The world has been playing an international game of blind man's buff, with two blind men. If the game continues, they will eventually collide, and the game will be over. So long as we maintain the thermonuclear military establishment, we perpetuate the threat of thermonuclear war. In this case, mutual deterrence is mutual madness.

We need to dismantle the thermonuclear military establishment, and if that means total disarmament, so be it. Disarmament must become a national objective. We do not yet know how to achieve it. Only through widespread discussion on an international scale will we find the way. Social scientists and other intellectuals can contribute to that end by widening the scope of the discussion—by using their own tools of trade: reading, thinking, speaking, writing. Such discussions are more than an intellectual exercise. They can be a direct demonstration of how to take disagreements off the level of violent conflict and pursue them on the level of rational discussion among rational men.

Thomas Merton | Peace: A Religious Responsibility

Between 1918 and 1939 religious opposition to war was articulate and widespread, all over Europe and America. Peace movements of significant proportions were active in Germany, Britain, and the United States. Yet they were crushed without difficulty and almost without protest by totalitarian regimes on the one hand, and silenced by the outbreak of a clearly defensive war on the other. Since 1945 there has been nothing to compare with the earlier movements of protest. Instead we have witnessed the enormous and crudely contrived fiction of the Communist Peace Movement which has been accepted with disillusioned resignation on one side of the Iron Curtain while, on the other, it has managed to make almost all efforts of independent civilian or religious groups to oppose nuclear war seem dishonest or subversive.

Yet never was opposition to war more urgent and more necessary than now. Never was religious protest so badly needed. Silence, passivity, or outright belligerence seem to be characteristic official and unofficial Christian reactions to the H-bomb. True, there has been some theological and ethical debate. This debate has been marked above all by a seemingly inordinate hesitation to characterize the uninhibited use of nuclear weapons as immoral. Of course the bomb has been condemned without equivocation by the "peace Churches" (Quakers, Mennonites, etc.). But the general tendency of Protestant and Catholic theologians has been to consider how far nuclear war could be reconciled with the traditional "just war" theory. In other words the discussion has been not so much a protest against nuclear war, still less a positive search for peaceful solutions to the problem of nuclear deterrence and ever increasing Cold War obsessions, but rather an attempt to justify, under some limited form, a new type of war which is tacitly recognized as an imminent possibility. This theological thought has tended more and more to *accept* the evil of nuclear war, considering it a lesser evil than Communist domination, and looking for some practicable way to make use of the lesser evil in order to avoid the greater.

But it would seem that a genuinely religious perspective, especially a Christian perspective, should be totally different. Therefore the purpose of the present article is to stand back from the imminent risks of the Cold War crisis, seeking to judge the problem of nuclear war not in relation to what seem to be our own interests or even our own survival, but simply in the light of moral truth. A Christian ought to consider whether nuclear war is not in itself a moral evil so great that it *cannot* be justified even for the best of ends, even to defend the highest and most sacrosanct of values.

This does not imply a purely pacifist rejection of war as such. Assuming that a "just war" is at least a theoretical possibility and granting that in a just war Christians may be bound to defend their country, the question we want to examine here is whether or not the massive and unlimited use of nuclear weapons, or the use of them in a limited first strike which is foreseen as likely to set off a global cataclysm, can be considered under any circumstances just.

The great problem is in fact that both in the East and in the West nuclear weapons are taken for granted. Nuclear war is now assumed to be a rational option or at least nuclear deterrence is accepted as a reasonable and workable way of "preserving peace." The moral issue is generally set aside as irrelevant. But if in all these cases, a use of nuclear weapons even to threaten total or quasi-total destruction of an enemy is immoral, then we are living in a completely noxious situation where most of our political, economic, and even religious thinking is inseparably bound up with assumptions that may ultimately prove criminal. And if this is so, we must be prepared to face terrible consequences. For moral truth is not a sentimental luxury. It is as much a necessity to man and his society as air, water, fire, food and shelter.

This essay takes the stand that the *massive and uninhibited use of nuclear weapons,* either in attack or in retaliation, is contrary to Christian morality. And the arguments will be drawn particularly from Catholic sources. Recent Popes have declared ABC warfare (that is, atomic, biological and chemical warfare) to be a "sin, an offense and an outrage" (Pius XII). It may be quite true that these Popes have also affirmed a nation's right to defend itself by *just means,* in a *just war.* It may also be true that a theological argument for the use of "tactical nuclear weapons" may be constructed on the basis of some of the Popes' statements. But when we remember that the twenty kiloton A-bomb that was dropped on Hiroshima is now regarded as "small" and a "tactical device" and when we keep in mind that there is every probability that a force that is being beaten with small nuclear weapons will resort to big ones, we can easily see how little moral value can be found in these theorizings.

"Tactical nuclear weapons" and "limited war" with conventional forces are of course proposed with the best intentions: as a "realistic" way to avoid the horror of total nuclear warfare. Since it is claimed that men cannot get along without some kind of war, the least we can do is to insure that they will only destroy one another in thousands instead of in millions. Yet curiously enough, the restraint that would be required to keep within these limits (a restraint that was unknown on either side after the early phases of World War II), would seem to demand as much heroism and as much control as disarmament itself. It would therefore appear more realistic as well as more Christian and more humane to strive to think of total peace rather than of partial war. Why can we not do this? If disarmament were taken seriously, instead of being used as a pawn in the game of power politics, we could arrive at a workable agreement. It might not be ideal, but it would certainly be at once safer, saner and more realistic than war, whether limited or total. But we make ourselves incapable of taking either disarmament or peace with total seriousness, because we are completely obsessed with the fury and the fantasies of the Cold War. The task of the Christian is to make the thought of peace once again seriously possible. A step towards this would be the rejection of nuclear deterrence as a basis for international policy. Nuclear war is totally unacceptable. It is immoral, inhuman, and absurd. It can lead nowhere but to the suicide of nations and of cultures, indeed to the destruction of human society itself.

We must now face the fact that we are moving closer and closer to war, not only as a result of blind social forces but also as the result of our own decisions and our own choice. The brutal reality is that, when all is said and done, we seem to *prefer* war; not that we want war itself, but we are blindly and hopelessly attached to all that makes war inevitable.

I THE DANCE OF DEATH

No one seriously doubts that it is now possible for man and his society to be completely destroyed in a nuclear war. This possibility must be soberly faced, even though it is so momentous in all its implications that we can hardly adjust ourselves to it in a fully rational manner. Indeed, this awful threat is the chief psychological weapon of the cold war. America and Russia are playing the paranoid game of nuclear deterrence, each one desperately hoping to preserve peace by threatening the other with bigger bombs and total annihilation.

Every step in this political dance of death brings us inexorably closer to hot war. The closer we get to hot war, the more the theoretical possibility of our total destruction turns into a real probability.

There is no control over the arbitrary and belligerent self-determination of the great nations ruled by managerial power elites concerned chiefly with their own self-interest. The UN is proving itself unable to fulfil the role of international arbiter and powerless to control the pugnacity of the nuclear club. Indeed, the big powers have been content to use the UN as a forum for political and propagandist wrestling matches and have not hesitated to take independent action that led to the discrediting of the UN whenever this has been profitable to them. Hence the danger that the uncontrolled power of nuclear weapons may break loose whenever one of the belligerents feels himself sufficiently strong and sufficiently provoked to risk an all-out war. Repeated threats to use the bomb have doubtless been mostly bluff, but one day somebody's bluff is going to be called, perhaps in a very drastic fashion.

Meanwhile the United States alone possesses a stockpile of nuclear weapons estimated at 60,000 megatons. This is enough to wipe out the present civilized world and to permanently affect all life on the planet earth. These nuclear bombs can be delivered by some 2,500 planes. It is no secret that such planes are constantly in the air, ready to strike. There are 200 missiles available to U.S. forces, mostly of intermediate range, and this does not suggest the immediate likelihood of a purely push-button war. But it is estimated that by 1963 there will be two thousand more of them, of which a large proportion will be intercontinental missiles based in "hard" installations. Attack on hard installations means ground bursts and therefore more fallout as well as more bombs. Hence even an attack concentrated on our missile bases is bound to have a destructive effect on many population centers.

An ICBM can carry an H-bomb warhead to a destination five thousand miles away, twenty times faster than the speed of sound. Intermediate range missiles can be fired from submarines and deliver H-bombs which could reduce the eastern United States to a radioactive wasteland. H-bombs will soon be fitted to satellites and will be able to reach a target within a few minutes, without hope of interception.

It must be remembered that H-bombs are relatively cheap to produce, and it is not difficult to build and deliver big ones. Poison gas can also be delivered by long-range missiles. One such gas is manufactured in quantity by the U.S. Army Chemical Corps and it can exterminate whole populations of men as if they were insects. A similar nerve gas, originally developed by the Nazis, is manufactured in Soviet Russia.

This gas is considered to be more effective against civilian populations than any nuclear agent. It leaves industry and property intact and there is no fallout! Shelters offer no protection against chemical agents.

In a word, the logic of deterrence has proved to be singularly illogical, because of the fact that nuclear war is almost exclusively offensive. So far there is no indication that there can be any really effective defense against guided missiles. All the advantage goes to the force that strikes first, without warning. Hence the multiplication of "hard" weapon sites, and of "deep shelters" becomes provocative and instead of convincing the enemy of our invulnerability, it only invites a heavier preemptive attack by bigger bombs and more of them. The cost of moving a significant portion of industry, business and the population underground is prohibitive and the whole idea is in itself nonsensical, at least as a guarantee of "peace."

Far from producing the promised "nuclear stalemate" and the "balance of terror" on which we are trying to construct an improbable peace, these policies simply generate tension, confusion, suspicion, and paranoid hate. This is the climate most suited to the growth of totalitarianism. Indeed, the cold war itself promises by itself to erode the last vestiges of true democratic freedom and responsibility even in the countries which claim to be defending these values. Those who think that they can preserve their independence, their civic and religious rights by ultimate recourse to the H-bomb do not seem to realize that the mere shadow of the bomb may end by reducing their religious and democratic beliefs to the level of mere words without meaning, veiling a state of rigid and totalitarian belligerency that will tolerate no opposition.

In a world where another Hitler and another Stalin are almost certain to appear on the scene, the existence of such destructive weapons and the moral paralysis of leaders and policy makers combined with the passivity and confusion of mass societies which exist on both sides of the Iron Curtain, constitute the gravest problem in the whole history of man. Our times can be called apocalyptic, in the sense that we seem to have come to a point at which all the hidden, mysterious dynamism of the "history of salvation" revealed in the Bible has flowered into final and decisive crisis. The term "end of the world" may or may not be one that we are capable of understanding. But at any rate we seem to be assisting at the unwrapping of the mysteriously vivid symbols in the last book of the New Testament. In their nakedness they reveal to us our own selves as the men whose lot it is to live in a time of possibly ultimate decision. In a word, the end of our civilized society is quite literally up to us and to our immediate descendants, if any. It is for us to decide whether we are going to give in to hatred, terror and blind love of power for its own sake, and thus plunge our world into the abyss, or whether, restraining our savagery, we can patiently and humanely work together for interests which transcend the limits of any national or ideological community. We are challenged to prove we are rational, spiritual and humane enough to deserve survival, by acting according to the highest ethical and spiritual norms we know. As Christians, we believe that these norms have been given to us in the Gospel and in the traditional theology of the Church.

II THE CHRISTIAN AS PEACEMAKER

We know that Christ came into this world as the Prince of Peace. We know that Christ Himself is our peace (*Eph. 2:14*). We believe that God has chosen for Himself, in the Mystical Body of Christ, an elect people, regenerated by the Blood of the Savior, and committed by their baptismal promise to wage war upon the evil and hatred that are in man, and help to establish the Kingdom of God and of peace.

This means a recognition that human nature, identical in all men, was assumed by the Logos in the Incarnation, and that Christ died out of love for all men, in order to live in all men. Consequently we have the obligation to treat every other man as Christ Himself, respecting his life as if it were the life of Christ, his rights as if they were the rights of Christ. Even if the other shows himself to be unjust, wicked and odious to us, we cannot take upon ourselves a final and definitive judgment in his case. We still have an obligation to be patient, and to seek his highest spiritual interests. In other words, we are formally commanded to love our enemies, and this obligation cannot be met by a formula of words. It is not enough to press the button that will incinerate a city of five million people, saying in one's heart "this hurts me more than it hurts you," or declaring that it is all for love.

As Pope John XXIII pointed out in his first encyclical letter, *Ad Petri Cathedram*, Christians are obliged to strive for peace "with all the means at their disposal" and yet, as he continues, this peace cannot compromise with error or make concessions to it. Therefore it is by no means a matter of passive acquiescence in injustice, since this does not produce peace. However, the Christian struggle for peace depends first of all upon a free response of man to "God's call to the service of His Merciful designs." (Christmas message, 1958.) Christ Our Lord did not come to bring peace to the world as a kind of spiritual tranquilizer. He brought to His disciples a vocation and a task, to struggle in the world of violence to establish His peace not only in their own hearts but in society itself. This was to be done not by wishing and fair words but by a total interior revolution in which we abandoned the human prudence that is subordinated to the quest for power, and followed the higher wisdom of love and of the Cross.

The Christian is and must be by his very adoption as a son of God, in Christ, a peacemaker (*Matt. 5:9*). He is bound to imitate the Savior who, instead of defending Himself with twelve legions of angels (*Matt. 26:55*), allowed Himself to be nailed to the Cross and died praying for His executioners. The Christian is one whose life has sprung from a particular spiritual seed: the blood of the martyrs who, without offering forcible resistance, laid down their lives rather than submit to the unjust laws that demanded an official religious cult of the emperor as God. That is to say, the Christian is bound, like the martyrs, to obey God rather than the state whenever the state tries to usurp powers that do not and cannot belong to it. We have repeatedly seen Christians in our time fulfilling this obligation in a heroic manner by their resistance to dictatorships that strove to interfere with the rights of their conscience and their religion.

Hence it must be stated quite clearly and without any compromise that the duty of the Christian as a peacemaker is not to be confused with a kind of quietistic inertia which is indifferent to injustice, accepts any kind of disorder, compromises with error and with evil, and gives in to every pressure in order to maintain "peace at any price." The Christian knows well, or should know well, that peace is not possible on such terms. Peace demands the most heroic labor and the most difficult sacrifice. It demands greater heroism than war. It demands greater fidelity to the truth and a much more perfect purity of conscience. The Christian fight for peace is not to be confused with defeatism. This has to be made clear because there is a certain complacent sophistry, given free currency by the theologians who want to justify war too easily, and who like to treat anyone who disagrees with them as if he were a practical apostate from the faith who had already surrendered implicitly to communism by refusing to accept the morality of an all-out nuclear war. This, as any one can easily see, is simply begging the question. And one feels that those who yield to this temptation are perhaps a little too much influenced by the pragmatism and opportunism of our affluent society.

There is a lot of talk, among some of the clergy, about the relative danger of nuclear war and a "communist takeover." It is assumed, quite gratuitously, that the communist is at the gates, and is just about to take over the United States, close all the churches, and brainwash all the good Catholics. Once this spectral assessment of the situation is accepted, then one is urged to agree that there is only one solution: to let the Reds have it before they get our government and our universities thoroughly infiltrated. This means a preemptive strike, based not on the fact that we ourselves are actually under military attack, but that we are so "provoked" and so "threatened" that even the most drastic measures are justified.

If it is argued that there can be no proportion between the awful destruction wrought by nuclear war and the good achieved by exorcising this specter of communist domination, the argument comes back: "better dead than red." And this, in turn, is justified by the contention that the destruction of cities, nations, populations, is "only a physical evil" while communist domination would be a "moral evil."

It must be said at once that this has no basis in logic, ethics, politics or sound moral theology. Two quotations from Pope Pius XII will suffice to establish the true Catholic perspective on these points.

The destruction of cities and nations by nuclear war is "*only a physical evil?*" Pope Pius XII calls aggressive ABC warfare a "sin, an offense and an outrage against the majesty of God." And he adds: "It constitutes a crime worthy of the most severe national and international sanctions." (Address to the World Medical Congress, 1954.) Fr. John Courtney Murray, S.J., whom no one can accuse of being a "pacifist" (he favors the liceity of "limited nuclear war" and also believes that such a war would have practical value) has stated, "The extreme position of favoring a war . . . simply to kill off all communists, cannot be a legitimate Catholic opinion."

The real issue here is not actually a moral principle so much as a state of mind. This state of mind is the one which we find in the American mass media. It is made up of a large number of very superficial assumptions about what is going on in the world and about what is likely to happen. We are in a sorry state, indeed, if our survival and indeed our Christian faith itself are left entirely at the mercy of such assumptions!

III BEYOND EAST AND WEST

We are no longer living in a Christian world. The ages which we are pleased to call the "ages of faith" were certainly not ages of earthly paradise. But at least our forefathers officially recognized and favored the Christian ethic of love. They fought some very bloody and unchristian wars, and in doing so, they also committed great crimes which remain in history as a permanent scandal. However, certain definite limits were recognized. Today a non-Christian world still retains a few vestiges of Christian morality, a few formulas and clichés, which serve on appropriate occasions to adorn indignant editorials and speeches. But otherwise we witness deliberate campaigns to oppose and eliminate all education in Christian truth and morality. Not only non-Christians but even Christians themselves tend to dismiss the Gospel ethic of non-violence and love as "sentimental." As a matter of fact, the mere suggestion that Christ counselled non-violent resistance to evil is enough to invite scathing ridicule.

It is therefore a serious error to imagine that because the West was once largely Christian, the cause of the Western nations is now to be identified, without further qualification, with the cause of God. The incentive to wipe out Bolshevism with H-bombs may well be one of the apocalyptic temptations of twentieth century Christendom. It may indeed be the most effective way of destroying Christendom, even though man may survive. For who imagines that the Asians and Africans will respect Christianity and receive it after it has state, indeed if our survival and indeed our Christian faith apparently triggered mass-murder and destruction of cosmic proportions? It is pure madness to think that Christianity can defend itself by nuclear preemption. The mere fact that we now seem to accept nuclear war as reasonable and Christian is a universal scandal.

True, Christianity is not only opposed to Communism, but in a very real sense, at war with it. However this warfare is spiritual and ideological. "Devoid of material weapons," says Pope John, "the Church is the trustee of the highest spiritual power." If the Church has no military weapons of her own, it means that her wars are fought without violence, not that she intends to call upon the weapons of nations that were once Christian, in defense of the Gospel. Whatever we may think of the ethics of nuclear war, it is clear that the message of the H-bomb is neither salvation nor "good news."

But we believe, precisely, that an essential part of the "good news" is that spiritual weapons are stronger than material ones. Indeed, by spiritual arms, the early Church conquered the entire Roman world. Have we lost our faith in this "sword of the Spirit?" Have we perhaps lost all realization of its very existence?

Of course we must repudiate a tactic of inert passivity that purely and simply leaves man defenseless, without any recourse whatever to any means of protecting himself, his rights, or Christian truth. We repeat again and again that the right, and truth, are to be defended by the most efficacious possible means, and that the most efficacious of all are precisely the spiritual ones, which have always been the only ones that have effected a really lasting moral change in society and in man. The Church tolerates defensive use of weapons only in so far as men are unable to measure up to the stricter and more heroic demands of spiritual warfare. It is absolutely unchristian to adopt, in practice, a standard of judgment which practically rejects or ignores all recourse to the spiritual weapons, and relegates them entirely to the background as if they had no efficacy whatever, and as if material weapons (the bigger the better) were the ones that really counted.

It seems that a great deal of the moral discussion about nuclear war is based, in fact, on the assumption that spiritual weapons are quixotic and worthless and that material weapons alone are worthy of serious consideration. But this attitude is precisely what leads to a fundamental vitiation of the Church's traditionally accepted doctrine on the use of violence in war: it seeks in every possible way to evade the obligation to use war only as a last resort, purely in *defense*, and with the use of *just means only*.

Inevitably, as soon as the obsession with bigger and bigger weapons takes hold of us, we make it impossible for ourselves to consider the just rights of non-combatants. We twist and deform the truth in every possible way in order to convince ourselves that non-combatants are really combatants after all, and that our "attack" is in reality "defense," while the enemy's "defense" really constitutes an "attack." By such tactics we disqualify ourselves from receiving the guidance of light and grace which will enable us to judge as spiritual men and as members of Christ. Obviously, without this special gift of light, we remain utterly incapable of seeing or appreciating the superiority of spiritual weapons, prayer, sacrifice, negotiation, and non-violent means in general.

This results in the unhappy situation that non-Christians with rather dubious doctrinal support in irreligious philosophies have been able to take over characteristically Christian spiritual methods, appropriating them to themselves and thus further discrediting them in the eyes of the orthodox believer who is already confused by the now instinctive justification of war and weapons as the "normal" Christian way of solving international problems.

We must remember that the Church does not belong to any political power bloc. Christianity exists on both sides of the Iron Curtain and we should feel ourselves united by very special bonds with those Christians who, living under Communism, often suffer heroically for their principles.

Is it a valid defense of Christianity for us to wipe out those heroic Christians along with their oppressors, for the sake of "religious freedom?"

Let us stop and consider where the policy of massive retaliation and worse still of preemptive strike may lead us. Are we to annihilate huge population centers, at the same time showering vast areas around them with lethal fallout? Do we believe it is necessary to do this in order to protect ourselves against the menace of world communism?

In these countries which we may perhaps be ready to annihilate, the vast majority is not communist. On the contrary, while the people have resigned themselves passively to communist domination, and have become quite convinced that there is no hope to be looked for from us because we are their declared enemies, and intend to wipe them out, they are by no means communists. They do not want war. They have, in many cases, lived through the horrors and sacrifices of total war and experienced things which we are barely able to imagine. They do not want to go through this again.

We, in the name of liberty, of justice, of humanity, are pursuing a policy which promises to crush them with even greater horror, except that it may be perhaps "merciful" that millions of them will simply be blown out of existence in the twinkling of an eye. Merciful? When many of them have a Christian background, many are faithful Christians?

What good will our belligerent policy do us in those countries? None at all. It will only serve to reinforce the fatalistic conviction of the necessity of armament and of war that has been dinned into these populations by the Communist minority which dominates them.

How do we justify our readiness to wage a war of this kind? Let us face the fact that we feel ourselves terribly menaced by Communism. Certainly we believe we have to defend ourselves. Why are we menaced? Because, as time goes on, the Communists have gained a greater and greater advantage over us in the cold war. Why have they been able to do this? This is a question of historic fact, which however is not absolutely clear, but anyone will admit that our very reliance on the massive power of the bomb has to a great extent crippled us and restricted our freedom to maneuver, and the Communists have been operating under the *protection* of this massive threat that is too enormous to let loose for any but the most serious causes. Hence, instead of the serious provocation, the massive attack, we are confronted with a multiplicity of little threats all over the world, little advances, little gains. They all add up, but even the total of all of them does not constitute a sufficient reason for nuclear war.

But we are getting mad, and we are beginning to be thoroughly impatient with the humiliation of constant defeat. The more humiliated we become, the worse we compromise our chances, the greater errors we make.

We used to have an unrivalled reputation among the backward peoples of the world. We were considered the true defenders of liberty, justice and peace, the hope of the future. Our anger, our ignorance and our frustration have made us forfeit this tremendous advantage.

IV   MORAL PASSIVITY AND DEMONIC ACTIVISM

One of the most disturbing things about the Western world of our time is that it is beginning to have much more in common with the communist world than it has with the professedly Christian society of several centuries ago. On both sides of the Iron Curtain we find two pathological varieties of the same moral sickness: both of them rooted in the same basically materialistic view of life. Both are basically opportunistic and pragmatic in their own way. And both have the following characteristics in common. On the level of *morality* they are blindly passive in their submission to a determination which, in effect, leaves men completely irresponsible. Therefore moral obligations and decisions tend to become practically meaningless. At best they are only forms of words, rationalizations of pragmatic decisions that have already been dictated by the needs of the moment.

Naturally, since not everyone is an unprincipled materialist even in Russia, there is bound to be some moral sense at work, even if only as a guilt-feeling that produces uneasiness and hesitation, blocking the smooth efficiency of machine-like obedience to immoral commands. Yet the history of Nazi Germany shows us how appalling was the irresponsibility which would carry out even the most revolting of crimes under cover of "obedience" to "legitimately constituted authority" for the sake of a "good cause." This moral passivity is the most terrible danger of our time, as the American bishops have already pointed out in their joint letters of 1960 and 1961.

On the level of political, economic and military activity, this moral passivity is balanced, or over-balanced by a *demonic activism*, a frenzy of the most varied, versatile, complex and even utterly brilliant technological improvisations, following one upon the other with an ever more bewildering and uncontrollable proliferation. Politics pretends to use this force as its servant, to harness it for social purposes, for the "good of man." The intention is good. The technological development of power in our time is certainly a risk and challenge, but it is by no means intrinsically evil. On the contrary, it can and should be a very great good. In actual fact, however, the furious speed with which our technological world is plunging toward disaster is evidence that no one is any longer fully in control—least of all, perhaps, the political leaders.

A simple study of the steps which led to the dropping of the first A-bomb on Hiroshima is devastating evidence of the way well-meaning men, the scientists, generals and statesmen of a victorious nation, were guided step by step, without realizing it, by the inscrutable yet simple "logic of events" to fire the shot that was to make the Cold War inevitable and prepare the way inexorably for World War III. This they did purely and simply because they thought in all sincerity that the bomb was the simplest and most merciful way of ending World War II and perhaps all wars, forever.

The tragedy of our time is then not so much the malice of the wicked as the helpless futility of the best intentions of "the good." There are warmakers, war criminals, indeed. They are present and active on *both sides*. But all of us, in our very best efforts for peace, find ourselves maneuvered unconsciously into positions where we too can act as war criminals. For there can be no doubt that Hiroshima and Nagasaki were, though not fully deliberate crimes, nevertheless crimes. And who was responsible? No one. Or "history." We cannot go on playing with nuclear fire and shrugging off the results as "history." We are the ones concerned.

In plain words, in order to save ourselves from destruction we have to try to regain control of a world that is speeding downhill without brakes because of the combination of factors I have just mentioned: almost total passivity and irresponsibility on the moral level, plus demonic activism in social, political and military life.

First of all we must seek some remedy in the technological sphere. We must try to achieve some control over the production and stockpiling of weapons. It is intolerable that such massive engines of destruction should be allowed to proliferate in all directions without any semblance of a long-range plan for anything, even for what is cynically called "defense." To allow governments to pour more and more billions into weapons that almost immediately become obsolete, thereby necessitating more billions for newer and bigger weapons, is one of the most colossal injustices in the long history of man. While we are doing this, two thirds of the world are starving, or living in conditions of subhuman destitution.

Far from demanding that the lunatic race for destruction be stepped up, it seems to me that Christian morality imposes on every single one of us the obligation to protest against it and to work for the creation of an international authority with power and sanctions that will be able to control technology, and divert our amazing virtuosity into the service of man instead of against him.

It is not enough to say that we ought to try to work for a negotiated disarmament, or that one power bloc or the other ought to take the lead and disarm unilaterally. Methods and policies can and should be fairly considered. But what matters most is the obligation to travel in every feasible way in the direction of peace, using all the traditional and legitimate methods, while at the same time seeking to improvise new and original measures to achieve our end.

Long ago, even before the A-bomb, Pope Pius XII declared it was our supreme obligation to make "war on war" (1944). At that time he stressed our moral obligation to ban all wars of aggression, stating this duty was binding on *all* and that it "brooks no delay, no procrastination, no hesitation, no subterfuge." And what have we seen since then? The A-bomb, the H-bomb, the ICBM, the development of chemical and bacteriological weapons, and every possible evasion and subterfuge to justify their use without limitation as soon as one or the other nation decides that it may be expedient!

Therefore a Christian who is not willing to envisage the creation of an effective international authority to control the destinies of man for peace is not acting and thinking as a mature member of the Church. He does not have fully Christian perspectives. Such perspectives must by their very nature, be "catholic," that is to say world wide. They must consider the needs of mankind and not the temporary expediency and shortsighted policy of a particular nation.

To reject a "world wide" outlook, to refuse to consider the good of mankind, and to remain satisfied with the affluence that flows from our war economy, is hardly a Christian attitude. Nor will our attachment to the current payoff accruing to us from weapons make it any easier for us to see and understand the need to take the hard road of sacrifice which alone leads to peace!

Equally important, and perhaps even more difficult than technological control, is the restoration of some moral sense and the resumption of genuine responsibility. Without this it is illusory for us to speak of freedom and "control." Unfortunately, even where moral principles are still regarded with some degree of respect, morality has lost touch with the realities of our situation. Modern warfare is fought as much by machines as by men. Even a great deal of the planning depends on the work of mechanical computers.

Hence it becomes more and more difficult to estimate the morality of an act leading to war because it is more and more difficult to know precisely what is going on. Not only is war increasingly a matter for pure specialists operating with fantastically complex machinery, but above all there is the question of absolute secrecy regarding everything that seriously affects defense policy. We may amuse ourselves by reading the reports in mass media and imagine that these "facts" provide sufficient basis for moral judgments for and against war. But in reality, we are simply elaborating moral fantasies in a vacuum. Whatever we may decide, we remain completely at the mercy of the governmental power, or rather the anonymous power of managers and generals who stand behind the facade of government. We have no way of directly influencing the decisions and policies taken by these people. In practice, we must fall back on a blinder and blinder faith which more and more resigns itself to trusting the "legitimately constituted authority" without having the vaguest notion what that authority is liable to do next. This condition of irresponsibility and passivity is extremely dangerous. It is hardly conducive to genuine morality.

An entirely new dimension is opened up by the fantastic processes and techniques involved in modern war. An American President can speak of warfare in outer space and nobody bursts out laughing—he is perfectly serious. Science fiction and the comic strip have all suddenly come true. When a missile armed with an H-bomb warhead is fired by the pressing of a button and its target is a whole city, the number of its victims is estimated in "megacorpses"—*millions* of dead human beings. A thousand or ten thousand more here and there are not even matter for comment. To what extent can we assume that the soldiers who exercise this terrible power are worthy of our confidence and actually realize what they are doing? To what extent can we assume that in passively following their lead and concurring in their decision—at least by default—we are acting as Christians?

V THE MORAL PROBLEM

In all-out nuclear war, there is no longer question of simply permitting an evil, the destruction of a few civilian dwellings, in order to attain a legitimate end: the destruction of a military target. It is well understood on both sides that all-out nuclear war is purely and simply massive and indiscriminate destruction of targets chosen not for their military significance alone, but for their importance in a calculated project of terror and annihilation. Often the selection of the target is determined by some quite secondary and accidental circumstance that has not the remotest reference to morality. Hiroshima was selected for atomic attack, among other reasons, because it had never undergone any notable air bombing and was suitable as an intact target to give a good idea of the effectiveness of the bomb.

It must be frankly admitted that some of the military commanders of both sides in World War II simply disregarded all the traditional standards that were still effective. The

Germans threw those standards overboard with the bombs they unloaded on Warsaw, Rotterdam, Coventry and London. The Allies replied in kind with saturation bombing of Hamburg, Cologne, Dresden and Berlin. Spokesmen were not wanting on either side to justify these crimes against humanity. And today, while "experts" calmly discuss the possibility of the United States being able to survive a war if *"only fifty millions"* (!) of the population are killed, when the Chinese speak of being able to *spare* "three hundred million" and "still get along," it is obvious that we are no longer in the realm where moral truth is conceivable.

The only sane course that remains is to work frankly and without compromise for a supra-national authority and for the total abolition of war. The pronouncements of the Holy See all seem to point to this as the best ultimate solution.

The moral duty of the Christian is by no means simple. It is far from being a neat matter of ethical principle, clear cut, well defined, and backed by a lucid authoritative decision of the Church. To make the issue seem too simple is actually to do a great disservice to truth, to morality and to man. And yet now more than ever we crave the simple and the clear solution. This very craving is dangerous, because the most tempting of all "simple" solutions are the ones which prescribe annihilation or submit to it without resistance. There is a grim joke underlying all this talk about "red or dead." The inherent destructiveness of the frustrated mind is able to creep in here and distort the whole Christian view of life and of civilization by evading the difficult and complex way of negotiation and sacrifice, in order to resort, in frustrated desperation, to "magic" power and nuclear destruction. Let us not ignore this temptation, it is one of the deepest and most radical in man. It is the first of all temptations, and the root of all the others. "You shall be as gods. . . ." (*Genesis* 3:5).

On the contrary, our Christian obligation consists in being and remaining men, believing in the Word Who emptied Himself and became man for our sakes. We have to look at the problem of nuclear war from the viewpoint of humanity and of God made man, from the viewpoint of the Mystical

Body of Christ, and not merely from the viewpoint of abstract formulas. Here above all we need a reasoning that is informed with compassion and takes some account of flesh and blood, not a legalistic juggling with principles and precedents.

In the light of these deep Christian truths we will better understand the danger of fallacious justifications of every recourse to violence, as well as the peril of indifference, inertia and passivity.

It is not a question of stating absolutely and infallibly that every Christian must renounce, under pain of mortal sin, any opinion that the use of the bomb might be legitimate. The H-bomb has not been formally and officially condemned, and doubtless it does not need to be condemned. There is no special point in condemning one weapon in order to give casuistical minds an opportunity to prove their skill in evasion by coming up with another, "licit" way of attaining the same destructive end. It is not just a matter of seeing how much destruction and murder we can justify without incurring the condemnation of the Church.

But I submit that at this time above all it is vitally important to avoid the "minimalist" approach. The issue of nuclear war is too grave and too general. It threatens everybody. It may affect the very survival of the human race. In such a case one is not allowed to take any but unavoidable risks. We are obliged to take the morally more secure alternative in guiding our choice. Let us remember too that while a doubt of the existence of an obligation leaves us with a certain freedom of choice, the doubt of an evil fact does not permit such freedom.

We may well dispute the legitimacy of nuclear war on principle: but when we face the *actual fact* that recourse to nuclear weapons may quite probably result in the quasi-total destruction of civilization, even possibly in the suicide of the entire human race, we *are absolutely obliged to take this fact into account and to avoid this terrible danger.*

It is certainly legitimate for a Catholic moralist to hold in theory that a limited nuclear war, in defense, is permitted by traditional Christian moral principles. He may even hold the opinion that the strategic use of nuclear, bacteriological and chemical weapons is theoretically permissible for defense, provided that there is a possibility that what we are defending will continue to exist after it has been "defended."

But when we come face to face with the terrible doubt of fact, *dubium facti,* the absolutely real and imminent probability of massive and uncontrolled destruction with the annihilation of civilization and of life, then there is no such latitude of choice. We are most gravely and seriously bound by all norms of Christian morality, however minimal, to choose the safer course and to try at all costs to avoid so general a disaster.

Let us remember that even if one were to admit the theoretical legitimacy of nuclear weapons for purposes of defense, that use would become gravely unjust, without a shadow of doubt, as soon as the effects of nuclear destruction overflowed upon neutral or friendly nations. Even though we may feel justified in risking the destruction of our own cities and those of the enemy, we have no right whatever to bring destruction upon helpless small nations which have no interest whatever in the war and ask only to survive in peace. It is not up to us to choose that *they* should be dead rather than red.

Pope Pius XII said in 1954 (concerning ABC warfare, described above as a sin, an offense and an outrage against God): "Should the evil consequences of adopting this method of warfare *ever become so extensive as to pass entirely beyond the control of man, then indeed its use must be rejected as immoral.*" He adds that uncontrolled annihilation of life within a given area "IS NOT LAWFUL UNDER ANY TITLE."

Nor is it moral to overindulge in speculation on this dangerous point of "control." A lax interpretation of this principle would lead us to decide that a twenty megaton H-bomb dropped on Leningrad is "fully under control" because all its effects are susceptible to measurement, and we know that the blast will annihilate Leningrad while the fallout will probably wipe out the population of Helsinki and Riga, depending on the wind. Obviously what the Pope meant was much more strict than that. He meant that if there was uncontrolled annihilation of everybody in Leningrad, without any discrimination between combatants and non-combatants, enemies, friends, women, children, infants and old people, then the use of the bomb would be "not lawful under any title," especially in view of the "bonus" effects of fallout drifting over neutral territory, certainly without control. And I do not think "clean" bombs are going to get around this moral difficulty either.

Hence though nuclear warfare as such has not been entirely and formally condemned, the mind of the Church is obviously that every possible means should be taken to avoid it; and John XXIII made this abundantly clear in his Christmas Message of 1961 where he pleaded in most solemn terms with the rulers of all nations to "shun all thought of force" and remain at peace. The words of Pope John in this connection imply grave reservations even with regard to limited war which might possibly "escalate" and reach all-out proportions.

There can be no doubt whatever that the absence of formal condemnation cannot be twisted into a tacit official approval of all-out nuclear war. Yet it seems that this is what some of our theologians are trying to do.

On the contrary, our duty is to help emphasize with all the force at our disposal that the Church earnestly seeks the abolition of war; we must underscore declarations like those of Pope John XXIII pleading with world leaders to renounce force in the settlement of international disputes and confine themselves to negotiations.

Now let us suppose that the political leaders of the world, supported by the mass media in their various countries, and carried on by a tidal wave of greater and greater war preparations, see themselves swept inexorably into a war of cataclysmic proportions. Let us suppose that it becomes morally certain that these leaders are helpless to arrest the blind force of the process that has irresponsibly been set in motion. What then? Are the masses of the world, including you and me, to resign themselves to our fate and march to global suicide without resistance, simply bowing our heads and obeying our leaders as showing us the "will of God?" I think it should be evident to everyone that this can no longer, in the present situation, be accepted unequivocally as Christian obedience and civic duty.

It is true that Pope Pius XII in his Christmas Message of 1956 declared that a Catholic was bound in duty to help his country in a just war of defense. But to extend this to all-out nuclear war is begging the question because Papal pronouncements on nuclear war cast doubts upon its justice. No theologian, however broad, however lax, would insist that one was bound in conscience to participate in a war that was *evidently* leading to global suicide. Those who favor nuclear war can only do so by making all kinds of suppositions concerning the political and military facts: that it will be only a limited war or that the destructive effects of H-bombs are not as terrible as we have been told. However much they limit the scoresheet of megacorpses, it is difficult for us to admit the morality of all-out nuclear war.

This brings us face to face with the greatest and most agonizing moral issue of our time. This issue is not merely nuclear war, not merely the possible destruction of the human race by a sudden explosion of violence. It is something more subtle and more demonic. If we continue to yield to theoretically irresistible determinism and to vague "historic forces" without striving to resist and control them, if we let these forces drive us to demonic activism in the realm of politics and technology, we face something more than the material evil of universal destruction. We face *moral responsibility for global suicide*. Much more than that, we are going to find ourselves gradually moving into a situation in which we are practically compelled by the "logic of circumstances" deliberately *to choose the course that leads to destruction.*

The great danger is then the savage and self-destructive commitment to a policy of nationalism and blind hate, and the refusal of all other policies more constructive and more in accordance with Christian ethical tradition. Let us realize that this is a matter of *choice*, not of pure blind determinism.

We all know the logic of temptation. We all know the confused, vague, hesitant irresponsibility which leads us into the situation where it is no longer possible to turn back, and how, arrived in that situation, we have a moment of clear-sighted desperation in which we freely commit ourselves to the course we recognize as evil. That may well be what is happening now to the whole world.

The free choice of global suicide, made in desperation by the world's leaders and ratified by the consent and cooperation of their citizens, would be a moral evil second only to the crucifixion. The fact that such a choice might be made with the highest motives and the most urgent purpose would do nothing whatever to mitigate it. The fact that it might be made as a gamble, in the hope that some might escape, would never excuse it. After all, the purposes of Caiphas were, in his own eyes, perfectly noble. He thought it was necessary to let "one man die for the people."

The most urgent necessity of our time is therefore not merely to prevent the destruction of the human race by nuclear war. Even if it should happen to be no longer possible to prevent the disaster (which God forbid), there is still a greater evil that can and must be prevented. It must be possible for every free man to refuse his consent and deny his cooperation to this greatest of crimes.

VI THE CHRISTIAN CHOICE

In what does this effective and manifest refusal of consent consist? How does one "resist" the sin of genocide? Ideally speaking, in the imaginary case where all-out nuclear war seemed inevitable and the world's leaders were evidently incapable of preventing it, it would be legitimate and even obligatory for all sane and conscientious men everywhere in the world to lay down their weapons and their tools and starve and be shot rather than cooperate in the war effort. If such a mass movement should spontaneously arise in all parts of the world, in Russia and America, in China and France, in Africa and Germany, the human race could be saved from extinction. This is indeed an engaging hypothesis—but it is no more than that. It would be folly to suppose that men hitherto passive, inert, morally indifferent and irresponsible might suddenly recover their sense of obligation and their awareness of their own power when the world was on the very brink of war.

In any case, as has been said above, the ordinary man has no access to vital information. Indeed, even the politicians may know relatively little about what is really going on. How would it be possible to know when and how it was necessary to refuse cooperation? Can we draw a line clearly, and say precisely when nuclear war becomes so dangerous that it is suicidal? If a war of missiles breaks out, we will have at the most thirty minutes to come to our momentous conclusions— if we ever know what is happening at all. It seems to me that the time to form our conscience and to decide upon our course of action is *NOW*.

It is one thing to form one's conscience and another to adopt a specific policy or course of action. It is highly regrettable that this important distinction is overlooked and indeed deliberately obfuscated. To decide, in the forum of conscience, that one is obligated in every way, as a Christian, to avoid actions that would contribute to a world-wide disaster, does not mean that one is necessarily committed to absolute and unqualified pacifism. One may start from this moral principle, which is repeatedly set before us by the Popes and which cannot be seriously challenged, and one may then go on to seek various means to preserve peace. About these different means, there may be considerable debate.

Yet it seems clear to me that the enormous danger represented by nuclear weapons and the near impossibility of controlling them and limiting them to a scale that would fit the traditional ethical theory of a just war, makes it both logical and licit for a Catholic to proceed, from motives of conscience, to at least a relative pacifism, and to a policy of nuclear disarmament.

In so doing, however, he has a strict obligation to see that he does not take a naive and oversimplified position which would permit him to be ruthlessly exploited by the politicians of another nuclear power. The logic of all serious efforts to preserve peace demands that our very endeavors themselves do not help the war effort of the "enemy," and thus precipitate war. There is sometimes a danger that our pacifism may be somewhat shortsighted and immature. It may consequently be more an expression of rebellion against the status quo in our own country than an effective opposition to war itself.

In a word, there are three things to be considered: (1) Christian moral principles, which by their very nature favor peace, and according to which nuclear war remains, if not absolutely forbidden, at least of exceedingly dubious morality; (2) The facts about weapons systems and defense policies. Our moral decision, and the morality of our participation in the economic and political life of a society geared for nuclear war, demand imperatively that we realize the real nature of the military policies to which we contribute by taxation and perhaps also by our work in industry. So much in our national life is today centered on the most intense and most overwhelming arms race in the history of man. Everything points to the fact that these frightful weapons of destruction may soon be used, most probably on the highest and most expanded scale; (3) We must finally consider factors by which these military policies are dictated.

The Christian moral principles are relatively clear. While there is still intense debate over details, no Christian moralist worthy of the name can seriously defend outright a nuclear war of unqualified aggression.

The facts about ABC warfare are also clear enough. There is no question of the immense destructiveness of the weapons available to us. There is no question that the destruction of civilization and even global suicide are both possible. There is no question that the policies of the nuclear powers are geared for an all-out war of incredible savagery and destructive force.

What remains to be explored by the Christian is the area that is least considered, which also happens to be the area that most needs to be examined and is perhaps the one place where something can be done.

By what are our policies of hatred and destructiveness dictated? What seems to drive us inexorably on to the fate which we all dread and seek to avoid? This question is not hard to answer. What started the First World War? What started the Second World War? The answer is, simply, the rabid, short-sighted, irrational and stubborn forces which tend to come to a head in nationalism.

Christopher Dawson has said:

The defeat of Hitlerism does not mean that we have seen the end of such movements. In our modern democratic world, irrational forces lie very near the surface, and *their sudden eruption under the impulse of nationalist or revolutionary ideologies is the greatest of all the dangers that threaten the modern world. . . .* It is at this point that the need for a reassertion of Christian principles becomes evident. In so far as nationalism denies the principle (of higher order and divine justice for all men) and sets up the nation and the national state as the final object of man's allegiance, *it represents the most retrograde movement the world has ever seen,* since it means a denial of the great central truth on which civilization was founded, and the return to the pagan idolatries of tribal barbarism.

Dawson then goes on to quote Pope Pius XII who distinguishes between "national life" and "nationalistic politics." National life is a combination of all the values which characterize a social group and enable it to contribute fruitfully to the whole policy of nations. Nationalistic politics on the other hand are divisive, destructive, and a perversion of genuine national values. They are "a principle of dissolution within the community of peoples."

This then is the conclusion: the Christian is bound to work for peace by working against global dissolution and anarchy. Due to nationalist and revolutionary ideologies (for Communism is in fact exploiting the intense nationalism of backward peoples), a world-wide spirit of confusion and disorder is breaking up the unity and the order of civilized society.

It is true that we live in an epoch of revolution, and that the breakup and re-formation of society is inevitable. But the Christian must see that his mission is not to contribute to the blind forces of annihilation which tend to destroy civilization and mankind together. He must seek to build rather than to destroy. He must orient his efforts towards world unity and not towards world division. Anyone who promotes policies of hatred and of war is working for the division and the destruction of civilized mankind.

We have to be convinced that there are certain things already clearly forbidden to all men, such as the use of torture, the killing of hostages, genocide (or the mass extermination of racial, national or other groups for no reason than that they belong to an "undesirable" category). The destruction of civilized centers by nuclear annihilation bombing is genocide.

We have to become aware of the poisonous effect of the mass media that keep violence, cruelty and sadism constantly present to the minds of unformed and irresponsible people. We have to recognize the danger to the whole world in the fact that today the economic life of the more highly-developed nations is in large part centered on the production of weapons, missiles and other engines of destruction.

We have to consider that hate propaganda, and the consistent heckling of one government by another, has always inevitably led to violent conflict. We have to recognize the implications of voting for politicians who promote policies of hate. We must never forget that our most ordinary decisions may have terrible consequences.

It is no longer reasonable or right to leave all decisions to a largely anonymous power elite that is driving us all, in our passivity, towards ruin. We have to make ourselves heard.

Every individual Christian has a grave responsibility to protest clearly and forcibly against trends that lead inevitably to crimes which the Church deplores and condemns. Ambiguity, hesitation and compromise are no longer permissible. We must find some new and constructive way of settling international disputes. This may be extraordinarily difficult. Obviously war cannot be abolished by mere wishing. Severe sacrifices may be demanded and the results will hardly be visible in our day. We have still time to do something about it, but the time is rapidly running out.

Gordon C. Zahn | The Case for Christian Dissent

> There is no hiding the fact that it is much harder to be a
> Christian today than it was in the first centuries, and there
> is every reason to predict that it will be even more difficult in
> the near future. When it becomes the "sacred duty" of a
> man to commit sin, the Christian no longer knows how he
> should live. There remains nothing else for him to do but
> bear individual witness. And where such witness is, there is
> the Kingdom of God.   —REINHOLD SCHNEIDER

It would be hard to find a more telling statement of the fear-
some challenge facing us all than these words of a great
German poet and scholar. Living as we are in the shadow of
a gathering conflict which, for many, has already taken the
shape of a simple and decisive confrontation between the
powers of Good and Evil, we are poised on the brink of a
moment when it could seem to become a "sacred duty" to
unleash unimaginable destruction and sorrow upon other helpless and essentially inculpable men. To Schneider the issue
was quite clear: "Every man who decides in favor of sin—as
he who takes up arms must decide—will find it ever harder to
defend the Kingdom, for it is no longer in him." This then is
the issue, and it is an old and familiar one. Do Christians *really*
believe it better to suffer the loss of the whole world (or even
that small part of it they happen to call theirs) than to risk
the loss of their immortal souls? Old and familiar as the issue
is, however, it presents us with an utterly new challenge
today; for never before has the choice been set in terms of
such immediacy and finality, never before has the decision so

clearly involved the continued existence of human life itself together with all that man has wrought and dreamed.

Schneider's words do more than state a challenge for the future. In an even stronger sense they present an indictment of the past. Most specifically this indictment concerns those who failed to resist and to refuse when they were ordered to take up arms in Hitler's wars; yet it can and should be applied much more widely than that. It indicts all who did not bother to question the moral licitness of the duties to which they were called. It indicts—and much more severely—those who *did* question and *did* recognize or even only suspect the moral evil in those actions and who nonetheless complied with the orders out of considerations of an exaggerated prudence or a far-too-willing submissiveness to the authority of secular rulers. Nor is the indictment limited according to national boundaries. It indicts the British airman who participated in the horrendous strategic bombings of Hamburg just as surely as it indicts his German counterpart who helped devastate Coventry—and the American whose atomic experiments at Hiroshima and Nagasaki may be regarded as the peak atrocities of World War II. In short, the indictment extends to all everywhere who failed to bear the individual witness, however limited the degree of participation required of them, however remote the possibility that their witness would have had any significant effect upon the ultimate outcome. There are times when the stones cry out, and in such a time man may not be silent.

It would be a mistake, too, to see this indictment limited to the actions (or the failures to act) of the past. To the extent that the nations of the world are engaged in preparations for a newer and far more murderous war, every Christian who is a citizen of those nations has the moral obligation to question *now* and to protest *now*, regardless of how faint and futile that protest may seem. In this connection, it is utterly incomprehensible that Christians in our own country have not risen as one in an outburst of moral indignation against the recent proposals to create the weapon which will represent the ultimate in the denial of human worth and dignity, the projected neutron bomb which spares the buildings and other material artifacts of man's creation while destroying the life which is the handiwork of God.

Thus we all stand under indictment. But the bill of particulars is perhaps most clearly applicable to the German Christians who knowingly conformed to the orders of Hitler's Third Reich by participating in its unjust wars of aggression. In this it does not distinguish between Christians of the Catholic or Protestant preferences. The heroic Protestant leader, renowned for his open opposition to the Nazis, who volunteered to resume his World War I submarine service from the concentration camp in which he was then being held, is touched by its bitter implications just as surely as are the masses of Protestant believers of more humble rank. And both find their parallels in the behavior recorded for the German Catholic community, shepherd and faithful alike. If the present paper stresses the latter record, the universality of the indictment should not be forgotten or overlooked. All of us, whatever our nationality, whatever our religious identification, must face the charge that—now as well as then—we have failed to bear the witness and, by failing, have abandoned or even betrayed the Kingdom.

Narrowing the focus to the failure of German Catholicism in World War II is justified, however, by the fact that Schneider was himself a Catholic and would be most likely to have Catholics most in mind when he stated the ideal against which the actual record must be measured: "Though the enemies of the Kingdom of God nail one and those he loves to the Cross, he would be a Christian to the extent that he feared such martyrdom less than sin." An even more imperative reason for this more specific interest in the wartime record of German Catholicism lies in the fact that the research investigations upon which these observations will be based were limited to the question of German Catholic support for Hitler's wars [1] and, therefore, would not support more than occasional and

[1] These researches, conducted in Germany under a Fulbright grant, have been reported in a more detailed and extensively documented form in *German Catholics and Hitler's Wars: A Study in Social Control*, Sheed & Ward, New York, 1962. See also "The German Catholic Press and Hitler's Wars," *Cross Currents*, v. X, no. 4 (Fall 1960), pp. 337-53.

highly tentative extensions into the record of German Protestantism.

There is no denying the most immediate and essential fact, namely that German Catholics with but the rarest of exceptions did support the Hitler war effort. This is not to say that they did so voluntarily—though it is obvious that many did— or with any great measure of enthusiasm on the part of the majority. In the course of research interviews, the point was repeatedly stressed that the respondent had limited his personal degree of participation as much as possible, by seeking the least direct forms of service, shooting into the air instead of at the enemy soldiers, and employing many other avoidance devices. The fact that they served at all was usually explained in terms of a desire to escape the certain and drastic penalties exacted for any open refusal (or, as in the case of a Catholic editor who volunteered for military service to escape impending imprisonment in a concentration camp, to avoid some "greater evil"). However, even granting such limitations of participation and the sincerity of the intentions behind them, this does not alter the fact that the overwhelming majority of Germany's Catholics did knowingly accept *some* degree of participation in what most of them will now agree was an unjust war. And what is even more significant, most of the research informants were quite definite in insisting that the majority of Germany's Catholics were never deluded as to the true nature of Hitler's wars.

This fact assumes particular importance when we realize that they were encouraged in their participation, indeed *called* to it, by their spiritual leaders. A review of episcopal wartime pastorals and other directives offers a wealth of evidence that any German Catholic who would have been in doubt as to the moral licitness of the behavior required of him and who turned for guidance to these writings of his religious superiors (or, as in one case at least, to the bishop himself in a personal visit) for guidance would have learned that he had "a Christan duty" to fight for the German *Volk* and *Vaterland*. Perhaps the most explicit and official illustration of this is the 1941 pastoral letter issued by the combined

Bavarian hierarchy which frankly stated its intention to exhort everyone "to fulfill his duty fully and willingly and loyally" and "to devote your full efforts to the service of the *Vaterland* and the precious *Heimat* in conscientious fulfillment of duty and serious awareness of your mission." Cardinal Faulhaber's vicar-general greeted the opening of hostilities against Poland with an official diocesan directive declaring that "in such difficult times when everything is at stake, it is absolutely imperative that everyone faithfully discharge his religious, patriotic, and civic duties at whatever post he is assigned." Even so famous an opponent of Hitler as Bishop (later Cardinal) von Galen, in the course of one of his most heroic anti-Nazi sermons, took pains to declare that "we will continue to do our duty in obedience to God, out of love for our German *Volk* and *Vaterland*" and that "bravely we continue the fight against the foreign foe." It is a legitimate assumption that, if such outspoken opponents of Hitler and his regime were so openly committed to the war effort, other churchmen who were less ardent in their opposition (or who, like Military Bishop Rarkowski, were favorably inclined toward the Nazi New Order) must have done likewise.

Of course, there were some German Catholics who did "bear individual witness" and who, with but one known exception, paid for it with their lives. Franz Reinisch, a Pallotine priest active in the *Schönstatt* Movement, refused to take the required military oath of unconditional obedience to Hitler. Dr. Max Josef Metzger, founder of *Una Sancta* and of the *Christkönigsgesellschaft* (a religious order which described itself as "one of the sources of Catholic pacifism"), was caught trying to initiate private "peace feelers" through some of his contacts with Scandinavian Protestant leaders. Two of his disciples in the *Christkönigsgesellschaft* were executed for refusing to bear arms, though they had accepted the call to non-combatant service. An Austrian peasant, father of three infant daughters, went beyond this, refusing to perform even non-combatant service and was beheaded in 1943. The lone survivor among these witnesses, a lawyer by profession, was also sentenced to death but somehow "escaped" by being confined in a military mental hospital for the duration of the war. Here, then, was the Kingdom of God; and we can rejoice while giving thanks and due honor to their memory. But we must also acknowledge the tragic fact that their stand was not appreciated [2] and certainly not supported by their fellow Catholics and their religious leaders. Thus, while Archbishop Groeber of Freiburg did appeal for clemency for his priest (Metzberg), he did so in terms which characterized him as a hopeless "idealist" who had become ever more estranged from the practical realities of life. Even this was more considerate than the stand taken by Bishop Fliesser of Linz. *After the war was over,* this prelate twice intervened personally to block publication in his diocesan paper of articles praising the peasant's stand; and his grounds for doing so were that he considered those men who fought and died (as did the early Christians serving in the armies of the pagan Emperor!) to be "the greater heroes."

It would, of course, be pointless to review this whole tragic pattern of failure were it not for the fact that we must seek and somehow find an explanation which will enable us to guard ourselves against some future repetition. If fault there was, where did it lie? Are we to place the blame on the weaknesses of the men who acted in this fashion—or is the real weakness to be traced to the principles according to which they acted? Or were there perhaps some intervening factors which muddied the principles or confused the actors?

Certainly human weakness played its part. No one looks with indifference (and few are heroic and saintly enough to look with joyous gratitude) upon a course of action which would involve almost certain martyrdom. Even assuming the unlikely, that the man in the street was well-enough informed and sufficiently objective in his judgment to recognize what

[2] The summer of 1961 was spent doing research in the Austrian village which was the home of Franz Jägerstätter, the peasant mentioned above. It is significant in this connection that his friends and neighbors do not even yet appreciate his stand, that virtually all of them regard his sacrifice as a "tragedy" in the sense that his "religious fanaticism" disturbed his mental balance. The community, one must add, is completely Catholic in population.

was required of him, he would undoubtedly cast about for any prudential consideration which would justify participation in the war effort and thereby enable him to save his neck. There can be no doubt that the official pronouncements of his responsible spiritual leaders would have more than served that purpose for the ordinary German Catholic. Those leaders, in turn, faced the same prospect of martyrdom had they decided to take a contrary stand; but, more than that, they were obliged to consider the institutional welfare of the Church in Germany and the persecution that any opposition to the war would have unleashed. To say then that human weakness was a factor is but to admit that German Catholics —bishops, priests, and faithful alike—were men and, as men, were subject to the subjective distortions and blockages of the truth which should have compelled a different pattern of behavior on their part as Christians. For this reason, too, it is better to speak in terms of "fault" rather than of sin and to proceed on the charitable assumption that most of them "did their duty" and supported the war in subjectively good faith. At the same time, however, the willingness to understand how this could be should not be permitted to grow into a blanket justification of their actions. Franz Jägerstätter's bishop adjudged him to be "in erroneous conscience," but historical perspective should make it clear that the reverse was true: the bishop, not the peasant, was objectively wrong however confident he may have been of the moral soundness of his stand.

The fact that such error could have been so widespread and manifested even in such high places forces us to consider the question of the moral principles which should have been operative in this area of decision. Catholic moral tradition has produced an extensive formulation of the so-called "just war." Since it represents one of the three "exceptions" to the otherwise universal prohibition of killing stated in the Fifth Commandment, the conclusion should logically follow that *only in such a just war* is the Christian permitted (some would prefer to say required) to take part. The "just war" teaching incorporates a set of conditions, all of which are to be simultaneously fulfilled before a war can be so regarded. These conditions include (a) the requirement that the cause be just; (b) a "right intention" on the part of those responsible for declaring and conducting the war; (c) declaration and prosecution of the war by rightful authority; (d) a reasonable assurance of a successful outcome; (e) a proportionality in which the good effects must certainly outweigh the evil; and (f) the exclusive use of legitimate means of warfare.

Faced with orders to participate in an actual war, one could expect that the Catholic could turn to these enumeraed principles and find there the help and guidance that would enable him to overcome the weakness imposed by a too-demanding concern for his own life and wellbeing and to make a responsible assessment of his personal moral obligations. So, at least, it would seem. However, as history has consistently demonstrated, this traditional morality of war has apparently failed to provide the help and guidance it promises. How else can we explain the fact that it has been used by Catholics on both sides of virtually every international conflict to justify their actions in support of their nations' cause? We are left with the scandal which has found the living members of the Mystical Body of Christ destroying one another throughout all the generations since the time of Christ. And the scandal has grown progressively worse and ever more pressing as each new war spreads in scope and magnifies in intensity. The "just war" theology and its deceptively convenient set of conditions did not keep German Catholics from actively supporting what one German theologian described as "the classic example of the unjust war." For this reason the grim prospect of World War III, with its as yet uncharted potential for evil should and must force a thorough reassessment of the traditional moral teachings concerning war and of its relevance, if any, to modern—and particularly nuclear—war. If this is not done, it is a foregone certainty that we will find ourselves every bit as helpless to meet the challenge of World War III as was the German Catholic in 1939.

It should be noted that such a reassessment was begun after World War I and that it made some of its most significant advances within German Catholicism. In 1932, for instance, the same Cardinal Faulhaber whose name headed the list of the Bavarian bishops signing the 1941 pastoral quoted earlier delivered a sermon in which he called for a "new ethic" of war and active preparation for peace. The cardinal voiced his confidence then that "even moral theology will speak a new language. It will remain true to the old principles, but in the question of war, new facts will be taken into account." Among these new facts were the great advances in communications technology which, he felt, would pave the way for amicable settlement of disputes before they could develop into wars; advances in military technology which made war "no longer human, not to mention Christian" and thus assured its own elimination; and, finally, the awareness that all participants would stand to lose in war, a fact which would make it possible for any future war to meet the traditional requirement of "proportionality" as one of the conditions of the just war. Overly optimistic though he certainly was—even he had not learned to speak a "new language" when war came—this eminent churchman's appeal has lost none of its validity and, if anything, has gained tremendously in urgency in the three decades which have passed since it was voiced.

Faulhaber was not the only one to speak in this vein. Archbishop Groeber, the man who later would write so condescendingly of Metzger's "idealism," had addressed the annual meeting of the Peace League of German Catholics (*Friedensbund deutscher Katholiken*) in November 1931 admonishing all that true international peace was to be assured not by preparations for war but, instead, "on the universal and open intention to block a new murderous war at any price." He could see "no justification before man or God for devoting billions to armaments while millions of people in virtually every country on earth suffer from unemployment and physical as well as spiritual hunger." The peace organization itself and the theologian Franziscus Stratmann, O.P., one of its founders and leaders (Dr. Metzger was another), did much to awaken interest in the need for a new formulation of Catholic moral teachings on the subject of war; the official monthly publication of the *Friedensbund* for March, 1932, carries the report of an international conclave of theologians at Freiburg (Switzerland) which took a sharply anti-war position.

Thus, by the time National Socialism came to power in Germany, a substantial number of Catholics had been made aware of this growing body of theological opposition to war as something incompatible with Christian teachings. Many had answered Faulhaber's call for Catholic "apostles and front-line soldiers for peace" to enroll in the *Friedensbund*. In the face of all this, how are we to explain the almost total absence of Catholic opposition to Hitler's wars and the open support given them by the leaders of the Catholic hierarchy, including Faulhaber and Groeber? The most obvious answer lies, of course, in the repressive controls of the Nazi State. The *Friedensbund* had the distinction of being the first Catholic organization to be suppressed by the Nazis and, even later, it remained one of the three or four organizations specifically mentioned in the statement of non-affiliation (a kind of loyalty oath) required of all aspirants to civil service in the Third Reich. A raid upon the organization's Frankfurt headquarters led to several arrests and culminated in a showcase trial of two *Friedensbund* leaders, Friedrich Dessauer and Josef Knecht, in the closing months of 1933. The statement of formal charges included the accusations that the organization had set for itself the task of killing every "defense readiness" on the part of Germany's Catholics; that a 1932 policy statement called for renunciation on the part of the Weimar Republic of any right to depart from the path of disarmament; that one of its leaders had declared conscientious objection to be a Christian duty; that still another leader, a priest, had designated the German national anthem as "the greatest heresy of the twentieth century." The repressive actions taken against this German Catholic peace organization testify to the Nazis' respect for it as representing a significant pacifist potential and, as such, a threat to their plans to make the Third Reich the dominant military world power.

These external social controls exerted by the secular authority must be given the lion's share of the credit for the elimination of the *Friedensbund* and for the suppression of any effective Catholic opposition to Hitler's wars. But this does not tell the whole tale. Had there been an active internal commitment to the moral principles set forth or implied in the just war teachings, one might still have expected that German Catholics, or at least a far more impressive number of them than proved to be the case, would have accepted martyrdom in preference to violating the Fifth Commandment by supporting and participating in an unjust war. That such a pattern of refusal and resistance did not emerge must be traced to the presence of other and stronger commitments to the competing values of personal and national survival. The effect of the former will be discussed later; at this point consideration must be given to the latter by raising the question of nationalism and its impact upon moral judgments.

John Eppstein, in a major work published before World War II, spoke of the "national bias of many Catholic theologians and publicists" before, during and after World War I and of the "meagre and indeed contemptible" response to the pacific leadership of the Holy See. A reading of the documents issued by the German bishops and of the far less restrained contents of the remnants of the Catholic diocesan press still publishing into the war years would justify extending that bitter judgment to cover the events of World War II as well. These official wartime pronouncements are pervaded by an almost reverent commitment to the national mythology of *Volk, Vaterland* and *Heimat* and abound in laudatory references to the fighting men and their heroic dedication to their sacred duties. Although the writings of the military bishop deserve special prominence, this nationalistic commitment is clearly evidenced in the wartime statements of Galen (Münster), Faulhaber (Munich), Groeber (Freiburg), and Ehrenfried (Würzburg) and the other leading bishops as well. If "national bias" may be said to have colored or distorted the moral judgments of such eminent and responsible leaders of the German Catholic community, it may be taken for granted that the average Catholic citizen of the Third Reich would have been similarly affected by it.

Perhaps the most direct (and by far the most disturbing) evidence of nationalism's impact is found in the pamphlet written by a well-known German Catholic theologian. The pamphlet, prepared for the practical guidance of the layman, addressed itself to the question, "What is to be done?" and resolved the whole question most simply by informing the reader, "Now there is no point in raising the question of the just war . . ." Such a question could only be answered in a scientific way *after* the war was over when the documents of both sides became available. Now, the writer continued, the individual had but one course open to him: "To do his best with faith in the cause of his *Volk*."

This statement serves to reveal in almost brutal clarity certain weaknesses inherent in the traditional just war teachings which render them almost useless in any actual wartime situation. These weaknesses reflect, in the first instance, the implied distrust of the competence of the individual to make a personal moral judgment coupled with a virtual denial of his moral responsibility in this critical area of behavior. This is matched by an exaggerated definition of the scope of authority proper to the secular ruler and of the quality and extent of the citizens' obligation to obey. These factors then combine in the principle which grants the "presumption of justice" (or "faith in the cause of his *Volk*") to the warring authority, a principle which, in effect, surrenders the moral autonomy of the individual Christian to the state.

The first component is evidenced by the assumption that, since the ordinary citizen does not have (and obviously can not have) full access to all the relevant facts, he has no basis for judging the necessity or the legitimacy of the acts required of him in a war. Archbishop Groeber was particularly disdainful of the scope of individual competence in his 1935 declaration that "Catholic theologians have always distinguished between the just and unjust war and have never left it to the judgment of the individual, with all of his shortsightedness and emotionalism, to decide the justice of any given war. Instead, the final decision has been left to the legitimate authority." Such a formulation, and one must admit that it is the formulation that generally prevails, can only lead to a theological "dead end." The individual Christian who is called to service in a war—service which will directly or indirectly involve him in the killing of other human beings—can always claim (indeed, he will be told!) that he has insufficient information to justify a refusal on his part to comply. Moreover, even if he did have all the facts, the implication is clear that he could not be trusted to make a decision as to the justice or injustice of the war because of the inherent intellectual and emotional shortcomings identified by the archbishop. We end up with the kind of moral helplessness offered in the theologian's pamphlet; there is "no point" in even raising the question of the justice or injustice of any given war, and there is no alternative for the individual but to make an act of blind faith "in the cause of his *Volk*."

This tendency to distrust the individual judgment reached in the light of a conscience formed according to whatever information is available is compounded further by the exaggerated conception of the nature of secular authority and its proper scope. Beginning with the unchallengeable principle that all authority finds its source in God, the argument usually proceeds through a series of deductions and ramifications tracing the origin of the state to the social nature of man and asserting the moral indifference of all forms of government (as well as of the particular ruler's virtues or lack of them). The whole sequence finally ends in the conclusion proclaiming the binding moral obligation of the citizen to honor and obey his government, to "give unto Caesar the things that are Caesar's." Stated in their pure and abstract generality, these principles are in themselves sound; but, again, in their actual application to the practical order they too easily lead to the kind of absurdity encountered in the wartime pamphlet (this time one of American origin) which instructed Catholic servicemen that by listening carefully to the voice of their blustering sergeant they would be hearing the voice of God. (One assumes that the "voice of God" would be heard, too, in the person of superior officers like the well-known admiral whose order to "kill Japs—kill Japs—kill more Japs!" were emblazoned on a billboard overlooking Tulgai Bay and whose assurances that "we are drowning and burning the bestial apes all over the Pacific, and it is just as much pleasure to burn them as to drown them" were intended to inspire the men under him to an ever more efficient performance of their duty.)

All authority does indeed find its origin in God—but only His authority is unbounded; only His authority is not prone to distortion and abuse. It is likewise true that no one form of government should be viewed as the "right" form or "divinely instituted" in the strict theological sense; but human history should have made it amply clear by now that it is all too possible for *some* forms to degenerate to the point where they do incorporate an intrinsic evil. And one may certainly hold that such a point is reached in the modern totalitarian state with the denial of the true nature and dignity of the human person implied in its conception of the individual citizen as nothing more than a "cell" in the body politic of the folk community. When such a form of government does obtain—or, for that matter, when the reins of any government fall into the hands of a wicked or antireligious regime—it seems far more consistent with the teachings and the example of Christ that the individual Christian regard the secular authority and its commands with a note of prudent suspicion and restraint lest, by too automatic a granting of obedience to objectively immoral orders, he find himself led into at least materially sinful acts. Thus, if Hitler's wars were indeed unjust wars, it must be admitted that the millions of German Catholics who supported them did offend against the Fifth Commandment, that their exaggerated idea of the proper scope and binding quality of the "legitimate authority" represented by the Third Reich did seduce them into patterns of obedience which ended up with them all too willingly giving unto Caesar that which was not rightfully Caesar's due.

In the specific problem facing us in this paper, the morality of war and its particular application to World War II (and a possible World War III), this combination of the distrust or denial of the individual's competence to determine his own right course of action and the exaggerated notion of the individual's obligations in obedience to the commands of secular authority become especially evident in the familiar "presumption of justice" teaching. This doctrine, a contribution of the probablist theologians, operates as the joker which reduces the whole elaborate formulation of the "just war" and its carefully developed conditions to little more than a meaningless copybook exercise. Intended to meet the problem faced by the Christian who is in doubt as to the justice or injustice of a given war, it simply resolves his problem in such a way that he is not only freed to participate in the war he suspects may be unjust, but he is actually expected to suppress his doubts and serve in the war if ordered to do so. Since, as we have seen, the situation will always be such that the individual will not have access to all the essential and definitive facts which might have bearing upon the question of the justice of a war, some vestige of doubt must always remain—even for those whose level of conviction has led them to the point of conscientious objection. To say, then, that any and all such doubt must be resolved in favor of the legitimate authority is to guarantee the unending repetition of that scandal which has always led to brothers-in-Christ killing one another in the firm confidence that they were fulfilling a Christian obligation in doing so. Add to this the knowledge we now have that the facts of such a situation are always under some control of the war-making authority and that they can be released, suppressed, and distorted to suit the purposes of that authority, and the "presumption of justice" doctrine actually places a premium upon the manipulation of the facts to assure the wholehearted support of the citizen who is also a Christian. Nothing more clearly exposes the utter bankruptcy of the doctrine and its disastrous effects upon any expectation that Catholics might be able to make a responsible judgment in this most vital problem of modern war than the grotesque situation which placed the German Catholic citizen under a moral obligation to give the "presumption of justice" to Adolf Hitler in his campaigns to impose an intrinsically anti-Christian ideology upon the entire world.

The net result of all this is something akin to a total denial of individual moral responsibility. Like Pilate washing his hands before the mob, or Eichmann pleading his case before the tribunal of Israel and the world, we end up with the situation in which the individual actor assigns the responsibility for his personal misdeeds to others who, he can claim, forced or commanded him to commit them. Franz Jägerstätter's bishop set this pattern before him in embarrassing clarity, telling him he had no right to refuse to serve in Hitler's armies; and he was apparently annoyed by the peasant's unwillingness to be convinced: "In vain I spelled out for him the moral principles concerning the degree of responsibility of the citizen and private individual for the deeds of the ruler and reminded him of his much higher responsibility to his own private state of life and, in particular, to his family." Not only was this man, one of the few to bear the individual witness, denied the moral support he sought from his spiritual leader; he was actually troubled throughout the months of his imprisonment while awaiting the executioner's axe by the haunting fear that he was committing a sin in refusing to serve in the war he recognized as unjust.

But, the realist will object, this man was an exception. Most Christians would have welcomed the bishop's advice because they would not have been ready or able to follow the peasant's lead; they would have feared such martyrdom more than sin. This may well be true; but if it is, if the values of personal survival are given priority over considerations of justice and morality, this fact should be a matter of grave concern to those responsible for the Church and the role it is supposed to play in the modern world. Can it be a matter of slight moment, for instance, that the same theologian who instructed the German Catholics not to trouble their heads over the justice or injustice of Hitler's wars was later to voice the opinion that Max Josef Metzger was a "fool" for acting as he did, that a man *does not have the right* to follow a course of action he knows will lead to his death? Or that another prominent German Catholic, an editor, could speak in much the same vein, insisting that the leaders of the Church may never impose impossible burdens upon the faithful or even themselves pursue a policy which will jeopardize the institutional functionings of the Church? To this man, the *summum bonum* of the Church lies in the distribution of the sacraments to the greatest possible number and this, he felt, must always be the overriding consideration in any episcopal decision.

Of these two limiting considerations—the fear that individual Catholics will fall away if the burdens become too much for them to bear and the fear that the secular power will engage in reprisal actions should the Church leadership fail to give sufficient support to its programs and policies—the second undoubtedly carries the greater weight. Certainly in other matters of individual morality, the responsible Church leadership is much more confident about spelling out obligations that might constitute serious burdens for the faithful. In the matter of sexual and family morality, for instance, there is no comparable pattern of caution; instead, the theologian, perched as it were on the edge of the marriage bed, is always quite ready to elaborate upon the inflexible and sometimes seemingly unbearable moral obligations associated with this most intimate area of individual behavior—and there is little or no inclination to modify these teachings or obligations or to maintain a prudent silence in the interests of reducing the "leakage" attributable to them.

When the secular authority is involved, however, things are usually quite different. The compulsion to reach and maintain a comfortable *modus vivendi* has apparently grown so strong that one might well suggest that the familiar separation-of-Church-and-state issue now requires a restatement. The problem is no longer so much one of efforts on the part of the religious authority to insinuate itself into the area of state prerogative by exploiting its influence over its members; rather it is one of the Church being reduced—or, more often, reducing itself—to little more than an agency for channelling or reinforcing the controls of the state in those matters it, the state, defines as crucial to its wellbeing. Thus, while the individual communicant can be dealt with rather easily when it comes to telling him what proportion of his income should be devoted to religious purposes, what movies he is to avoid, and what

books he may not read, the spokesmen of the Church are likely
to be much more inclined toward a policy of expedient silence
when it comes to passing open judgment upon the actions he
is commanded to perform by the state. Again the history of
the Third Reich is illustrative. There were leading Catholic
bishops who have received, and deservedly so, great honor
for their heroic stand against euthanasia; yet it cannot be
denied that in other areas involving objective violations of
the Fifth Commandment—and, incidentally, bearing more directly upon more vital objectives of the Nazi rulers—they
either maintained official silence (as in the case of the liquida-
tion of the Jews) or, as in the case of Hitler's aggressive wars,
openly called for support on the part of Germany's Catholics.

But they were not alone in this picking and choosing of
issues on which to speak out. The bishops of the nations
ranged against the Third Reich showed the same expedient
silence in their failure to pronounce upon the immorality of
the strategic bombings of German cities or the even more
murderous fire-bombings and, later, atomic bombings of Japanese cities. Starvation blockades directed against civilian
morale fully as much as, perhaps even more than, against
military forces provoked no protest. Papal appeals for a speedy
peace received no echo in their wartime messages; nor did
they even go so far as to take public issue when the "unconditional surrender" objective became the formally announced
policy in direct opposition to those appeals.

Circumspection remains the order of the day. Today, too,
one hears thundering denunciations of obscenity and heroic
appeals from the pulpit calling upon the faithful to (as one
pastor recently put it) "have the guts" to refuse to attend
movies violating the Legion of Decency codes; but one listens
in vain for even the merest whisper of public criticism of
officially proclaimed military policies based upon *retaliatory*
(a "right intention?") second-strike strategies or the proposal
to invest tax monies, contributed in part by the Catholic faithful, in the development of newer and more fearful weapons
of highly doubtful morality.

In short, while the record of German Catholic support for

Hitler's wars is valuable as an illustrative case history of the utter inadequacy and almost total irrelevance of our traditional morality of war, it holds far greater value for us as a warning example for the future. The day may be near when it will again become "the 'sacred duty' of a man to commit sin," and it is, therefore, of most urgent importance that we begin to develop the new ethic of war called for by Cardinal Faulhaber so that the Christian may be furnished a more useful guide to enable him to determine how he should live and act in such a tragic situation. One may take some hope in the fact that there is a growing body of writers, priests and theologians as well as laymen, entering into an active discussion of this vital issue of the morality of war. Not all are in agreement; but one may take confidence that the new formulation will finally emerge which will preserve the old and immutable principles of the Christian faith but will apply them to the world in which we live, a world from which the so-called "Christian prince" has long since vanished (if, indeed, he ever was anything more than a philosophical abstraction).

Such a new formulation, the writer would insist, requires a recognition of a far wider scope of competence and responsibility for the individual believer as well as a far greater readiness on the part of the Church to detach herself from the temporal interests and objectives of the national state. It would require, too, a greater measure of fortitude and perhaps a lesser concentration of prudence in determining when and in what terms the religious leaders should speak out on matters of public concern. Perhaps, though, what is needed most of all is the readiness to reawaken the ascetic ideal that so strongly marked the early period of Church history, to realize that, in Schneider's words, "Persecution and suffering will ever be the lot of the Christian" and to translate this into a readiness to return to the catacombs and to accept martyrdom if need be.

For the greatest temptation of all may lie ahead in the gathering conflict which promises to be at one and the same time a struggle for national survival and a crusade against the forces of an open and aggressively anti-Christian ideology.

This past summer a German bishop spoke to this writer of his overriding concern for the Communist threat; and, to make his point most effectively, the bishop quoted a former Communist who reportedly once heard his associates boast of their willingness to "go through a sea of blood" to gain their ends. What apparently escaped the notice of the bishop, however, was the fact that this could just as easily serve as a statement of the Christian answer; that the followers of Christ, too, must be prepared to go through a sea of blood to achieve their objectives. There is, though, one all-important difference: the blood the Christian must be ready to shed is his own. But he can always take heart in the certainty that the ultimate victory will be his—unless, of course, he secretly fears that the Gates of Hell can prevail after all.

The developing discussion is encouraging, but it must continue to expand until it engages all levels of the Catholic community. The beginnings made by the Faulhabers and the Groebers in the 1930's have been greatly overshadowed by the even more forthright statements of prelates like Cardinal Ottaviani and Archbishop Roberts made since the end of World War II. The appearance of a growing number of books and periodical articles dealing with the question of the morality of modern war is another hopeful sign. And all this activity is crowned, and to a great degree inspired, by a steady stream of papal messages which, though they are not entirely unambiguous in their statement nevertheless do lend clear and direct support to those who have rejected modern war, and especially nuclear war, as something incompatible with the basic truths and distinctive spirit of Christianity.

Even the apparent "ambiguities" disappear when the two major themes stressed in these papal messages are fitted into a single context and not, as is usually the case, advanced as argument and counter-argument by those who, on the one hand, advance a pacifist interpretation and those who use these same messages to refute that interpretation and support their own position favoring the continuation of programs of military preparedness. One cannot ignore or deny the unmistakable pattern of outright denunciation of war and its means these messages contain just as one should not overlook the equally undeniable affirmations of the licitness of an active defense of national rights and the obligations of the individual Christian to support such defense efforts. Instead of regarding these as contradictions, however, one can and should combine them into a single and coherent position which at the very time it acknowledges such defense to be a legitimate objective makes it quite clear that war is no longer to be considered a permissible means of accomplishing that objective. Once this statement of the case is accepted, it will necessarily follow that some alternative to war must be sought and found by which the thoroughly legitimate end will be accomplished through equally legitimate means.

Most Catholic pacifists would accept this as a statement of their essential position. Many would go further and suggest that such an alternative already exists in the complex of means and techniques known as nonviolence. But, encouraged though he is by the trend of the developing discussion and his confidence that the pacifist implications of the Christian faith will ultimately win their due recognition, the pacifist is also acutely conscious of the urgency of the need and the special responsibility borne by those who claim to subscribe to that faith. He would insist that time is running out; that we must finally free ourselves from the restraints and incapacities imposed by theological formulations that have proved to be tragically inadequate and have opened the way to the hideous scandal of support given by well-intentioned Catholics (actually *required of them* as "a Christian duty!") to what may well have been history's most unjust war. Certainly he would share John XXIII's concern over "the severe judgment of God and of history" and make his the Pope's Christmas appeal to the rulers of nations to "shun all thought of force; think of the tragedy of initiating a chain reaction of acts, decisions and resentments that could erupt into rash and irreparable deeds."

The issue is terrifyingly simple. If, as Catholics believe, their Church possesses the fullness of the Christian truth and the sacramental means to bring that truth to its realization among men, it must provide other and better answers than it has to this problem of war, and it must inspire and manifest in all its members the spirit of dedication such answers may require. If we fail again; if, like the salt which has lost its savor we lose our identity and purpose in a new surrender to the temptations of conformism and accommodation, humankind may never have another chance.

Walter Stein | The Defense of the West

Everybody detests the H-bomb. Few are prepared to do without it. No H-bomb, no Western freedom, remains the dominant verdict. And this may well be right. Our military security rests on nuclear defense.

Indeed, it seems improbable that it will ever be safe for the West to relinquish these weapons. Even if, through mutual fear, a serious agreement for disarmament and control were achieved, we should not have achieved security. Britain alone has long possessed enough nuclear explosive to destroy every large city in the world; the United States and Soviet stockpiles are vastly larger. Does anyone imagine that a foolproof system of inspection could be worked out which would guarantee that none of this stock has been hidden away? Much could be done (especially by controlling the means of delivery) to diminish the consequent risks, but vast risks would remain to be lived with. Leaving the H-bomb aside, it would not need many Hiroshima-type bombs, wielded by one side alone, to determine the outcome of any conflict. Can the West, then, afford to trust Moscow's word in this matter? Or Moscow to trust the West's? And—in the long run, even more challenging—how, if we were stripped of these weapons, how, in the last resort, could we balance the increasingly explosive pressure of Chinese numbers?

It is in a general East-West *rapprochement*—the radical treatment of international infections, together with general

Editor's note: This essay has been slightly abridged. The complete text, together with related statements by other British Catholics, will be found in *Nuclear Weapons: A Catholic Response*, New York, Sheed & Ward, 1962.

disarmament arrangements—that our hopes have come to center. Men must have hope; and, no doubt, the gathering urge towards international co-operation in these days, in spite of the bitterest setbacks, reasserts our humanity across immensities of terror and estrangement. Yet, where it would reach for *security*, this urge may itself be blinkered. We may indeed hope that the necessary gestures of trust might not be abused. . . . The fact remains that anything short of a World State would leave us so far from "secure" that it might actually seem more hazardous to risk betrayal after disarming than to risk betrayal whilst one remains armed.

It does not follow that we should not continue to seek agreed disarmament, only that we should be serious in striving to bring this about—and that we should be serious in facing the risks. . . . We may then find that there is in fact only one realistic basis for such a policy (however rarely this may be confessed or perceived): a readiness, if need be, to disarm unilaterally, or, in the last resort, to fall back on non-violent resistance, *as if* we had thus unilaterally disarmed.

1 THE ARGUMENT FROM EXPEDIENCY

A strong case can be made for a basic commitment to non-violent defense in present circumstances on strategic and political grounds. This case is becoming increasingly familiar.

Like the demands for unilateral nuclear disarmament, to which it is related, this case has a special relevance to Britain and Western Europe; though some of these arguments are no less relevant to the position of the United States. . . .

The case has a positive and a negative aspect. Negatively, it rests on the three facts that no amount of nuclear power can guarantee Western security; that no military means at all can shield us against communism as an ideological force; and that the concept of nuclear war has indeed obliterated the concept of military defense. . . .

That nuclear power cannot guarantee Western security is evident both in theory and from experience. It did not, for

instance, prevent Soviet infiltration into the Middle East, nor
—in spite of Western reactions—the suppression of the Hungarian revolt. The very enormity of strategic nuclear weapons
disqualifies them as instruments of limited defense. What they
do provide is an over-all "balance of terror" that discourages
naked large-scale aggression, plus a tremendous general stiffening of the risks attending local coups. Now, apart from the
fact that strategic nuclear power cannot provide effective local
protection, there are at least three sorts of situation in which
a nuclear war might be unleashed. . . . (i) A local conflict—in
Central Europe, for instance, or in Africa—might in spite of
the great stiffening of risks already mentioned, set off a chain-
reaction towards total war. (ii) In the atmosphere of fear and
strain generated by a prolonged nuclear stalemate, one side
or the other may eventually suffer a failure of nerve. A rumor
of enemy war preparations or a mistake relating to radar sig-
nals, might thus easily precipitate a plunge into actual war.
(iii) And it is not necessary to rehearse the fantastic hazards
that would result from the imminent diffusion of more and
more nuclear weapons among more and more governments
throughout the world. We may take it as established that the
"security" provided by nuclear weapons is far from complete
—and is achieved at the price of the most radical insecurities
men have ever been exposed to.

It is, moreover, self-evident that no military means at all
can shield us against communism as an ideological force.
Ideologically, communism is an infection that can only be
arrested by better health. Military strength is as irrelevant
from this point of view as it is to the destruction of cancer.
Even a defeat of Russia and China might actually be followed
by a resurgence of communism throughout the world. The
enormous sums spent on nuclear armaments might be used
more effectively to combat communism by a world-wide campaign against poverty and the evils that make the communist
solution attractive.

But not only is nuclear defense unable to guarantee
security; not only are military means incapable of stemming
communism as an idea: "nuclear defense" is simply a con-

tradiction in terms. This has been shown again and again in recent discussions—and indeed is presupposed in official N.A.T.O. thinking. The policy of "deterrence" recognizes that our best hope, in a full-scale nuclear war (short of actually starting it) is to inflict similar feats of annihilation upon our enemy as our enemy has just inflicted upon ourselves. Worries about technological breakthroughs, vulnerability of bases, "credibility" and so on, are all primarily worries about the capacity of "the deterrent" to *deter:* few of our leaders are apparently troubled by the question whether the hope of annihilating even though one has already been annihilated can amount to a rational concept of defense.

It is clear that the security provided by nuclear weapons has its limits. In the light of this consideration—and its corollary, that without nuclear weapons military security is now altogether unthinkable—the alternative of non-violent resistance acquires an unprecedented practical attraction. What we used to dismiss as the panacea of political enthusiasts, now imposes itself as a strategy for the tough-minded. At the least, it can no longer be precluded from serious thought.

Yet it must be admitted that the force of these arguments is negative. They show that military security is now absurd. It is only when this fact has been grasped—really assimilated into our image of the world—that we are likely to cease chasing after such "security." But even when we have thus broken through what Sir Stephen King-Hall calls "the thought-barrier in defense thinking," there remain enormous intractable problems when it comes to a positive advocacy of non-violent defense. There is quite a lot of available information about historical uses of non-violence. There is the outstanding achievement of Gandhi. And Sir Stephen himself outlines some interesting plans for non-violent action in our situation, towards the end of his *Defence in the Nuclear Age.*[1] Yet does any of this really measure up to the problems of a life-and-death struggle of the kind we are concerned with, a world-wide struggle for ideological survival—with the men who "saved Hungary from the fascists"—and whose ritual clamor for

[1] Gollancz (London), 1958.

peace is punctuated by outbursts of savage diplomatic aggression and threats of nuclear punishment? Or with the men who "liberated Tibet"—and who openly continue to believe in the efficacy, if not the inevitability, of international violence?

This, too, must be faced: the positive case for non-violent resistance, in our situation, appears to be as implausible in terms of prudence, as the negative arguments seem compelling.

2 THE MORAL ARGUMENT

Nuclear defense cannot provide security; and in this sense we do not surrender our security if we renounce it. Yet there are important senses in which we should nevertheless be less "secure" without nuclear weapons, especially in view of what has just been admitted about non-violent resistance. Secure or insecure, however, there is now no *moral* alternative to an unconditional renunciation of "the deterrent."

In essence, the plea is very simple indeed: (i) that some things are intolerable, irrespective of circumstances; that total war is thus absolutely intolerable; and that "nuclear defense" means total war; (ii) that the mere willingness to *risk* a war that could annihilate civilization, poison the whole of this planet, and forever violate the life of the future, if life survives, is a wickedness without parallel, a blasphemy against Creation; and (iii) that the policy of "deterrence" involves a conditional willingness to unleash such a war—and is therefore not only wicked in what it risks, but in terms of implicit *intention*.

Nearly two decades after Hiroshima and Nagasaki, and a decade after the testing of a bomb whose destructive power is fifteen times greater than the total weight of bombs dropped on Germany during the last war, this plea is still struggling to gain so much as a serious hearing. There is now a thought-race, over against the arms-race, to master the new facts of death. But the perception that things like these *simply must not be*—the simple acknowledgement of our status as human beings—remains strangely muddled and muffled. Even those whose thought and attitudes clearly spring from this kind of perception, often prefer to clothe themselves in elaborate pragmatic expertise (as if to acknowledge such claims as decisive must be a little embarrassing in its naïvety). And elsewhere, there are vast and complicated ranges of resistance to this plea—if only the resistance of silence. It thus becomes necessary to restate this essentially simple plea in precise, analytic detail, in the hope of driving out mistaken analyses. (One cannot, of course, hope to drive out a determination to by-pass or irrationally overwhelm it.)

Certainly, there are strong logical and psychological difficulties that may obstruct clear vision. One reason, for instance, why this case has made so little headway is that the notion of total war is one to which we have been steadily acclimatized. There is, it seems, a long unbroken ascent of military developments towards Hiroshima, with no footholds for moral distinctions. Before Hiroshima, there was saturation bombing; and before that, more haphazard raids on civilians. In the background of these is the combined raiding of military and civilian targets—and, for that matter, heavy artillery shellings. The whole concept of conscript armies already implies a large measure of "totality." . . .

Now it is no doubt difficult to insert a line into this sort of progression; and there may be much discussion about where precisely it should be drawn. What is certain is that a line must be drawn somewhere, and that nuclear warfare stands far to the wrong side of it.

There is nothing odd about this combination of open-mindedness and certainty. There may be much discussion about whether Strasbourg is really a French or German town, and I may be unwilling to commit myself; but this does not mean I have any doubt about whether Paris is French or German. It is common, indeed usual, to be uncertain of a boundary but quite certain of what lies well to the east or west of it. This is especially the case when we are dealing with something that shades off from one extreme to another. We all know when a man is clean-shaven, and we know what it is for a man to be bearded. But what is it that makes a man bearded?

Is it having one hair? or two? or three? or thirty? We can imagine a man saying that if it is impossible to settle for some definite number, if there is no such thing as the exact number of hairs which make a man bearded, then there is no such thing as the difference between having a beard and not having one. Of course, this is a simple and notorious logical fallacy. But while nobody is likely to commit this in cases such as this text-book example's, we may easily slip into fallacies of this kind where we are dealing with matters involving us more deeply. Thus the fallacy is especially prevalent in discussions of defense ethics. The existence of an unbroken chain of "degrees" between the primitive warrior's club and the modern man's H-bomb should not, however, obscure the difference between them.

Here the line has to be drawn between killing enemy combatants in a just war, which may be legitimate, and the deliberate killing of non-combatants (or "harmless"), which is murder.

We recognize that some such line can be drawn, and we show that we recognize it, by the fact that (unless we are pacifists or cynics) we think it is one thing to be a soldier and another to be a murderer. We do not seriously think of soldiers as "licensed murderers" or of murderers as unlicensed soldiers. We think that it is possible, or at least that it used to be possible, for a soldier to do his job without moral guilt.

The primary job of a soldier is to defend the community against a particular form of attack—direct physical violence. In order to fulfil this important and honorable purpose he may use certain extreme measures; for example, he may, of course, kill enemy troops if this is the only practicable way of protecting the community against them. It is important to see that the right to kill is not something that belongs to a soldier because he has a uniform but because he has a certain job to do. Troops may be used for many other purposes—quelling riots, or policing a conquered country, for example: in these circumstances they do not have the same right to use extreme measures. Similarly, the man who may be killed is not just any man who wears enemy uniform but a man who cannot

otherwise be prevented from carrying out his present activity
of violence; thus to shoot prisoners of war who are not engaged
in hostilities is just ordinary murder. If we may not kill a man
simply because he wears enemy uniform, still less may we kill
him simply because he belongs to the enemy country or sub-
scribes to the enemy's religion or political ideology. On the
other hand, if a man is directly engaged in hostilities against
the community, we may prevent him by killing, whether or
not he is wearing a uniform. Any such man, in or out of uniform, is for the time being a combatant; he ceases to be a
combatant as soon as he presents no immediate danger of
physical violence.

Now, of course, the line between combatants and non-
combatants is one of those which it is difficult to fix exactly,
particularly is it difficult to draw it in the heat of action; yet,
nevertheless, there are large areas which unquestionably lie
on either side of the line. If it is right to kill enemy troops,
what about civilians supplying their weapons? If it is right to
kill munitions-workers, what about those supplying the forces
with food? What, moreover, of all those who—in coal mines
or steel plants or laboratories—stand behind the immediate
war-suppliers? And of those who, simply by performing the
most unaggressive jobs, right down to hospital nursing and
haircutting, keep the economy in being and thereby assist
the war-effort? Is "totality" not implicit in modern societies?

At this point it is only necessary to repeat that difficulties
about the drawing of lines do not dispense from conscientious-
ness; to suggest that, when all has been said, there remains
a qualitative abyss between a pilot's or munitions-worker's
job and a barber's; and that a high proportion of any population consists of children, full-time mothers, pensioners and sick
people. Of course, if someone is so inclined, he can reply
that mothers rear children and are good for their husbands,
that children will one day be workers or even soldiers—and
are, in fact, already knitting socks for the troops—that pensioners can do all sorts of things in a crisis, and that sick
people frequently get well again. Moralizing can have its
moments.

Here we should perhaps pause to observe that the legitimate killing of combatants is something horrible. War would be full of horrors even without the murder of non-combatants. It is important to say this because many people suppose that the objection to killing non-combatants is simply that the horrors of war ought to be kept within some conventional bounds. But the objection to murdering non-combatants is not simply that it makes war a degree more horrible, but that it is wicked. The killing of combatants is indeed a necessary evil—something ghastly which we may find ourselves bound to do; the killing of non-combatants is a *moral* evil, something which we have never the right to do.

Even when we have drawn some kind of line between combatants and non-combatants, there remains a further problem. Granted that we may never deliberately seek to kill an innocent man, must we always refrain from killing combatants if there is a danger of killing non-combatants as well? Clearly not. I may sink an enemy submarine even though I am sure there are prisoners on board. I may destroy an enemy arms dump even if I am sure that nearby civilians will be killed. In such cases I have a definite and justifiable military purpose and it is this that I seek to achieve. I do not deliberately try to kill the non-combatants, their death is a circumstance attendant upon the achieving of my purpose. In the case of combatants, on the other hand, I do *deliberately seek their death as a means* for protecting the community. It seems, then, that I may sometimes take action which issues in the death of non-combatants, provided that their death is *merely a circumstance attendant upon the thing I am trying to do*.

But, clearly, the consequences of an act can be "unintentional" in this sense only (i) if there is a reasonable proportion between the intended good and the unintended evil, (ii) if the evil effects do not become too vast in themselves (for there comes a point when sheer scale must deprive the concept of "unintended effects" of meaning), and (iii), above all, if the evil effects do not constitute a foreseen *means* of the *good ones* (for, of course, if they did, they themselves must needs be intended). And to intend an evil is evil, whatever the ultimate aim: the end does not justify the means.

Thus, suppose that a raid is aimed directly at the houses or hospitals or schools of a city, or is to cover a center of population so extensively that military and non-military targets are indiscriminately affected, there can no longer be any justification in terms of "double effect." Even if one allowed that the criterion of reasonable proportion might be satisfied; even if one could hold on to the notion of "unintended effects" in view of the massiveness of the circumstances involved: there can be no getting round the fact these evils would be *directly aimed at.* Whatever the ultimate aim (i.e. victory for a just cause), the immediate aim would include the deliberate destruction of non-combatants—would include a commitment to *mass-murder.*

This is why nuclear warfare is immoral. It could hardly achieve a just balance of consequences; and the hugeness of its evils—which of course might extend to the entire destruction of civilization, grave and permanent harm to future generations, and, potentially, even the total extermination of our species—reduces the notion of "unintended effects" to parody; whilst it is, above all, absolutely clear that its indiscriminate terrors must in fact be directly willed, since "deterrence" ultimately rests on the possibility of "massive retaliation."

Nuclear warfare dramatizes the concept of total war in a uniquely compelling way, though what it dramatizes is not altogether new. Though there are aspects of nuclear war that take it utterly beyond anything man has ever yet inflicted upon himself, there are others that are continuous with previous history. As regards its immediate results, an H-bomb dropped on a city clearly does not differ in principle from, for instance, air raids in which 100,000 people, including refugees, were killed in a single night. It is simply as if we had stumbled against a mutilated body on our doorstep, or had suddenly witnessed an administrative atrocity. Such experiences may rock one into a new alertness—opening one's eyes to things hitherto unnoticed; or they may be neutralized by recalling that, after all, they are not unique. We may see the H-bomb and other atomic weapons as a final revelation of total war—and, in the light of this, revise many of our past judgments and tolerances. Or we may swallow this *reductio ad absurdum* for the sake of absurdities swallowed long ago. How often do we hear of the Allies' saturation raids of the last war, or, say, of the behavior of mercenary armies of the Middle Ages—triumphantly pointed to as brutal and atrocious—as though they were bullseye proof of the righteousness of the H-bomb!

3 THE MORALS OF DETERRENCE

Let it be quite clear what we are *not* saying. We are not saying that war can never, in principle, be justified. Nor that there are not powerful motives in justice—and even charity —to protect our countries against communist aggression. We can envisage situations in which, other things being equal, we *ought* to defend our countries—our liberty, our institutions—by force, even at enormous sacrifice. The point is that other things are not equal: their name is "massive nuclear bombardment" and "virtual annihilation."

These names are not of our invention; they are the names, respectively used by the 1958 British Government White Paper on Defense and by President Eisenhower, in his State of the Union Message of 9 January 1958, which—in spite of important modifications, intended to make the "ultimate deterrent" more genuinely *ultimate*—continue to define the basis of Western defense policy in the Kennedy era. The British White Paper, alluding to "the balancing fears of *mutual annihilation*" (my italics), reaffirms that "the democratic Western nations will never start a war against Russia."

> But it must be well understood that, if Russia were to launch a major attack on them, even with conventional forces only, they would have to hit back with strategic weapons. In fact, the strategy of N.A.T.O. is based on the frank recognition that a full-scale Soviet attack could not be repelled without resort to a *massive nuclear bombardment* of the sources of power in Russia. (My italics.)

And President Eisenhower:

> The most powerful deterrent to war lies in the retaliatory
> power of our Strategic Air Command and the aircraft of
> our navy. They present to any potential attacker the
> prospect of *virtual annihilation* of his own country. Even
> if we assume a surprise attack on our own bases, our
> bombers would immediately be on their way in sufficient
> strength to accomplish this *mission of retaliation*. (My
> italics.)

One does not need to be a Christian—nor indeed any sort
of theist at all—to recognize in these threats a deracination
from humanity, and from the humanity within ourselves. But
we have the Prophets and the Gospels; and we have a full
and precise tradition of the Church's thinking, evolved over
the centuries, about the tolerable limits of war. Can it reasonably be claimed that commitments like these do not transgress
the traditional limits?

In this tradition, there are three principles that have decisive
implications in a world of H-bombs:

1. Only just uses of violence may be employed.
2. There must be good hope of success.
3. There must be good hope that the ultimate gains will
outweigh the evil effects of the war.

Can it really be supposed that a war of "massive nuclear
bombardment," of "virtual annihilation"—of "mutual annihilation"—might somehow be justified in terms of these conditions? [2]

A rhetorical question should never be too sure of itself: there
is no doubt that this has been supposed.

For the most part, however, participants in this discussion
do not deny the claim that a total nuclear war would be immoral. Instead, those who nevertheless defend the stockpiling
of nuclear weapons tend to base themselves on a distinction
between "using" and "possessing" these weapons, or between

[2] cf. E. I. Watkins, in *Morals and Missiles*. (Edited by Charles Thompson;
James Clarke, London, 1959).

a possible "total war" and the actuality of "nuclear deterrence."

This position is important because of the wide, and at times highly authoritative, support it commands. It usually relies on one of three arguments—or a combination between these arguments—which might be called: (i) the argument from bluff, (ii) the argument from military targets, and (iii) the argument from the enforcement of peace.

(i) *The argument from bluff* simply asserts that, if it came to the point, Western governments would not in fact make good their threats, so that nuclear deterrence does not imply a conditional commitment to total war. Thus it is one thing to "have" these bombs; quite another to "use" them. And, immoral as it may be to engage in total nuclear war, there is nothing immoral about nuclear deterrence.

But are there any grounds at all for assuming that governments are merely bluffing? (And if there were, would the deterrent be a deterrent?) Was it not, in fact, Western governments who initiated the atomic era with Hiroshima and Nagasaki—and never expressed any regret about these acts? Are we to discount the categorical statements of our statesmen and soldiers, and credit them with the certainty of being liars? And even if it should, in spite of everything, turn out that all this apparatus of bombs and threats was vain, can we, as voters in democratic states, underwrite their commitment to admittedly wicked acts, in the hope that this commitment might perhaps be dishonored?

It is, moreover, widely recognized that there can be no guarantee that governments will, at the critical moment, be fully in control of the situation. Can anyone claim that there is any infallible way of preventing a minor incident from "escalating" into all-out war? And the speed with which military decisions now have to be taken means that vital decisions might be taken at a subordinate level, leading uncontrollably to catastrophe. (One cannot even rule out the possibility of some deliberate defiance of government authority, during a crisis, on the Algerian model—but with powers of destruction and provocation beyond the reach of the Algerian extremists.) Everybody also knows that some technical accident, such as envisaged in the Mershon Report, could bring about a fatal series of reactions, leaving no adequate scope for control. It follows that, even if we could assume that governments only "intended" their threats as bluff, they are in no position to guarantee the arrest of their policy at the level of bluffing. And there can be no "mere bluff" without absolute control over one's own hand. So long as there is the remotest possibility that the situation might get out of control, the bluffer is responsible for what might result—in this case the genocide he has threatened, without adequate power to contain his own threat. In fact, however, such a possibility is anything but remote. So that, even if governments firmly set out to confine themselves to bluff, they —and those who support their policies—could not evade responsibility *here and now* for their acceptance of such a possible outcome, through circumstances which (they here and now know) might *by then* be beyond their control.

But the policy of deterrence not only involves genocidal threats by civil and military leaders, which we have every reason to think express real intentions—and involves acceptance of genocidal risks, even if the immediate purpose were simply to bluff: it also requires that those who actually operate the deterrent must, *at this moment*, be ready, if called upon, to carry out acts of genocide. As Air Commodore Magill said at the British Official Secrets Trial, in February 1962, in reply to the question "Would you press the button you know is going to annihilate millions of people?": "If the circumstances demanded it I would." Quite apart from such solemn public confessions, it is clear that anyone involved in the operation of the deterrent, however humble his job, must be similarly ready to contribute toward mass-annihilation: bomber and missile crews could not fulfil their functions without a constant, split-minute readiness to perform unhesitatingly whatever acts of genocide may be commanded.[3] Such a readiness— as insistent as it is dreadful—to be instantly available for automatic genocidal responses, presupposes a long-matured resolve

[3] cf. N. M. L. Wharton, *The Tablet,* 18 November 1961, and the subsequent correspondence.

to acts of mass-annihilation "if the circumstances demanded it." Can such Eichmann-like commitments—imposed by governments and peoples upon thousands of their servants—be meaningfully reduced to the language of bluff?

(ii) One must take much more seriously *the argument from military targets*, if only because it is so often taken seriously. It is hardly going too far to suggest that, if this argument had to be withdrawn, the attempt to drive a wedge, morally, between "deterrence" and total war would be fatally impaired. There are several important expositions of this argument. Here I shall rely on an article by Fr. Paul Crane, S.J., from *The Month*, October 1959.[4] The article submits that we cannot assume

> that the use of nuclear weapons by a just defendant is necessarily to be identified with the direct massacre of the innocent through the indiscriminate hydrogen bombing of an unjust aggressor's cities and towns. It need not be, for there are now in existence controlled nuclear devices which can be restricted to military targets. At the same time, one can conceive of military targets on which a certain type of nuclear bomb could be used whilst remaining discriminate in its effects: such, for example, could be a fleet at sea. One concludes . . . that nuclear war is not necessarily indiscriminate war and that, in consequence, the use of nuclear weapons by a just defendant is not necessarily immoral.

This argument, it will be noted, does not directly depend on submissions concerning *deterrence*, but on submissions concerning nuclear *warfare* itself. The "wedge," that is, does not seek a point of entry between "deterrence" and actual "use" (it implicitly recognizes that there is here no relevant distinction), but seeks to effect a division within nuclear warfare itself—a division between "controlled," as opposed to "indiscriminate" nuclear war. (On this basis, it is wholly consistent to claim, as Fr. Crane does, that not only "deterrence"

---

[4] cf. Dr. L. L. McReavy's formulation in *The Tablet*, 29 March 1958 and the *Clergy Review*, February 1960. Cf. also "Falconer's" articles, "Should We Disarm?", in *The Catholic Times*, 17 February—10 March 1961.

but nuclear war itself need not violate the conditions for a just war.)

In a sense this argument is absolutely invulnerable. It is proof against objection, in the same sense in which it would be unobjectionable to assert that the mass-production of pornographic photographs need not necessarily be identified with the direct debauchery of the public, since one can conceive of persons who would find a certain type of pornography of indubitable professional value: such, for example, could be a moral theologian. One certainly might thus conclude that pornography is not necessarily pornographic and that, in consequence, the mass-production of dirty pictures by a patriotic company is not necessarily immoral.

Such arguments are unanswerable. All one can do, perhaps, is to mention a few relevant considerations. One might, for instance, indicate that whilst "controlled nuclear devices" are no doubt very ingenious inventions, it is difficult to restrict governments to controlled nuclear devices. This, one might add, would seem all the more important where governments have in fact categorically proclaimed "to any potential aggressor the prospect of virtual annihilation of his own country." Then there is that "fleet at sea" (it is remarkable how this fleet keeps turning up in this connection): one has to admit, "a certain type of nuclear bomb" *could* be used against it—and used with impressive efficiency—whilst remaining discriminate in its effects; though this still leaves the question how many of these fleets, or armies concentrating in deserts, perhaps, are likely to be about. What we do, on the other hand, know with some directness is that many hundreds or thousands of "a certain type of bomb," and many thousands or ten-thousands of bombs of other types (not necessarily negligible) are accumulating in various parts of the globe. We do know that, already in April 1957, Admiral Burke, United States Chief of Naval Operations, felt confident that "enough nuclear weapons for 'complete destruction' of the Soviet Union" were available in the United States.[5] And we do know that American civil defense specialists have found it convenient

5 Philip Noel Baker, *The Arms Race,* p. 174; Stevens (London), 1958.

to give a new word—a unit—to our language: "megacorpse":
one million dead bodies.

Moral theologians concerned to fence off criticisms of
nuclear weapons may choose to affirm theoretical possibilities
no longer found relevant by strategists, statesmen or common
sense, but it is time to match gravity with gravity. Pope John
XXIII, in his encyclical *Ad Petri Cathedrum*, of June 1959,
chose to speak not of how one might still "conceive" of "military targets," of fleets at sea, of a nuclear war "not necessarily
indiscriminate," but of the dangers of "drifting"

> in utter blindness towards a new and frightful war. In
> utter blindness, we say, for if indeed (which may God
> avert!) a new war should break out, the power of the
> monstrous new weapons is such that all the nations, vic-
> tors and vanquished alike, would be left with nothing but
> a scene of universal ruin and destruction.

(iii) The last of these three arguments, *the argument from
the enforcement of peace,* is sometimes associated with one or
the other, or both, of the preceding arguments, sometimes it is
offered by itself. It is the most popular of all these arguments,
being also the standard *secular* apologia for "deterrence." . . .
Rightly or wrongly, the maintenance of "the deterrent" is thus
held to be not only necessary for Western defense but necessary for present peace—as also for the establishment of international arrangements that would secure the peace of the
future.

In its own terms, this is a strong argument. . . . But even if,
for discussion's sake, we assume that, on balance, the deterrent may support peace, this would not necessarily justify it.
It would justify it *if, and only if, in employing this threat, we
were not already involved in immoral risks—and in immoral
hypothetical decisions.* The two preceding arguments purport
precisely to meet this condition; they are meant to demonstrate
that no evil *need* attach to the threat of nuclear war. If this
could indeed be shown, then the goods of security and peace
might undoubtedly justify the maintenance of the deterrent—
and indeed might oblige us to maintain it. As we have seen,
the arguments fail to support their claims. And nothing, not

even the alleged interests of peace itself, can save murderousness from evil.

4 A "NECESSARY EVIL"?

In the end, however, the discussion may shift to another plane. Sooner or later, someone will return to the plea that we simply have *no choice*. If nuclear deterrence is evil, it is a necessary evil; it is the lesser of the two evils confronting us. What could be a greater evil than to be conquered by communism—not only to lose our liberties and suffer persecution but to see our children exposed to this immensely efficient parody of Faith?

This argument has the dignity of speaking with the voice with which it thinks. And it matches the gravity of the challenge we are facing. It is, moreover, an argument that probes deeply into our ultimate commitments. It is conscious that behind the phrase "the defense of the West" lies a meaning more deep-seated than any connected with military strategy. And in this awareness, it exposes itself to real questions.

One might, for instance, consider once more whether the potential destruction of mankind is indeed so surely a "lesser evil" than a military triumph of communism. If we are liberal humanists, we might ask ourselves just how deeply we believe in man. If we are Christians, we might take this opportunity to reconsider what it is we believe.

And we could check on that potently ambiguous phrase "no choice." Do we mean that there literally is *no alternative* to this course? Or do we mean that we have *lost our freedom to choose*? Or do we actually mean to claim, with some part of our minds, that a decision to do without the evil of nuclear "defense" would be so *morally* outrageous as to be unthinkable?

We are thus finally led to ask whether, when we speak in this way of "necessary evils," we are not doing more from within to harm what we defend than any enemy could do from outside. The word "evil" can, of course, be used in either a moral or a non-moral sense; and it is disastrously easy to slip from one sense into the other, especially when speaking of "necessary evils." We may say, for instance, that—in certain situations—war may be a necessary evil. This can only mean that, though intrinsically *dreadful,* war may sometimes be the lesser of two dreadful things. For to be the lesser of two evils, it must certainly be *morally* good, or at least avoid being morally evil: since, whatever is *morally evil* is *ipso facto* absolutely to be dreaded. A "necessary evil" can thus only be evil in a non-moral sense. Yet again and again people slip into ways of speaking which assume that "necessary evils" may include necessary *moral* evils, so that the choice between two evils may be a choice between two morally repugnant courses.

This fallacy is, unfortunately, much more than logical. For to regard a "necessary evil" as the lesser of two *moral* evils is, quite literally, to surrender to evil. It assumes a world that is morally self-contradictory, a world that obliges one to morally evil acts. And, in assuming such a world, it ensures that one's choices will actually be evil choices.

It ensures this by obliterating any sense of moral roadblocks. Where everything is tainted with moral evil, nothing is absolutely barred. Once you believe that wickedness can be forced upon you, not because of your cowardice or human weakness but because of the way the world is, then morality is shifted to another world. "In an ideal world, no doubt, it would be possible to observe absolute prohibitions of such things as the murder of children, but of course in the real world these things can be forced upon us." This kind of moral sell-out is, of course, commonly masked by high-sounding phrases. Often these are variations on the theme of "realism" and common sense. Or men who simply suffer from panic can pose as tragic heroes driven to evil by forces outside their control. They believe that they are "morally earnest"—almost conscientious objectors to conscience—because they have a certain nostalgia for the ideal world. They can even fool themselves into thinking that they are bringing it into being —that their habitual moral squalor is the price they must pay for the well-being of future generations. . . .

But the fact is, the H-bomb is calling our bluff. The *defense*

of the West, it seems to ask. What West? The West of the
rationalist movement that gave birth to Marxist thought and
now seems distinguishable from its offspring only by its
lingering inconsistencies? Or the West of a Christianity so
thin as to have called down upon its world the revolt of the
betrayed, and that now protests it has no choice but to do evil
to prevent evil? . . .

In the normal run of the world, force is a right and necessary condition of order and humane existence. We cannot
imagine a world that would not, man being what he is, require a measure of physical power, to restrain abuses of
physical power. . . . Yet it is precisely at this moment of extreme need for physical protection that effective physical
force seems to elude us, beyond its ultimate tolerable limits.

Even so—even as we recollect the annunciations of Christmas
Island, or celebrate satellite epiphanies—there is this to hold
on to: We cannot now help seeing where we are. Where force
will no longer do, we shall have to do without it. A policy of
unconditional disarmament could break through the closed
circle of terror within which we co-exist. It could form the
basis of reciprocal disarmament without illusions. It could free
our resources to fight world-poverty and world-resentment.
Should we, however, be invaded, there is the ultimate weapon
of meaningful suffering. "If we believe we should defend our
civilization and our way of life, then we should be prepared
to defend it at whatever the cost."

Those to whom all this seems madly unrealistic might perhaps reconsider where *realpolitik* has brought us. May not the
ultimate meaning of the H-bomb be just this, that "realism"
is under judgment—that it is time to return to reality? At the
root of our civilization there are, after all, sources of hope
and resources of defense sufficient for every human situation.
Heaven and earth will pass away, but no "necessity," however
extreme, can divorce us from these sources: so long as we
acknowledge that there is, after all (whatever the cost) only
one thing necessary in the end.

Herbert Butterfield | Human Nature and the Dominion of Fear

Fear is a thing which is extraordinarily vivid while we are in its grip; but once it is over, it leaves little trace of itself in our consciousness. It is one of the experiences that we can never properly remember—one also which, since we may be ashamed of it, we may have reason for not wishing to remember.

Because it is so hard for us to recapture the feeling in our imagination, we can be thoroughly nonparticipating when there is question of a fear that is not our own. If another person is the victim of it, we may fail—or it may never occur to us to try—to apprehend either the thing in itself or the range of its possible consequences. It would seem that we are not always easily convinced of the existence of fear in other people, especially when the other people are political rivals or potential enemies. At any rate historians are not easily convinced when they deal at a later time with former enemies of their country. Above all, if the thing which the other party dreaded is a danger that never materialized, it becomes easy to be sceptical about the genuineness of the fear itself. When the historian cannot escape recording the terror that Napoleon inspired, or the German dread of Russia at one time and another, or the apprehension of a people in the face of imminent attack, he may produce a factual statement that gives little impression of the force and the effect of the emotion actually experienced. Sometimes he is jolted into a realization of his deficiency as he finds himself confronted by an event and sees that the rest of his picture provides only an inadequate context for it. It turns out that there was some standing factor in

the story—a terrible feeling of thunder in the atmosphere—
which he had imperfectly apprehended or merely failed to
keep in mind.

The student of history needs to consider this question, therefore. Some aspects of the past—and these perhaps the ones
most related to men's minds and moods—are particularly difficult to recapture. The atrocities of our own day, for example,
are naturally more vivid to us than those of a century ago. The
world tends to judge a present-day revolution merely by its
atrocities and an ancient one much more by its ideals and purposes. This is partly because the sufferings and terrors of a
former generation are more easily overlooked. We need to
possess something of the art of the dramatist in order to enter
into the sensations of other people—to recover, for example, the
"feel" of some terror that once possessed a nation or a ministry.
And it must not be said that we ought to leave our imagination
out of our history, for the minds of men, and even the mood
of society, may have their part in accounting for human conduct. Even when the student of the past is really bent on
analysis, he must recapture the fear, and the attendant high
pressure, which so greatly affect the actions of men and the
policy of governments. Yet the historical imagination is never
so defective as when it has to deal with the apprehension and
insecurity of frightened people. It is a point to remember,
therefore, that the historian, surveying the past (like the statesman surveying rival powers in his own contemporary world),
is apt to do less than justice to the part played by fear in politics, at any rate so far as concerns governments other than
his own.

We do not always realize—and sometimes we do not like to
recognize—how often a mistaken policy, an obliquity in conduct, a braggart manner, or even an act of cruelty, may be
traceable to fear. What is true of individual people is likely to
be still more true of great agglomerations of humanity, where
further irrational factors always come into play. With nations,
even more than with individuals, in fact, the symptoms of fear
may be unlike fear—they may even be the result of an attempt
to convince us of the reverse. Apart from all this, fear may

exist as a more constant and less sensational factor in life, perpetually constricting very reasonable people in their conduct in the world. It may curb their natural desire to react against injustice, or (if only by the production of wishful thinking) prevent them from recognizing the crimes of their own government. It can lead to small compliances and complicities, the production of "yes men," the hardening of inherited orthodoxies and accepted ideas. There can also be a generalized fear that is no longer conscious of being fear, and hangs about in the form of oppressive dullness or heavy cloud, as though the snail had retreated into its shell and forgotten the reason, but had not the spirit to put out its feelers any more.

The extreme case, however, is the situation that Hobbes seems to have had in mind—a situation in which men are not absolutely brutish, and do not want to be brutish, but are made brutish by their fear and suspicion of one another. Each may be wanting peace above all things, but no single one of them can be certain about the intentions of the rest. They are like two men in a room, both anxious to throw their pistols away, but in a state of deadlock because each must be sure that he does not disarm himself before the other.

In other words, fear and suspicion are not merely factors in the story, standing on a level with a lot of other factors. They give a certain quality to human life in general, condition the nature of politics, and imprint their character on diplomacy and foreign policy.

It is the realm of international affairs, however, which comes closest to the last situation that has been mentioned, the situation of Hobbesian fear. Since the war of 1914 our predicament in this respect has become worse, not better, because, till that time, a considerable region of Europe had long enjoyed the benefit of stability and traditional acceptance. Here frontiers had been comparatively settled and a country like Norway had not needed to be greatly pre-occupied with its security. Much of that region has now been thrown into the melting pot. It is doomed to suffer further dislocations if ever there is a change in the distribution of power. The demand for security, and the high consciousness that we now have of this problem of security, have increased the difficulty, and increased the operation of fear in the world. Hitler demanded security for Germany, and I am not sure that he did not show more discernment about this matter than many other people. It was impossible, however, for Germany to acquire the degree of security she thought she ought to have, without herself becoming a menace to her neighbors. This universe always was unsafe, and those who demand a watertight security are a terrible danger in any period of history. I wonder if it could not be formulated as a law that no state can ever achieve the security it desires without so tipping the balance that it becomes a menace to its neighbors. The great aggressors of modern times, France, and then Germany and then Russia began by resisting aggressors, then demanding guarantees and more guarantees until they had come almost imperceptibly to the converse position. Then the world (always rather late in the day) would wake up and find that these powers were now aggressors themselves.

One of the most terrible consequences of fear and war fever is a melodramatic kind of myth-making which has been the curse of international relations since 1914. This is the source of the blight which makes compassion wither out of the world; and its results are before our eyes. Because we thought that there could never be an aggressor so wicked as Germany under the Kaiser, we determined to fight the First World War to the point of total surrender. We thereby conjured into existence two menaces still more formidable for ourselves—the Communist on the one hand, and Nazi on the other. Some men realized, even in 1914, that all we needed to do was to hold off Germany till the Russian Bear became a more formidable threat to all of us. To judge by the writings of some leading members of the British Foreign Office at the time, the intervening period would not have had to be long. In general, however, we can say that, until 1914, the world was perhaps proceeding very tolerably, save that it was beginning to get a little fevered, because, already, it had come somehow under the dominion of fear. Those who made dark and dismal prophecies about Germany could claim in the days of Hitler that their predictions had come true. But these people had their part in the producing of that nightmare situation in which their prophecies were almost bound to come true.

Fear, then, plays a greater part in life and in the course of history than we often realize, and sometimes we know that it is fear which is in operation when individuals and nations are bullying or bragging, or taking a crooked course. It may even be fear that is at work when a nation is desperately engaged in trying to convince us that it is not afraid. In spite of this (or perhaps rather because of it) one may feel a little anxious about the way in which the great powers of the earth appear to be relying on fear today. On the one hand, statesmen ought never to be too sure about the efficacy of fear in the last resort. On the other hand it is always dangerous to assume that fear can be used to cast out fear. The mere dread of having to suffer the consequences of the hydrogen bomb is not going to deter governments and peoples from starting warlike action, or intensifying this, once it has begun. In the critical instance— the case of the ruthless man who knows that he is beaten—the mere fear of retaliation will not in itself prevent desperate policies, including the actual use of the bomb.

The world can hardly ever have been so apprehensive as since the days when statesmen proclaimed that by victory in war they could bring about "freedom from fear." Those who can boast of their stocks of hydrogen bombs are not exempt from this fear, which numbs people and makes them think that they must take their fate passively, that their opinions and resolves can make no difference. We must not imagine that all is well if our armaments make the enemy afraid; for it is possible that, at least in the twentieth century, it is fear more than anything else which is the cause of war. Until very recently we ourselves had not lost the realization of the fact that mounting armaments, because they intensified fear and poisoned human relations, operated rather to provoke war than to prevent it. Under the high pressure which fear induces, any minor and peripheral issue can seem momentous enough to justify a great war.

Those who refuse to recognize squarely the dominion of fear

and the play of necessity in the world (especially during times
of war, revolution and unsettlement) are often the very ones
who refuse to do justice to man's freedom when they are called
upon for an act of will. It is for this reason that a world as
intellectually advanced as ours stands mute and paralyzed
before a great issue; and we grind our way, content to be
locked in historical processes, content just to go digging our
thought deeper into whatever happens to be the accustomed
rut. There comes a moment when it is a healthy thing to pull
every cord tight and make an affirmation of the higher human
will. When we seem caught in a relentless historical process,
our machines enslaving us, and our weapons turning against
us, we must certainly not expect to escape save by an unusual
assertion of the human spirit. The intensified competition in
armaments embodies movements which have been mounting
through the centuries, and providing mankind with its chief
headache for a number of decades. Those who once thought
it cynical to imagine that any power save Germany could be
responsible for keeping the world still in arms, and now think
that only Communists could be so wicked do not realize that
if Russia and China were wiped out, the world would soon
be rearming again, and as likely as not, the United States
would be getting the blame for it. In other words, the problem of armaments is a bigger one than is generally realized,
and we cannot begin to put the initial check upon the evil—
we cannot begin to insert the first wedge—unless we make a
signal call upon every human feeling we possess. We wait,
perhaps, for some Abraham Lincoln who will make the might-
iest kind of liberating decision.

If it is possible to put a personal opinion without claiming
any authority for it, or asserting that it ought to have any
weight, but regarding it as one of the varied views that are
thrown up in a democracy, one might suggest that what is
most terrifying of all in the present situation is not to have
to keep discovering the crimes of the Communists; it is something much more inconvenient to us; namely, having to recognize the services which Communism has rendered in various
parts of the globe. Those services have been accompanied by

tyranny and oppression; but, again, it is terrifying to have to remember that this was once the chief objection to revolutionary democracy. It is not even clear that Communism, though it can be oppressive today, does not possess colossal potentialities for future liberty—a liberty that we must not expect to be achieved before an international detente has made it more possible to have a relaxation at home. I think that, in this modern world, which in some ways is worse than people think but in some ways is better, all systems are going to move in the direction of liberty, if only somebody will open a window so that the world can breathe a more relaxed air and we can end the dominion of fear. If, however, we are unable to achieve this, the very measures which we are taking to preserve liberty in the world are bound to lead to the loss of liberty even in the regions that most prize it. They are bound—if we go on intensifying them—to make us become in fact more and more like the thing we are opposing. Even those who customarily try to guard themselves against a facile and unrealistic idealism in politics might well wonder whether—now that the hydrogen bomb has been super-added—their antidoctrinairism is not becoming too doctrinaire. When there is a question of a weapon so destructive, the risk which accompanies one kind of action has to be balanced against the risks involved in the opposite policy, or attendant upon inaction itself. When the hazard is very great in either case, it may be useful to take account also of the end for the sake of which one chooses to accept the hazard.

The hydrogen bomb will presumably always have at least a potential existence in our civilization, since the knowledge of how to make the weapon can hardly be unlearned, except in a disaster that would follow its drastic use. If we were to resort to the most destructive kind of bomb, we could hardly claim privilege for our generation or rely on any possibility of restricting the use of the weapon to a single war. We cannot argue still again that no generation past or future could possibly have to face an enemy as wicked as our present enemy. We should have to conclude that ours is a civilization that took the wrong turn long ago, and now, by the hydrogen bomb, had to be rolled back to its primitive stages, so that, in a second Fall of Man, the world could unload itself of knowledge too dangerous for human possession. It is not necessary to take a very high perspective on these matters; it is just too crazy and unseemly when a civilization as lofty as ours (pouring the best of its inventive genius into the task) carries the pursuit of destructiveness to the point at which we are now carrying it. Let us be clear about one important fact: the destructiveness which some people are now prepared to contemplate, is not to be justified for the sake of any conceivable mundane object, any purported religious claim or supermundane purpose, or any virtue that one system of organization can possess as against another. It is very questionable whether when it comes to the point, any responsible leader of a nation will ever use the hydrogen bomb in actual warfare, however much he may have determined in advance to do so. The weapon is dangerous to the world because it is a weapon only for men like the falling Hitler—desperate men making their last retreat. The real danger will come from the war leader who will stop at nothing because he knows that he is defeated and doomed in any case. He may be reckless even of his own nation, determined to postpone his own destruction for a week, or to carry the rest of the world down with him. As in the case of Germany when Hitler was falling, war may be protracted by the will of a handful of wicked and desperate men. On these terms we are going to be more afraid of defeating our enemy than of suffering ordinary military defeat ourselves.

It is not clear that there is much point in having the equality (or even the superiority) in terroristic weapons if, as is sometimes asserted, the enemy has the ruthlessness and the organization to carry on a war with less regard for the sufferings of his people than is possible in the democracies. If Communism is a monstrous sadistic system, the gentle and the urbane will not easily outdo it in the use of terroristic device. By a reversal of all previous ideas on the subject of armaments, however, some people have imagined that the hydrogen bomb is the climax of blessing, the magical "deterrent" which will paralyze the guns and neutralize the numbers of the potential enemy.

Such reasoning is precarious; and we ought to be very careful before we accept the view that ten years ago it was only the atomic bomb which deterred the Russians from a major war. A country in the position that Russia held after 1945 tends to seek to make use of its interim advantage up to any point short of a renewal of general war. It seeks to step in wherever there is a power vacuum and it probes for a power vacuum even where none exists—probes until it meets an uncomfortable degree of resistance. There seems to be no reason for believing that Russia would have meditated a full-scale war, even if she had to meet only pre-atomic weapons, the weapons of Hitler's war. Short of such a conflict, I wonder what power ever went further in the type of aggrandizement in question than Russia at a time when the West held the atomic bomb while the East was still without it. It is even possible that we hoaxed ourselves with the atomic bomb, which was too monstrous a weapon for peripheral regions and problems, too terrible to use in a cause that was in any way dubious, too cumbrous for dealing with a power that was ready to skirmish with any danger short of actual war. In such a case one can even conceive the possibility of the Russians realizing the situation in advance, and calling our bluff while we ourselves were not yet aware that we were merely bluffing. Whether this had already happened or not, it is just this situation—with the West deceived and the Russians undeceived—that we ought to be careful to avoid at the present day. We cannot contemplate—we cannot even plausibly threaten—a nuclear war over some of the mixed and mongrel issues which are arising (and are going to arise) in sundry sections of the globe. If it is argued that we can, and that the dread of this will be effective with the Russians, then, beyond question, the Russians are in a more general sense under the dominion of fear; for in such a case they have a right also to fear a wilful and capricious use of nuclear weapons.

Some men say that the world must perish rather than that Justice should fail—as though we were not leaving sufficient injustices unremedied on our own side of the Iron Curtain. The justice of man has less mercy than the justice of God, who did not say that because of the sins of some men the whole human race should lose even the chance of bettering itself in future. Even in peacetime the hydrogen bomb has made such a deep impression as to suggest enormous evils (greater than the evils of Communism itself) if the weapon is ever used by either party in a war. The demoralizing effect on the user as well as the victim might well include a hysteria beyond all measure, the dissolution of loyalty to the state, and anarchy or revolution of an unprecedented kind. Even the sense of the possible proximate use of the hydrogen bomb—short of an actual explosion—will have the effect of creating a deep separation between peoples and their governments. We may know that war is near by two signs: firstly, when people begin to say that the hydrogen bomb is not so terrible after all; and secondly, when we are told that it is better to destroy civilization than to tolerate some piece of barbarism on the part of that nation which happens to be the potential enemy at the moment. In fact, we have reached the point at which our own weapons have turned against us, because their destructiveness is so out of relation with any end that war can achieve for mankind.

There is so great a risk in having the hydrogen bomb that there can hardly be greater risk if we unplug the whole system, and if our governments refuse to have anything to do with the weapon. Even if there were, the radical difference in the quality of these risks would cancel it; for with modern weapons we could easily put civilization back a thousand years, while the course of a single century can produce a colossal transition from despotic regimes to a system of liberty. I am giving a personal view; but I am not sure that the greatest gift that the West could bring to the world would not be the resolution neither to use the hydrogen bomb nor to manufacture it any further. Certainly the East would hardly believe us (at least for some time) if we said we were not going to resort to this weapon for any conceivable end. We should have to take the line, therefore, that our determination was not dependent on anything that other people believed. Even if the East refused to join us in the assertion, we can declare that the hydrogen bomb is an unspeakable atrocity, not to be used in any war, and not even to be the basis of any form of threat. It is a thing not to be used even if the enemy has used it first, since the situation is a new one—the right of retaliation could mean no more than the right to multiply an initial catastrophe that could not be undone. While it is still open to us in time of peace, we might ask ourselves whether there is no conceivable weapon that we will brand as an atrocity, whether there is no horror that we should regard as impermissible for the winning of a war, because so incommensurate with the limited objects that can ever be secured by war. When we talk about using the hydrogen bomb to defeat aggression, we are using dangerous language. Some day, no doubt, a wiser world than ours will use the term "aggressor" against any people which enjoys rights, powers and possessions in a country that is not its own, and exploits these against the will of the population concerned. Sometimes we seem to be using the term in respect of peoples who are merely seeking to be freed from such oppression; in this sense I have seen the Algerian rebels described as aggressors, using violence for the purpose of securing a change in the status quo. The Anglo-French action at Suez should open our eyes to the fact that a so-called "invasion" (though it be by armies in full array) can arise from something much more complicated than a mere cruel lust for conquest. The United Nations condemned the Anglo-French enterprise; but, even so, a hydrogen bomb on London or Paris would have been an unspeakable form of punishment.

It is sometimes argued that those who refuse to resort to the hydrogen bomb may be declining to risk themselves for the liberty of others. But nobody can calculate—and perhaps only accidental circumstances would decide in a given case— whether the use of the bomb or its repudiation would carry the greater immediate risk. In any case, we cannot say that we will not receive the bomb—we can only say that we will not be responsible for the sin and the crime of delivering it. Supposing we do have to receive it, the one thing we can do is to choose the end for which we will consent to be sacrificed. We can choose the cause on behalf of which we will die if we are going to have to die. We can do this instead of being the blind victims of historical processes, which will end by making us more and more like the thing that we are opposing. However hard we have tried in the twentieth century to make allowances in advance for the unpredictable consequences of war, we have always discovered that the most terrible of these had been omitted from our calculations or only imperfectly foreseen. One of the examples of the fact is the loss of liberty in various countries in Eastern Europe and the Balkans—the very regions whose freedom was the primary issue for which we were supposed to have undertaken two world wars.

If it is wrong to tip the balance slightly in favor of humanity and faith at such a point as this, the fact is so monstrous as to imply the doom of our civilization, whatever decision we take on the present issue. If we picture a long line of future generations we can hardly help feeling that, even if wars of some sort continue (human nature remaining very much as it is now), we would want our successors not to hate one another so much as to think it justifiable to use the hydrogen bomb. The fact that we can contemplate such an atrocity is a symptom of a terrible degeneracy in human relations—a degeneracy which the predicament itself has no doubt greatly helped to produce. But if all this is not correct, and if we do not signally repudiate the hydrogen bomb, it is still true that in the last resort some strong human affirmation of a parallel kind may be the only way of stopping the tension and deflecting the course of development to which we are now enslaved. Some other kind of affirmation might serve a similar purpose; and amongst the possibilities at our disposal there is one which to many earnest people would come no doubt as a serious test. We have talked a great deal about the crimes of Communism, and those who are chiefly concerned with militaristic propaganda would like us to think of nothing else. We do not always realize what a tremendous area of our thinking is affected by the fact that we refuse to recognize also the services which Communism has rendered in various parts of the globe. At the very beginning of all our arguments and decisions, it matters very much if we consent to say that Communism is a benevolent thing gone wrong—it is not mere unredeemed and diabolical evil. For anything I know, its chief error may even be the same as that of both Catholics and Protestants in the age of the religious wars and persecutions—an error which has been responsible for terrible massacrings and atrocities in history—namely a righteousness that is too stiff-necked and a readiness to believe that one can go to any degree in the use of force on behalf of a cause that one feels to be exclusively right. In such a case it is possible that we ourselves are making even the identical error, especially in any contemplation of the use of the hydrogen bomb. When there is a terrible impasse, it is sometimes useless to go on battering against the obstruction—one must play a trick on fatality by introducing a new factor into the case. We seem unable to subdue the demon of frightfulness in a head-on fight. Let us take the devil by the rear, and surprise him with a dose of those gentler virtues that will be poison to him. At least when the world is in extremities, the doctrine of love becomes the ultimate measure of our conduct.

All this represents in any case the kind of way in which to assert the human will, against the machinery of relentless process, in history. It represents also the way in which one would like to see the Christian religion working softly and in silence upon the affairs of the world at large. It illustrates the way in which religious activity may get a purchase on the wheels of a human destiny which otherwise now appears to be directionless.

Allan Forbes, Jr. | An Essay on the Arms Race

The most recent academic discipline to achieve respectability is Strategics—the study of nuclear war. Since 1945 this territory had been inhabited solely by "natives," primitive, naive beings living in a state of purity and innocence, clinging to such unsophisticated beliefs as "nuclear war is unthinkable," "deterrence is immoral and unlikely to work." Their most cherished leaders declared that "there is no alternative to peace"; "if man does not abolish war, it will abolish him"; a nuclear war, they thought, might mean "the end of civilization," "end of man."

Some time in the 1950's a landrush to the new territory took place. Scholars and graduate students in physics, chemistry, government, economics and other fields abandoned their more conventional homesteads and headed for the virgin lands where they staked out theories and hypotheses as sourdoughs stake out claims. A landrush invariably raises hob with the natives. Within a short time they had been ousted from the more attractive, productive areas. A new language was introduced too complicated for them to fathom. The old landscape was renamed. They retreated in confusion, their beliefs challenged, values undermined. Such is the price of progress.

In January of 1959, a milestone in strategics was marked by the publication in *Foreign Affairs* of a study which pointed out that a qualitative change in the nature of deterrence had taken place.[1] The new weapons systems, the author stated, gave an enormous advantage to an aggressor. The Hiroshima

[1] Albert Wohlstetter, "The Delicate Balance of Terror," *Foreign Affairs*, (January 1959).

bomb—equivalent to 20,000 tons of TNT—had been replaced by the hydrogen bomb—20 million tons of TNT. SAC bombers had been outmoded by the ICBM traveling at 10,000 mph. Warning and decision times were reduced from several hours to a matter of minutes. The danger of accidental war through electronic or mechanical failure was substantially increased. Under certain conditions, a surprise attack might not be an irrational or insane act; in fact, compared to waiting for the enemy to strike, it could be the "sensible choice and the smaller risk." Deterrence was acknowledged to be "failure-prone." Thus the strategicians arrived, via the high road of methodology, at much the same point the natives had reached via the low road of intuition a decade or more earlier. This study turned out to be a bonanza to the profession, large numbers of which left their own diggings and hurried over to stake out adjacent claims.

Almost a year afterwards, in December of 1959, the Stanford Research Institute *Journal* published an article, "The Nature and Feasibility of War and Deterrence." [2] The life cycle of this paper is worth noting. On December 21, 1959, it reappeared in *U. S. News and World Report* in abridged form. In January, 1960, the RAND Corporation reissued it in a "slightly enlarged and revised version." Later it formed an important part of a series of lectures given to government officials, members of the military forces and defense industrialists in "more times and places than (the author) cares to remember." Eventually these lectures were published in a highly controversial book, *On Thermonuclear War*.[3]

"The Nature and Feasibility of War and Deterrence" began more or less where the previous study left off. It concurred in the definition of deterrence as "accident-prone" and went on to enumerate the ways in which it might fail. It examined the potential effects of a thermonuclear war on the nation and concluded that it was feasible to survive and restore the pre-

[2] Herman Kahn, "The Nature and Feasibility of War and Deterrence," *Stanford Research Institute Journal,* (Fourth Quarter 1959).

[3] Herman Kahn, *On Thermonuclear War,* Princeton University Press (1960).

war economy within five-to-fifteen years, provided certain preparatory measures were taken.

It would be presumptuous for a "native" to criticize the work of a strategician who had spent many years studying thermonuclear war and its effects. However, since the concept of "feasibility" has assumed national, if not international, significance in recent months, it might be worthwhile to glance at some of the author's comments on his own work.

> In spite of the many uncertainties of our study we do have a great deal of confidence in some partial conclusions.
>
> The war may have some important and totally unsuspected ecological consequences.
>
> We have discussed at some length, but probably much too lightly, some of these postwar problems.
>
> The large numbers of other studies that have been done are relatively strong on details, but the integration provided by a comprehensive study is lacking. In general there are too many unexamined mechanisms and interactions which might produce considerably greater problems of recovery than the work done so far suggests.
>
> Some of these interactions are researchable and should be studied even though we did not do so. However, I believe, though admittedly on the basis of inadequate evidence and subject to the caveats I have already pointed out, that none of the problems encountered in the small attack would prove to be annihilating or even seriously crippling. No such judgment can be passed about the heavy attack without more research effort. Even then doubts may remain.

Whatever the merits of feasibility, it has played a major role in the formation of our current military posture. How, otherwise, could we have been able to talk seriously of thermonuclear war as a solution to the Berlin crisis? The Soviet Berlin gambit was a deliberate, provocative, destabilizing act of brinkmanship, but it was kept within purely political limits and our initial response should have been couched in precisely the same terms. We should have met the Russians with proposals, countercharges, countermoves, demands of every kind. Above all, we should have immediately prepared an aggressive position from which to negotiate. As Walter Lippmann commented after the 1961 German elections, "Incredible as it will seem to the historian, we have teetered on the brink of nuclear war without one paragraph, without one sentence, from any Allied leader seriously discussing the German problem . . . during this past summer."

The Russians did not find our war-talk "credible," thus we were forced into the humiliating position of sending government representatives in Washington and elsewhere to plead with Russian officials to accept our threats at face value. One of the first acts of the new administration had been to discard Foster Dulles' doctrine of "massive retaliation" as outmoded and unworkable; hence the Russians can hardly be blamed for their surprise at its sudden exhumation, particularly since the corpse had altered in appearance, the massive aspect being somewhat attenuated.

To assume our new posture gracefully has not been easy. The government and the mass media have felt constrained to deluge the public with a flood of claims about the feasibility of thermonuclear war, some of which can only be called misleading. *U. S. News and World Report* for September 25, 1961, claimed that "by comparison (to Hurricane Carla) an H-bomb is just a little puff." A photograph of an exploding H-bomb was captioned "Puff of an H-bomb." In a cover story on fallout shelters in its September 15th, 1961 issue, *Life* magazine stated that "97 out of 100 people can be saved." This was lifted out of context from a study based on a 300-megaton attack limited to military targets, a small and unlikely war. The *Boston Sunday Globe*, August 6, 1961, published a front-page feature on shelters. The headline screamed "You CAN Survive A-Blast (*sic*)." Boston's newly-appointed CD director was misquoted as saying "Whether you live or die depends on you."

Edward Teller, step-father of the H-bomb, wrote a series for a national syndicate in mid-September, 1961, on nuclear war. Dr. Teller said, "I firmly believe 90% of our population could be saved (from an all-out nuclear war)." This is the most optimistic estimate for an all-out war yet made.

The *New York Herald Tribune* of October 7, 1961, printed without comment or qualification a letter from a well-known New York clergyman which, among other things, stated that "fallout does not destroy food or water."

Letters to the editor columns last summer and fall were filled with cries of "Give Me Liberty or Give Me Death" and "Better Dead than Red." These are admirable as statements of personal conviction but as solutions to desperate world crises they somehow do not seem entirely adequate. Americans have always had a tendency to look at life in its simplest forms.

The Cold War is not the sort of weather for us. It leaves us frustrated and bellicose. The Russian is a political animal *par excellence*, weaned on dialectics and conspiracy. We equate politics with baby-kissing. The devious, rough-and-tumble, rabbit-punching, advancing, retreating, thrusting post-war world is not to our taste. Writing in the *U. S. Naval Institute Proceedings*, a Navy officer has expressed our sentiments perfectly.

> . . . the era of peace is far more dangerous to our ultimate survival than a time of war. In war the problem is simple—survive and win. In peace, however, world and home politics exert tremendous pressures. The problems become complex indeed, beset with imponderables and lashed by the spirit of nationalism and the battle of ideologies.[4]

This was written by an officer who had been a member of the Politico-Military Policy Division of the Office of Chief of Staff of Naval Operations and had attended the Armed Forces Staff College.

A nationally-syndicated columnist puts it this way: "My own convictions are that peace is a 'myth' word, that we are universally at war with Communism, that our generation or the

[4] Lt.-Commander John F. Riley, "Philosophy of Command in the Challenge of Our Time," *U. S. Naval Institute Proceedings*, (July 1960).

next will have to shoot it out and that there is a very good argument for do-it-now."

The man-in-the-street may be less eloquent with his "Better Dead than Red," but he is saying essentially the same thing— This is not our kind of world. We would like to "get it over with," "do it now." We are afraid of ourselves and of our society. We tremble at the prospect of a high-level conference. What will happen to our envoys? They'll be eaten alive by those diabolical foreigners. Negotiation is appeasement; talking is surrender; conferences are a sell-out.

Perhaps we can put enough thermonuclear pressure on the Soviets to make them behave. Perhaps not. The fact remains that we have a first-rate crisis still going. It may be possible to postpone once more a Berlin showdown; but sooner or later it will come up again. Crises are nasty affairs. They leave a permanent scar. They don't just go away. This crisis, even if it vanishes tomorrow, has done great damage. We called up 200,000 men. The Soviets halted demobilization. We started a CD program. They are procuring a 100-megaton weapon. They resumed testing in the atmosphere; we followed suit and they have threatened another round in which they will match us test for test.

Thus far the arms race has had relatively little effect on the everyday life of Americans. Taxes have gone up; a missile base or a bomber field is nearby. But in general, the American condition has not materially altered. Berlin has changed all this; from now on the arms race cannot fail to have an increasing impact on the life of every American and Russian. The "rumpus room" shelters we are now buying will be obsolete in a year or two. We will have procured a new generation of weapons and many more of them than we have now. We will need blast and thermal shelters, evacuation procedures, full-scale attack warnings and drills. In a few years we will be well on the way to a garrison state *underground*. We may be on the way already.

Most Americans have no idea what they are getting into. Massive shelter programs have not yet been discussed in the mass media. A study was made in 1958 on this subject. It bears the unlikely title, "Some Specific Proposals for Achieving Early Non-Military Defense Capabilities and Initiating Long-Range Programs." [5] It is really not much more than a list of suggestions for research projects, but it is worth looking at for the candid picture it gives of the future. Among its many recommendations are—

Mines as personnel shelters: $1 million. 2-90 day occupancy.

Psychological and Psychiatric Studies: $200,000: A study would be made of the preparation for family separation and of shelter techniques for handling this problem.

Studies of Very Austere Shelters and Long Occupations ($1.5 million): A study should be made of the survival of populations in environments similar to overcrowded shelters (concentration camps, Russian and German use of crowded freight cars, troop ships, crowded prisons, crowded lifeboats, submarines, etc. Some useful guiding principles might be found and adapted to the shelter program. Research projects might include: Study of available information that might suggest both reasonable standards and limits of human endurance, the latter to be used to determine overcrowding tolerances and for defining the early capability needed in personnel shelter studies ($200,000). Investigation of the use of sedation and chemical tranquilization for long periods and for possible use in shelters ($800,000).

Social Problems (Excerpt): ". . . Prolonged confinement in shelters will unavoidably produce emotional stress. Various measures (work therapy, sedation, recreation, segregated activity, or discipline areas, etc.) ought to be studied and prepared in order to maintain shelter discipline, to lessen the mental strain and to minimize the incidence of psychological aftereffects."

Food Problems (Excerpt): "Survival and emergency rations used by the Armed Forces are costly and are not designed to be used by a population for survival. An

[5] Herman Kahn *et al.*, "Some Specific Suggestions for Achieving Early Non-Military Defense Capabilities and Initiating Long-Range Programs," RAND Corporation RM 2206–RC, (January 1958).

army survival ration costing 75 cents per person per day would mean a total ration cost of $150 million per day. Based on a minimum cost diet, a suitable shelter ration might cost no more than 40 cents per person per day, a saving of almost 50% which would certainly make research in this area worthwhile."

The above gives us a glimpse of what a massive shelter program might be like in 1965–1970. It has the ring of unvarnished truth about it. No one is making claims of ninety-seven out of one hundred being saved. The population will be eating a ration one-half as good as the GI survival ration. We will not be in our rumpus room any more, but deep underground, tranquilized, sedated, separated, crowded, crushed.

So much for non-military defense measures. What sort of "hardware" will the weapons system analysts have presented to us? It is impossible to predict what we will actually end up with, but any combination of the following is at least conceivable. Begaton (1 billion tons of TNT) H-bombs; neutron bombs; cobalt bombs; manned and unmanned weapons satellites; third and fourth generation Polaris and Minuteman; ocean seeding with H-bombs; orbiting doomsday machines; chemical and biological warfare; weather control (meteorological warfare); disguised warfare (the use of CBR and weather control so subtly a nation does not realize it is being attacked; it will resemble natural catastrophes—plague, famine, drought and flood.)

A Naval expert talks about weather control:

Obviously, reduced rainfall adversely affects plant life in general and grain in particular. Eventually famine would result in the water-starved areas if corrective measures were not, or could not be taken, and famine in certain parts of the world could easily lead to political upheaval and perhaps the violent overthrow of current regimes. Conceivably, drastic ideological transformations might even result if adverse conditions persisted . . . Recent progress has been such that it is no longer visionary to discuss and plan for the eventuality of weather control. It will soon be a matter of survival . . . The question is no longer "Will mankind be able to modify

the weather on a large scale and control the climate?"
Rather the question is: "Which scientists will do it first,
American or Russian?" [6]

Weather control may be just around the corner, but there
is something pretty naive about the commander's thoughts
that "famine in certain parts of the world could lead to violent overthrow of current regimes, political upheaval . . .
drastic ideological transformations." What are the leaders of
these regimes doing while their people starve and riot? They
are getting ready to pre-empt obviously.

Some extremely fanciful schemes have been kicked about
by the weapons people for a number of years now and perhaps some of the following will be getting off the drawing
boards by 1970: melting polar ice caps; shifting continents by
5 feet, raising or lowering the ocean levels, including earthquakes, etc. Some of this will sound like science fiction to natives, but the strategicians are well acquainted with most of
these schemes and many are trying to discourage some of the
more outlandish ideas.

Until Khrushchev announced the procurement of a 100-
megaton weapon considerable restraint had been evident on
both sides of the arms race (this may come as a shock to many
natives but is a fact). However, Berlin has changed all this,
perhaps temporarily, perhaps not. It is clear that every crisis,
every serious outbreak of tension, every destabilizing event in
the Cold War is almost bound to touch off a new round of
threats, dangers and weapons, no matter how stable the period between crises is.

Late weapons systems will tend to be automated. They will
probably be linked to sensors and computers as a hedge
against a first missile wave knocking out command and control
centers or as a safeguard against the possibility of a failure of
will on the part of a decisionmaker, thus inhibiting retaliation.
If the enemy thought one had not bothered to take this step
he might be tempted to have a go at the command and control center; therefore the automatically-triggered retaliation

[6] Commander W. J. Kotsch, USN, "Weather Control and National
Strategy," *U. S. Naval Institute Proceedings*, (July 1960).

contributes to a more credible deterrent. Thus the late weapons will, in a sense, have independent capabilities. They will *not* be entirely under our control. In a way they will be superior beings; they will have infallible resolve; we will be able to trust them more than ourselves. And we will be almost as afraid of them as of the enemy's weapons.

Is this what the late 1960's have in store for us? If so, there would seem to be a striking resemblance to the final period of Aztec civilization. The Aztecs lived in what has been called a

> metaphysic of disaster . . . the continuation of the world, the rising of the sun, the falling of the rain, the growth of crops, were envisaged as permanently uncertain; every day the next day was in peril, and at the end of each "century" of 52 years, the whole universe was in jeopardy; disaster could be averted only by the continuous spilling of human blood and the sacrifice of human life . . . The whole of Aztec society was organized around this concept . . . the emperor and the warriors . . . were trained to stoicism and to regard death in battle or on the sacrificial stone as the most glorious death possible.[7]

It is difficult to believe that a responsible national leader would be willing to subject his people and his system to the risks of this sort of world. If it were apparent to him that nothing could be done to alter or reverse this situation, then it seems likely that one leader or the other will succumb to the temptation to launch an all-out pre-emptive strike as the last remaining possibility of halting the arms race. This sort of war—terminal war—will be regarded by its instigator as a service to humanity with—one might add—some justification.

This picture of the arms race may seem too apocalyptic. It should be remembered that it is not a prediction of what is going to happen; it is a forecast of what might happen if no appreciable amount of arms control or disarmament is achieved. It is a warning of where the arms race, advocated by millions of Americans and Russians, can take us.

Many strategicians are genuinely concerned about the arms

[7] Geoffrey Gorer reviewing "The Daily Life of the Aztecs," *Observer* (London), (October 8, 1961).

race. At Civil Defense hearings conducted by the House Subcommittee on Military Operations in August, 1961, the concept of an all-out thermonuclear war was revised. The possibilities of "controlled war" and "limited general war" were discussed. A new definition of deterrence was introduced—"intrawar deterrence"—the attempt to "make deterrence work after the war has started." [8]

A leading strategician explained these new categories: "It is perfectly possible for us or the Soviets to use force in a rational and reasonable fashion at least, in the sense, that we do not use it in a wildly irrational or wildly unreasonable fashion . . . having unreasonably decided to use force, one might still decide to use the force in a reasonable fashion."

This is the thermonuclear "new look." If you can't deter war, then perhaps you can deter it from being too bad. Measured retaliation replaces massive retaliation. What this means is that a non-nuclear provocation might well be met by a thermonuclear reprimand. We make the punishment fit the crime. Let's get mad at each other, but not too mad. A whole new range of possibilities for "scenarios" has been opened up. They subvert Iran; we H-bomb Kiev and Volgograd. They retaliate with Pittsburgh and Baltimore. Then we talk about it for a while—at Camp David maybe? Instead of losing fifty to one hundred cities in six hours we lose them over twenty years.

In the eyes of the Free World, the Soviets have subjected man to an unparalleled tyranny. The individual is nothing; the state is everything. We cherish, above all else, the belief that the individual has priority over the state. This is our reason for being caught up in an arms race and a Cold War. But if the cost of competing in this arms race means that we must bury our populations deep underground, tranquillize and terrorize them, expose them to casualties on the order of twenty-five million, fifty million, one hundred million, then where is

[8] U.S. Congress, House of Representatives, Hearings Before a Subcommittee of the Committee on Government Operations, *Civil Defense— 1961*, 87th Congress, First Session, U.S. Government Printing Office, Washington, D.C. (1961).

our rational means and what is our rational goal? Long before the bombs drop we will have forfeited our only justification for resisting the tyrants—the defense of democracy and democratic values. Both our means *and* our end will be unacceptable. Will there be any appreciable difference between our society and the Soviet world?

Many advocates of an all-out arms race contend that if we are to win out we must be prepared to match every move the Soviets make; we must be as immoral as they, as unethical as they, as ruthless, as tyrannical. If it is necessary to jettison every last value of our way of life, then we must do it. To follow such a course is to degrade the Cold War to the level of a death struggle between two monsters in a primeval swamp. If this is to be our course—and this is exactly where the Cold War is taking us—then we ought to join forces with the Soviets now and subject the rest of the world to our joint dominion.

Participation in the arms race will necessitate a gradual repudiation of all the values of Western society. This is one way we can lose the Cold War—just by running in the arms race. There are other ways to lose—the bombs go off and we are defeated. Or the bombs go off and we win. The sort of society we will have—win, lose, or draw—will not even remotely resemble what we have today.

Suppose, for a moment, that an accidental thermonuclear war has occurred. We have inflicted severe damage on the enemy and he has sued for peace. Although we have lost some twenty cities and thirty million people we have won a clear-cut victory in conventional military terms. What sort of post-war world will we be living in? Unlike previous wars, this will be followed by a total mobilization of national resources. Martial law will have been proclaimed during or shortly after the end of hostilities; the nation will have food rationing, price controls, wage ceilings, unprecedentedly high taxes, and unlimited control of manpower. We will have lost an enormous number of schools, universities, colleges, hospitals, homes, churches, financial and business establishments, museums, prisons, retailing installations, industrial and manufacturing plants, most of which will have low reconstruction priorities compared to the essential machine tools, telephone, telegraph, transportation and other communications systems. The post-war government may find it necessary to take over, at least on a temporary basis, key industries like television, railroads and airlines. An entire generation will have to sacrifice itself with total single-mindedness to reconstruction under a centralized, authoritarian government in much the same way the Chinese are doing today. It requires a considerable amount of optimism to assume that after several decades of this we will return to a benign, permissive system.

This scenario is for a moderate war; and it purposely leaves out all the complex post-attack social, psychological and moral problems. Scenarios for an all-out war, win *or* lose, will be grimmer by several orders of magnitude.

With literally hundreds of strategicians in different countries deeply involved in studying the arms race, writing papers, books, evolving tactics, attending symposia, lecturing, appearing on television, counselling generals, politicians and governments, one might expect that there would have been proposals produced for ending or changing the arms race. Yet, strangely enough, the only two plans we have both came from the "native quarter." They are based on unilateral action by the U. S. One calls for a program of "graduated unilateral acts"—the sharing of scientific information, stopping of atomic tests, troop reductions, evacuation of military bases. The idea is that through a number of individual, independent actions we can break the disarmament deadlock. These actions are to be taken by the U. S. without simultaneous Soviet compliance. There is great merit to this proposal. Unfortunately, if the Russians have failed to reciprocate after a number of U. S. steps, we return to the *status quo ante.*

The other proposal is for unilateral disarmament. It calls for the U. S. to reject deterrence completely and to scrap nuclear weapons. It is usually referred to as the "Better Red than Dead" position, and the most vehement opposition to it comes from the "Better Dead than Red" advocates who consider it tantamount to lying down and letting the Russians trample all over us. Unilateral disarmament does nothing of the kind. It calls for a protracted nation-wide struggle of non-violent resistance to the enemy demanding the utmost skill, courage, selflessness and devotion to country. Perhaps it is too complex for the general public to grasp; however, one has at least the right to demand of the strategicians that they have looked at it before they reject it. One well-known member of the RAND Corporation wrote of unilateral disarmament in a professional journal: "I do not believe that we came across the ocean of history these thousand years fighting tyranny, fighting Nazism, fighting concentration camps and fighting totalitarianism in order to drop onto the beach and say, 'We are not going to do anything now; we are just going to lie down and quit.'" This statement places the author firmly in the lowest category of "native."

What does the "Better Dead than Red" position have to offer us? An article in *Political Science Quarterly* sets forth the prospects in their most extreme terms: [9]

> What we are saying, then, is that America must be hardened so that if nuclear war comes and millions are killed, if millions more are sick and dying of radiation exposure, if the nation is fragmented into islands of survival, with remnants of state and federal authority, here a Naval District Commandant, there a member of the Federal Reserve Board, if food, power and transportation are inadequate, if commands are conflicting and come from enemy as well as from American authority, if invasions occur or are expected, if final annihilation is expected momentarily by those who have thus far survived, then the incredibly difficult mission is not only for the military to prosecute the war successfully, but for the civilian survivors to pull the U. S. together and start the long process of rebuilding segment by segment into a nation. Safety does not lie in abandoning our capacity to wage nuclear war but in improving it.

This is admittedly a graphic exegesis of the "Better Dead" position. It is less a prescription for survival than a wish for

[9] Gerhard C. Bleicken, "The Role of Nonmilitary Defense in American Foreign and Defense Policy," *Political Science Quarterly*, (December 1959).

death. It does not seem that either of the "better" positions ful-
fills the requirements of a viable national security policy. Ultimately, the unilateral disarmament idea seems to have something immoral about it; not because it avoids a good fight; it
doesn't, but because it is an abdication of responsibility. It
places the welfare of the U. S. above that of its allies and the
non-aligned nations. It does not solve the long-term problem
of nuclear war; it merely postpones the conflict which sooner
or later will probably occur, whether between Russia and
China, Israel and the Arab nations or South Africa and the
sub-Saharan countries.

When the strategicians took over from the natives they
claimed they were going to look at the problems in depth.
One grants that the natives had neither the technical background nor the stomach to do this; yet, the strategicians have,
although to a much lesser degree, of course, made the same
mistake. Deterrence has one basic flaw which even the most
superficial student immediately recognizes: It is at best a
device for buying time, a Mephistophelean bargain, the perfect contract for Faustian Man. In the preface to *On Thermonuclear War* the author states, "This book will concentrate on
the problem of avoiding disaster and buying time, without
specifying the use of this time." This seems to be the
consensus of the profession. Almost without exception the strategicians are committed to the status quo. They talk of tomorrow in precisely the same terms as of today. There are different weapons with different capabilities, but there is no real
change between 1962, 1965 and 1970. We'll have Bomarc B
and C, Nike-Zeus X or Y, B-47's phased out; later on there'll
be Skybolt Q, Bambi 56B, Regulus 103, better command
and control, earthquakes, doomsday machines whirling around
our heads, tourists with Leica-sized H-bombs, the best of all
possible worlds, and we'll try to be careful, too.

Our terms for ending the arms race are disarmament with
inspection and control; the Russians insist on disarmament
without inspection. The positions are irreconcilable. Unless
there is a drastic transformation in Soviet policy—almost incon-

ceivable under present conditions—there is little or no hope of progress towards disarmament.

Does this condemn us to an all-out, open-ended arms race? Two recent reports in the national press indicate that it may. *The Wall Street Journal's* Washington correspondent has written that

> A vastly accelerated nuclear arms race looms . . . with no end in sight . . . Key administration officials talk of the prospect of swarms of nuclear-armed satellites circling the earth . . . technological advance may, within a few years, permit one country to gain a near-monopoly of destructive nuclear capacity—leaving its enemy almost powerless.[10]

The Chairman of the State Department's Policy Planning Council has said that Americans will have to live with the "hard but necessary fact of the nuclear arms race" until the Soviets agree to disarmament on our terms. "We live on—and we shall probably continue to live over the foreseeable future —in a world of high tension." [11]

Two of the most responsible and distinguished strategicians have expressed their views on an all-out arms race. The author of *On Thermonuclear War* says in Chapter V that

> . . . purely military solutions to our security problem are likely to be grossly inadequate in the long run, and may prove to be so in the short run. If we are to reach the year 2000, or even 1975, without a cataclysm of some sort . . . we will almost undoubtedly require extensive arms control measures in addition to unilateral security measures.

Henry A. Kissinger, in his *The Necessity for Choice*, says:

> . . . in the present state of technology an arms race is [an extremely unstable form] of security. In the next few years we may have perhaps our last opportunity to stabilize the arms race by means of negotiation. Perhaps Communist obduracy will foil our most earnest efforts. But it would be unforgivable if we failed because we re-

[10] Henry Gemmill, *The Wall Street Journal*, (March 5, 1962).
[11] E. E. Asbury, *The New York Times*, (May 4, 1962).

fused to face either the importance or the complexity of the challenge.

Today we are pouring into the research, development and procurement of weapons systems some $25 billion a year; into devising the techniques, tactics and strategies for their use go scores of millions of dollars. Into peace—how much? The State Department's new Arms Control and Disarmament Agency has 105 employees and a budget of $2,017,000, substantially less than the amount allotted to the legislative program of the Defense Department—the Pentagon lobby. There are three small groups concerned with problems of arms control and/or disarmament—in the AEC, the White House and the Pentagon. "Billions for thermonuclear war, but hardly a penny for peace" is an appropriate slogan for the United States. Peace is the province of the amateur, the dilettante, the free-lancer. A handful of individuals are involved; some sail boats into nuclear testing areas; some parade with placards; some take time off from academic duties to write papers.

The great danger is that we will slip gradually into an all-out arms race, not so much because we will adopt it as our "grand strategy" but simply because it is the easiest course to pursue. We have the weapons and we can get more of them any time we want; we can continue to design systems which are increasingly more lethal and sophisticated. It is difficult to evolve alternative strategies; and it is easy to rely on the Russians to meet us halfway. But each year the price of a failure of deterrence goes up alarmingly. A war in 1950, 1955 or 1960 would have cost but a fraction of what a war in 1965 or 1970 will cost.

We will not achieve peace nor will we deserve it unless and until we—as a nation, as individuals, as politicians, as experts, as a society—make the most serious, dedicated, supreme effort to avoid war of which we are capable, unless we decide to surpass the Soviets not only in weapons, strategies, overkill capacity, but in the imagination, ingenuity, intellect, courage and resourcefulness we bring to bear on the problems of the arms race.

An arms race between two nations is governed by an inexorable law. The nation which is running second must try by all possible means to close the gap or to take the lead. Only the nation which is ahead is in a position to transform or halt this macabre competition. With our superiority in strategic striking power we are ahead of the Russians by a considerable margin today. Hence the responsibility and the initiative are ours. That our problems and difficulties are appalling even now is undeniable. The sooner we come to grips with them the better; they can only get worse if left alone.

Strategicians dismiss world law, world government and disarmament as naive Utopias. While they are genuinely concerned to keep the arms race within rational tolerances, they too make a number of hypotheses about the world based more on intuition than knowledge. In defiance of any sense of history, politics, humanity, psychology, they postulate a permanent gauntlet of brinkmanship which the world is condemned to run. Their energies and talents are almost exclusively devoted to minor palliative measures. The future does not exist for them.

Perhaps disarmament and world law are at present unattainable goals. Perhaps it is out of the question to get any sort of agreement with the Soviets. The new weapons may have made trust and confidence obsolete. Even if one grants all these claims, there still remains the question: Is there absolutely nothing we can do to halt the arms race? Are we to remain indefinitely a sort of Soviet overseas "satellite" run from Moscow, reacting to what Moscow says and does? This is the last remaining area of the virgin lands the strategicians have not yet explored. This is the "reservation" set aside for the natives.

At the House hearings on Civil Defense in August, 1961, a well-known strategician talked about lay attitudes to thermonuclear war:

> Most people do not want to face the reality of potential thermonuclear war as something which might be fought. They prefer deterring it, abolishing it, wishing it away, thinking it away, ignoring it or in some other way deny-

ing its existence as a problem worthy of consideration together with other programs.[12]

The strategician appears to equate deterring and abolishing nuclear war with wishing it away, thinking it away, ignoring it. In other words, all any reasonable and intelligent person can now do is prepare for it, speculate how it will happen, try to cut down losses. The natives are *not* denying the "existence of thermonuclear war as a problem worthy of consideration"; they are acutely aware of the danger and prefer to make every possible effort to deter and abolish it. How has it come about that deterrence and abolition of war are suddenly unrespectable? When did it happen? Who decided? It appears significant, somehow, that critics of Civil Defense were not invited to testify at the House hearings. The weeklong session consisted of a monotonous march-past of military and para-military witnesses beginning with Secretary of Defense McNamara and ending with the author of *On Thermonuclear War*. The agenda of the Subcommittee made no provision for questions, doubts, debate, misgivings or contrary views.

In 1962, the sophisticated don't worry about a nuclear war happening. They just worry about what happens when it happens. What will it be like? How many will survive? How long will it take us to get ready for another one—five years, fifteen twenty-five?

Every society gets the high priests it deserves. Ours are the strategicians. We created them; the fault is ours. Obviously it is necessary to examine the appalling consequences of the failure of deterrence. But even more obviously someone has to continue to make deterrence work if there is to be any real hope of avoiding thermonuclear war. And if deterrence is completely unworkable, then perhaps one ought to try to find a way out of the predicament altogether.

We are living in a ghoulish 1984 world some twenty-two years ahead of schedule where H-bombs are "puffs of wind," where ninety-seven per cent can be saved, where deterrence

[12] U.S. Congress, House of Representatives, *Civil Defense—1961*.

begins *after* war has started, fallout does not destroy, and the high priests—those "strange, sterile sons of Chaos"—move among us murmuring comforting phrases, mumbling incantations, and trafficking with disaster, blight and cataclysm. In the words of Goethe

> I tell you what: your groping theorist
> Is like a beast led round and round and round
> By evil spirits on a barren ground
> Near to the verdant pastures he has missed.

Man's problem is man himself—not his weapons. He can lay no claim to having created the world, but the temptation to destroy it—the next best thing—thus conferring some degree of godhood on himself, may prove irresistible. Somehow we are fascinated by the thought of the great unknown experience, the Universal Death, from which some of us will nevertheless emerge as survivors.

The Aztecs lived in mortal terror of a natural disaster—famine, flood, the end of the world. We live in terror of a man-made disaster. Drought, plague and thermonuclear war are inexorable processes of nature. Like primitive man, all we can do is store corn and build dikes. The die is cast; the storm approaches. We go underground. We take some food along and some medicine and some machine tools and some Miltown and we wait.

Joost A. M. Meerloo | Can War Be Cured?

I WHAT AILS OUR CIVILIZATION?

What ails our civilization? Our world is in crisis; not the world of the white race only, but the world of all races, all peoples. We are actually in the midst of a tremendous global convulsion, a process we cannot fully comprehend because our mental capacities are still warped and clouded by a postwar hangover. Hitler predicted that a defeated Germany would drag the world down to its final downfall. The illusion fits into the myths of the masochistic and sadistic fantasies of the infant: the push-button fantasy of a magic destruction. Hitler's prediction of downfall is the same idea that Spengler sold us after the first defeat of Germany in his *Decline of the West*.

Only pessimistic voices seem to echo through the postwar world. They announce with Spengler that Western civilization is on the decline. "The individual economic adventurer, the white Croesus has had his day." . . . "Every civilization comes and goes. The same old historical law is occurring again." The picture of cataclysmic horror at the end of our world is part of a Judaeo-Christian mythology of history, in which the days of Armageddon come before the final return to paradise.

Similar prophetic voices spoke of humanity's decline and the world's downfall during the Renaissance. It is a lively theme for pessimists.

Is ours a dying civilization? This self-condemnatory ques-

---

* A sequence of excerpts from Dr. Meerloo's recent book, *That Difficult Peace*, published by Channel Press, Manhasset, N.Y.

tion is being asked by a shocked and guilty world as it casti-
gates itself for producing a Hitler, a Buchenwald, world wars,
a Stalin, a hydrogen bomb. All those historians see as they
look at the world a development of evil principles only.

What has happened to the human being? Did he really
attempt a form of mass suicide in the last war, a war followed
by chaos, hunger, suspicion, and destruction? Is it reasonable
to be so pessimistic? Shall we be seduced into defeatism because of the difficult tasks of reconstructing the world? Or
should we accept the opposite simple dogma of inevitable
progress and a golden future?

Psychology teaches us that good and evil belong together
as an inherent polar development of growing and becoming.
This, then, remains our most crucial question: Is the human
being able to check and control his aggressive and self-destructive tendencies and give leeway to more peaceful behavior? Will man always identify civilization with wealth,
honor, status, prestige and influence and the power to fight
for these "goods"?

It has become increasingly possible for man to mold history
to suit himself, for history has developed gradually into a
product of human control and creation.

In ancient times civilizations died because of their isolation (e.g., the Mayan civilization), but today the world has
become one big crossroad of cultural exchange and diffusion.
Technically, influenced by our means of communication, we
already live in a world of enforced co-existence, although there
are still too many barriers and deep suspicion of opposing
ideas and viewpoints. Even the difference between Eastern
and Western psyche is a pseudo-difference. Nobody knows
better than the doctor that all men are equal. They come to
him with identical pains and problems, with the same sad-
ness and ecstasy. Man falls in love, children are born, a man
dies.

The fallacy of describing psychological differences between
East and West is that we tend to interpret them as contrasts

rather than as a more or less pronounced variant of universal human qualities.

Aggressive, competitive twentieth-century man has a better opportunity to become civilized and to form a permanent culture than man at any time before him. Moral training, through modern education, can bring human instincts of destruction and aggression under control. In spite of such bestial regression as Hitler's systematized criminalization of his followers, man has proved that he is capable of forming peaceful and stable communities. His need for dependency and his social needs force him to accept, no matter what the cost, the difficult and restrictive rules of his community.

Yet there is danger in over-emphasizing community ties. Bureaucratic planners, for instance, can have an inhibiting effect on human spontaneity and creativity. We have to be very careful with the selection of those who administer and govern us. They are those who finally touch the push-buttons. We have to be aware, too, how easily a powerloaded bureaucracy can show inner decay and promote the reign of aggressive morons. Nevertheless, the baffling hurdles that have to be taken can gradually help us to sublimate aggression and to turn the spirit of revolt within the mind into productive cooperation.

In his battle for security and serenity man must first learn to endure insecurity and uncertainty. It is the same with his battle for universal justice. Only when he is very consciously able to suffer and tolerate personal injustice will he be able to champion a movement promoting justice for others. But as long as his battle for justice is rooted in self-pity and a personal feeling of misery, no justice for others will be attained.

When we speak of our neurotic world we imply that people suffer nowadays from inner paradoxes, and from an awareness of the contrasting forces and motivations acting on them. Yet this very doubt can help them to become less dogmatic, less satisfied with their little strategic solutions. They will see their way to exchanging mechanical perfectionism for free creativity. The conscious choice between political extremes seems a difficult one because it requires honesty, not corrupted by either emotional histrionics or pedantic social theories. And then, suddenly, man discovers that the contrasts belong together as part of one immense polarity.

We must distinguish between man's contrasting inner forces and a passive cultural "horizontalism" aiming at limited goals of adjustment and security. Cultural "horizontalism" is leveling and vulgarizing. But alert, continual awareness of man's limitations and turbulent inner paradoxes challenges man's creativity. Horizontalism creates passive onlookers and bystanders. People, deprived of responsibility, become incapable of mental initiative or moral action. They are transformed into the shouting crowds at sports events or the cheering masses guided by totalitarian propaganda.

Nineteenth-century European civilization, although seemingly stable, was too smug, too sure and secure about itself, too comfortable for the few, too brutally competitive for the many. Men lived from it, but did not provide for it, and it became a perversion of civilization, a semi-culture. It was devoured from within.

Contemporary civilization is growing more complex by the day and seems even chaotic. Earthly goods are still divided unequally, creating a breeding ground for social struggle, scapegoatism, racism. The idol of technical production created the big metropolis, where man got lost in material competition. Now men feel naked and undefended; they tend to hide more and more in great cities for protection against loneliness and fear. Thus they cut themselves off from the inspiring challenge nature offers. Scientific techniques may put dangerous powers in the hands of incompetents: automobiles in the hands of aggressive neurotics, atomic bombs in the hands of political adventurers. Sports, films, dancing, and sex have become drugs offering artificial ecstasy and cheap intoxication —camouflage for empty lives. Sex is looked upon more often as a hungry need than as an erotic art. Shallow education may inflate men by providing empty factual knowledge without emotional foundation, making them into intellectual accumulations without experience. Our schools too often serve more as fact-factories than as training centers for individual thinking. Men are still so undecided about their own goals that any outside influence—whether a Stalin or a "yellow" newspaper columnist—can push their minds into some temporary malpractice. There is a general lack of awareness of these influences.

The veneration and over-evaluation of technique and material production covers up man's ever-present enervating and weakening need for security. Like the dictator, technique requires an infantile, servile attitude from people. The need for security increases our passivity and moral cowardice. The ancient myths cannot soothe mankind any more. Today, the myth of a perfect technocracy is replacing the older myths of powerful, protective idols. In urban culture, where people are always kept busy even during leisure time, the challenge to face the hard forces of nature outside and the subtle forces of instinct within us is hardly ever met. Only confrontation with these two forces can form sound character and personality. We have to turn the systematic breeding of dissatisfaction—as stimulated and suggested by technological production—into greater awareness of the processes going on inside man's mind.

Can we adjust and reconcile people to a rapidly changing world? Did Pandora unleash forces man can no longer control?

Clinical psychology is astutely aware of the fact that insight, knowledge, and the will to face problems have in themselves a curative and regenerative action. Mutual insight diminishes tension. It teaches people to live with their limitations and to accept their ignorance.

Unawareness of inward fears and panic breeds passive escapists, who consequently surrender to their doom in a mood of destructive fatalism. Perhaps the biggest psychological battle we have to fight is against such mental apathy, passivity and self-pity, as is proved by the study of panic and fear in man.

A free democratic world finds its own answers to problems

by building up through trial and error various legal and institutional controls, protecting society against its own foibles and failures.

At this very moment mankind knows enough about itself and its history, about man and the natural, social and intrapsychic factors guiding him, to be able to plan its future tentatively with scientific and philosophic wisdom and leadership.

Yet, such intelligent leadership has to be cultivated in small, selected teams, fortified by an inner wisdom as well as the critical knowledge that their very planning can breed the germ of new danger in that it may kill the spontaneity of higher wisdom. Such a leading group has to teach the world how to convert the manifold "isms," "principles" and "ideologies" into the patient wisdom of repetitious tactics and probable compromises. And let them not forget that the reasonable man is a lonely man. He cannot be too gregarious, since he must constantly defend his individual integrity.

The new Atomic Age has put before us enormous new challenges, asking of man unfamiliar forms of awareness in order to check the tremendous outer and inner forces which he has unleashed.

II   WAR IS CURABLE

The word peace is related to the Sanskrit root pac, meaning to bind. We find this meaning back in our word pact, a binding mutual agreement. To pay, paccare, means to appease those to whom you are indebted. The German word Frieden (vrede in Dutch) expresses more the passive connotation of being secure and protected.

As a binding pact in all religious and social systems, one finds in astonishingly similar form the same golden rule: Do naught unto others which would cause you pain if done to you.

Peace is war against aggressive hostile impulses—war is escape from the more subtle involvements and tensions of peace. I had never realized the paradoxical implications of peace quite so clearly as I did after my experience with penal camp inmates I had to judge, who incessantly fought their private battles and harbored grudges against society.

A great deal of so-called peace is not necessarily as peaceful as the fervent lover of peace presumes. Important are the inner motives, the realization of the warring contrasts in man, and the spiritual background of the condition we call "peace." Peace can be the very mask of aggression, and aggression the disguise of a peaceful mind. Perpetual armistice is possible between people—a constant state of unsolved tension, which erroneously is called peace. I've known so-called "peaceful" lovers, silent mates in marriage, who avoided every complication and conflict and thus every fruitful solution of controversies by escaping into tacit peacefulness. Among the naïve advocates of world peace, I know some who radiate aggression, who are white-hot with rage and the lust to fight the warmongers! Many a fanatical pacifist is merely fighting his own unsolved hostile tendencies.

Before we investigate the positive actions we can take against the atomic peril and atomic fear, we have to be deeply aware of man's contrasting attitudes toward danger and catastrophe. There is a tragic side to our personalities which accounts for our unconscious readiness to engage in war. Consciously—and truthfully—we say we hate war, we hate death and destruction. But deeply rooted in each of us is a primitive urge—a submerged personality level—that finds satisfaction in war's terrible destruction; indeed, it craves such a nemesis.

I remember a lecture I gave before a group of ultra-pacifists years before the outbreak of the Second World War. These pacifists thought they might still be able to prevent war. All sorts of idealistic actions were planned, and the aid of leading statesmen from different countries was recruited. "Moral Rearmament" was the slogan at that time. I warned my audience as emphatically as I could that they should not assume a passive attitude toward the political evils in the center of Europe. I pointed out that Hitler was trying to misuse the European pacifist movements to weaken the more militant anti-Nazi movements in the countries surrounding Germany, knowing, cynically, that the pacifism of the one might activate and fortify the aggressive potency of the other. Pacifism in our country might activate the potential enemy at the other side of the frontier, I said. Even in people who profess pacifism, deep aggressive and destructive drives have by no means disappeared, although they may have been channeled into more acceptable expressions of human action.

When I had finished, the pacifistic lambs had turned into most violent wolves. It was as if their pent-up hatred and aggression had been released and was now directed at me. I was almost thrown out. They themselves proved that they still nurtured various forms of violence.

Man's unconscious expectation of war and Armageddon is dangerous, indeed. It prepares the mind for what is justified as an "inevitable fact." It paves the way for passive surrender to the dreaded event. It is analogous to the thought-process of a thief who feels more secure when he finally surrenders to his pursuers. He cannot bear the growing insecurity of the feeling that he may be caught at any moment. He prefers the security of imprisonment. All of us are in some way the same kind of insecure criminals. Nemesis and downfall can free us from our pent-up primitive drives!

We can grow used to wholesale slaughter. After all, the population of the world is far too large ever to make an instantaneous total annihilation of mankind probable. Our primitive fantasy even tells us secretly that we will be among the few who will survive the radioactive dust, leaving us as inheritors of the remnants of the world. The truth is that somewhere in our minds we rather prefer the atomic show, especially when we have been hardened to suffering by fear and intensive war propaganda. Our technical age has insidiously made us much more self-destructive. Speed and motion have replaced feeling and emotion.

The primitive in us enjoys the turmoil of war; it admires the technical dream of human omnipotence and tremendous destruction. I once treated a conscientious objector who refused to carry weapons or wear a uniform. He presented the most ethical justifications for his refusal. After many therapeutic sessions, however, I learned that he had a terrific fear of militaristic symbols. He feared his own unconscious and deeply hidden criminal lust to kill and to destroy. He could not run the risk of carrying a deadly weapon nor of having such a perfect excuse for killing his fellow human beings.

Are we really full of panic about the atom bomb? How many among us are already thinking that we should drop atom bombs before our potential enemies attack us? A number of people daily write to the papers—see almost any "Letters to the Editor" column—to say that they think we should drop the bombs now—first. That was especially true when we smugly thought that the eventual enemy was not ready for reprisals.

Thousands of times we have in our dreams blasted away at all whom we hate. Behind the display of horror our primitive megalomaniacal wish for terrible devastation—a childish dream of revengeful omnipotence—is fulfilled. What a powerful gesture! What frustrated magicians we are! Imagine, one push of a button and a whole world may vanish! In our dreams we become as powerful as God. Man is a crazy dreamer. His technical toys fulfill his primitive dreams and compensate for his lack of inner strength and self-confidence. In science fiction we give vent in a romantic way to those primitive magic fantasies.

However, we are not only children and fighting dreamers. Apart from the phrases and the catchwords, we still possess positive, active drives for peace. There are constructive drives, too: for thinking, and for building a more harmonious society. But these drives have nothing to do with fear and the dread of attack. The compulsion to destroy is not the principal thing that motivates human beings, even though we often behave aggressively and destructively toward one another. Human love and purposefulness and intelligent social adaptation and cooperation exist too. These feelings cannot be regulated or channeled by diplomats, military staffs, or atomic scientists. These positive roots of civilization have nothing to do with the checking of aggressive behavior. International military strategy can only check the aggressive discharges of states and communities in much the same way that our police force tries to check the individual criminals among us. Positive peace, however, is built in a different atmosphere and with different means.

Some people today are certain that the one way to insure peace among men is to play up the tremendous horrors of the next war. Behind this sort of thinking is the notion that to picture the terrific destruction of an atomic war will create so deep a fear in all people that they will actually be persuaded by fear to build a constructive plan for peace.

But we know that people do not entirely abhor carnage and gruesomeness; they experience hidden pleasure even as they shudder. Anyone who sees movies, watches television, or listens to radio programs must be convinced of man's tremendous self-intoxication with destruction. Psychological studies tell us that fear never evokes peaceful reactions. On the contrary, people react to fear by preparing themselves instantly for defense and attack. Man reacts to danger and fright by becoming aggressive, not peaceful. After he gets out of his initial paralysis he tries to land the first blow. Involuntarily, man in fear looks for a means of counterattack, and by so doing prepares himself for the very fight he dreads so deeply.

This was brought home to me time and again among combat soldiers. The "green" troops indulged in all kinds of philosophical discussions on the "stupidity of war," but when they were really scared, when the enemy attacked, they fought like demons. For many a soldier the free release of aggression became the one ecstatic experience in his life, as if war were the only challenge to man's bravery and courage.

So when we read scare stories about a possible atomic war, about the unspeakable destruction it will cause, about the countless cities that will be turned into rubble, about the millions of casualties that will result, can we be expected to react by becoming so afraid of war that in self-defense we will outlaw it? I say no. We are afraid, true; but as soon as we become afraid we begin inwardly to mobilize ourselves for attack. Thus each of these scare stories leads us a little farther along the road to the acceptance of the atomic holocaust of a Third World War. And the culmination of these scares unwittingly builds up the primitive lust to fight, with its attraction of horror and terror lurking in each of us and waiting only to be discharged again. It costs us a lot of energy to keep our instincts under control.

History has shown us many times that war is not an unavoidable fate, and that hostility and aggression can be handled intelligently in a well-planned society. Hungary in the nineteenth century, Norway at the beginning of our century have been examples of this; the peaceful solution of the colonial tie between India and Great Britain is one of the more recent illustrious examples.

When individual drives are not in harmony, an integrative mental cure is necessary and possible. The same is true of group or state tendencies. In the future, serious, informed practitioners of social psychology are going to be forced to leave their desks and classrooms and go out into society to influence people in actual social groups. When they have helped mankind to recognize war as a curable discharge of frustrated instinctual, economic, and political tendencies of the masses, then therapeutic measures can be taken and peace re-established.

Intellect develops slowly. But there is hope for the human being if he will only grow toward greater awareness before an atomic war has annihilated our civilization.

The modern world has no common moral base. Each country, in justification of its deeds, speaks a different moral language. In World War II we did not even find an acceptable pretext of morality; it was a war against something—against Hitler and Mussolini, against Nazism and Fascism. It was not a war for anything.

A re-evaluation of moral values does command attention. The "Declaration of Human Rights" as formulated by the United Nations has tried to supply such common values. However, in place of a common moral faith, we have rival ideologies: marxism, fascism, totalitarianism, capitalism, liberalism, democracy, etc. Often these terms are used more to cover up private politics than to express well-formulated political ideas; they hardly ever express anything with semantic clarity. Historical materialism has become the voiced justification and disguising ideology for defense of one-sided totalitarian interests; so-called idealism can often be a disguise to perpetuate the old conservative ideas.

Long, sophisticated words, purporting to describe different ideologies, are often used to hide the realities behind them. The words merely cover up mythical concepts. Most of those who talk about marxism do not know what marxism is. To recognize mythological wishful thinking for what it really is, this conceptual deceit must be worked out and repeatedly shown to people. One hears, for instance, talk of a Third World War—Russia against America. But "Russia" is a collective myth, and so is America. People in these countries are not basically different. Those who are cheered by or those who suffer from the idea of a future war don't understand their own feelings.

In psychological terms we may say: Dark myth against dark myth makes for war; the deep unconscious complexes of hidden drives and the absence of clear insights impel man to war. The destructive but hypnotizing myth itself is created by the propaganda machine of the few who are in charge. If a Third World War breaks loose, it will be a war of warped ideologies, of fantastic myths that do not deal with the reality of human beings who are suffering and dying for it.

Is it possible to establish a common moral basis for all nations? Is it possible to make every nation a loyal member of a universal United Nations? Without such a moral basis it is useless to expect anything but misunderstanding to grow out of world conferences.

A common base is only possible when men are freed of their suspicions and fears, when the masses can be sure of certain economic minimums. The new civilization must have a broad material and psychological basis, spread evenly among the common people of the world, and a common moral basis as well. I hope fervently that the Declaration of Human Rights as formulated by the United Nations may gradually embody such a basic principle.

In order to become free, however, certain outside conditions must be prevented from hampering this moral development of self-control. We have to become increasingly aware of the internal dangers and ills of democracy: laxity, lack of discipline, laziness and unawareness. People have to be aware, for instance, of the tendency of technology to automatize their minds. They have to become aware of the fact that mass media and modern communication are able to bypass people's critical barriers and imprint all kinds of unwanted suggestions on men's brains. They have to know that education can turn us either into weak, uncritical fact-factories or strong personalities. A free democracy has to fight against "mediocrity" in order not to be smothered by mere numbers of automatic votes. Democratic freedom requires from the members of society a highly intelligent appraisal and understanding of the democratic system itself. This very fact makes it rather difficult to advertise or "promote" such a political system. Furthermore, inculcating democracy is just as dangerous as inculcating totalitarianism. It is the essence of democracy that it must be self-chosen; it cannot be imposed.

Freedom and social planning present no essential contrasts. In order to let freedom grow, we have to plan our controls over the forces that limit freedom. First, there has to be guidance and discipline to develop a strong inner nucleus with which to face the un-freedom of the world. Beyond this, however, people must have the passion and inner freedom to prosecute those who abuse freedom. They must possess the vitality to attack those who commit mental suicide, dragging down other persons in their wake of passive surrender. Suicidal submission is a kind of "subversion" from within; it is passive surrender to a mechanized world without vital personalities; it is the denial of the personality. There exists in our world too much urge for security and certainty. Such a goal finally leads to death and mental surrender, to automation and the mere existence of the computed man, because life in itself presumes an acceptance of uncertainty. People must have the fervor to stand firmly for freedom of the individual, and for mutual tolerance and dignity, and they must learn not to tolerate the destruction of these values. They must not tolerate those who make use of the glamor of worthy ideas and values—such as freedom and liberty—only to destroy these as soon as they themselves are in power. We must be intolerant of these abuses as long as the battle of mental life versus death of the free-existing personality goes on.

It cannot be emphasized too strongly that liberty is only possible with a strong set of beliefs and moral standards. Man must adhere to self-restrictive rules—moral rules—in order to keep his freedom. Where there is a lack of such internal checks, owing to lack of education or to wrong, stereotyped education, then external pressure or even tyranny becomes necessary to check unsocial drives. Then freedom becomes the victim of man's inability to live in freedom and self-control.

Mankind should be guaranteed the right not to hear and not to conform, and the more subtle right to defend himself against psychological encroachment and against intervention in the form of oppressive mass propaganda, totalitarian pressure and mental coercion. No compromise or appeasement is possible in dealing with such attitudes. However, we have to watch carefully lest our own mistakes in attacking personal freedom become grist for the totalitarian's mill. Even our denunciations may have a paradoxical effect. Fear and hysteria further totalitarianism. What we need is careful analysis and understanding of such soul-disturbing phenomena. Democracy is the regime fostering the dignity and decency of man and his right to think for himself; the right to have his own opinions and, even more than that, the right to assert his own opinion and to protect himself from mental invasion and coercion.

Jerome D. Frank | Breaking the Thought Barrier: Psychological Challenges of the Nuclear Age

My purpose in this paper is not to offer solutions to the political problems of our times, since these must in the last analysis be devised by politicians, but to bring together information and ideas arising out of my own area of interest which may stimulate thought and discussion about these problems. As a psychiatrist, I have been struck by an analogy between the behavior of policy makers today and the behavior of mental patients. That is, they see a problem or a threat and then resort to methods of dealing with it which aggravate it. The leaders of the world agree that nuclear armaments pose or soon will pose an insufferable threat to the existence of humanity. This is reflected in the unanimous United Nations resolution of November 2, 1959, that "the question of general and complete disarmament is the most important one facing the world today." Yet the preparation for war goes on feverishly.

The dilemma is sharply pointed up by two items which appeared in the same issue of the *New York Times*. The first was a statement by President Eisenhower:

> No other aspiration dominates my whole being as much as this: that the nations of the East and West will find dependable, self-guaranteeing methods to reduce the vast expenditure for armaments.

In the same issue appeared the following news item:

> United States armaments manufacturers have begun to pour massive amounts of capital and technical experience into the reviving West Germany arms industry. The motive . . . is the widespread conviction that the

Bonn republic is destined to become a major weapons producer.[1]

The psychiatrist will recognize here a pattern similar to that of the patient who has insight into his problems but is unable to act on it—for instance, the alcoholic who drinks in order to relieve himself of anxiety and depression, even though he knows that this will ultimately prove disastrous to him. He says, in effect, "I know this is killing me," as he takes another drink.

The psychiatrist must often first convince the patient that he is really ill; then try to help him understand the emotional blocks and faulty habit patterns which impede the solution of his problems, and even aggravate them; and finally help him to find more successful solutions. Applying the same approach to the predicaments of the nuclear age, I shall first try to demonstrate how mankind's present course leads inevitably to disaster, then consider some of the psychological blocks to finding a way out, and finally explore some possible solutions.

At this point an awkward question arises. To what extent is it possible to draw valid analogies from individual behavior to the behavior of groups of people? This question cannot be satisfactorily answered at this point. All one can do is to point out possible analogies and try to test their usefulness. Certainly I do not believe that information about personality quirks and personal motivations of national leaders helps much to understand the behavior of nations. True, Hitler's personality had something to do with the excesses of Nazi Germany, but in a conflict situation between two groups those in control of each group are *usually* the most responsible, talented, and exemplary members, who can withstand the strains of the conflict situation, as Sherif and Sherif point out.[2]

Thus leaders of nations in their official dealings are primarily motivated by their concept of national interest and by

[1] *New York Times,* October 14, 1959; pp. 20, 1.
[2] Muzafer and Carolyn W. Sherif, *An Outline of Social Psychology;* New York, Harper, 1956; p. 283.

the values of the groups they represent. Certain general prin-ciples of individual psychology, however, govern the behavior and attitudes of both leaders and followers and are, I believe, pertinent. Moreover, group psychological principles are obvi-ously relevant. I shall try to call upon concepts of individual and group psychology where each seems most appropriate, while recognizing that it is not always possible to distinguish sharply between them.

The core of the problem is that mankind is faced with a rapidly and drastically changing environment. More drastic changes in habits of thinking and behavior are required than have ever occurred in the history of mankind, and they must be made in a very short time. As Albert Einstein put it, "The unleashed power of the atom has changed everything save our modes of thinking, and thus we drift toward unparalleled catastrophe." [3] In a more erudite vein, Brewster Smith writes, ". . . irrationality proliferates when the challenge to a person's adaptation is too severe, or too obscure, to be met head on with the resources then at his command." [4] The challenge of the nuclear age is at once too severe and too obscure to be met head on with the resources now at our command.

One facet of this challenge is the growing interdependence of the world through improved communication and transport. While war has sometimes been an agent of progress, as Mar-garet Mead has pointed out,[5] this cannot occur any longer, because humanity is now one interdependent web. The prob-lems which this interdependence creates are immensely ag-gravated by the fantastic destructive powers of modern weap-onry. Mankind now has the power to destroy itself in three entirely independent ways. The first is by nuclear weapons. Enough uranium is available to the United States to make a

---

[3] Quoted on title page, Alice F. Bryant, *Radiation and the Race;* Phila-delphia, American Friends Service Committee, April 10, 1959.

[4] M. Brewster Smith, "Rationality and Social Process," presidential ad-dress, Society for the Psychological Study of Social Issues, Amer. Psycho-logical Assn., September 7, 1959.

[5] Margaret Mead, "Significance of the Individual," *What's New* (1959) 215: 2-7.

40-million megaton bomb [6]—that is, the United States alone has several thousand times enough fissionable material to wipe out all life. This conclusion is supported by a statement of the Federation of American Scientists, a highly responsible group: "With a stockpile . . . that now exists it is possible to cover the entire earth with a radiation level which for ten years would remain sufficiently intense to prove fatal to all living beings on land." [7]

The second means is by nerve gas; according to Representative Byron Johnson of Colorado there is now enough stockpiled in that one state to wipe out all of mankind and, of course, the Russians have at least as much, if not more.[8] Finally, bacteriological weapons of incredible virulence have been developed. A little more than a glassful of one strain of botulinus toxin would be enough to wipe out mankind if it could be distributed. While these chemical and biological agents are very easy to prepare and are produced in many countries, for simplicity's sake I shall not consider them further, since the problems they present are no different in kind from those of nuclear weapons, and the latter are at the moment by far the most menacing.

There is no defense against these weapons, and it is highly unlikely that there ever will be, for the same thought processes which perfect a defense against a weapon at the same time devise ways of thwarting the defense. For example, we are now trying to develop a system for intercepting missiles through plotting their trajectories, and at the same time developing missiles which do not follow predictable trajectories. We boast of our means of confusing Russian radar, but they, of course, will be able to confuse ours equally well.

In the days of conventional weapons, a defense which worked reasonably well was good enough. Because of the massive destructive power of nuclear weapons, this is no longer true. Now a defense would have to be at least ninety

[6] Thomas E. Murray, *New York Times*, December 10, 1959; p. 4.

[7] Federation of American Scientists, statement of November 23, 1958, New York City.

[8] *The Morning Sun*, Baltimore, February 5, 1960; p. 1.

per cent effective—a level of effectiveness never achieved in history; and the likelihood of its being achieved when technology is advancing at such a fantastically rapid rate seems extremely remote.

And the weapons are getting more deadly and more effective all the time. According to Herman Kahn, right now it would be possible to build a "doomsday machine," capable of literally blowing the earth into little pieces, at a cost between fifty and a hundred billion dollars. This machine—the ultimate deterrent—would be set to go off automatically in the event of an enemy attack. It will become ever cheaper to make such machines, and small nations will have a particular incentive for building them, because this would enable them to blackmail large nations.[9]

While it is unlikely that anyone will build such a machine, and unlikely that the stockpiles of nuclear weapons will go off in such a fashion as to wipe out mankind, a nuclear war is not at all unlikely. The exact amount of damage it would do is uncertain, but the most optimistic estimate of American casualties, based on the development of a full-scale civil defense program, is around six to twenty million people. As Bertrand Russell says:

> . . . the world which would emerge from a nuclear war would not be such as is desired by either Moscow or Washington . . . it would consist of destitute populations, maddened by hunger, debilitated by disease, deprived of the support of modern industry and means of transport, incapable of supporting educational institutions, and rapidly sinking to the level of ignorant savages.[10]

Some sophisticated defenders of nuclear armaments maintain that if certain drastic conditions are met—in itself highly unlikely—a country might survive a nuclear war with its so-

[9] Herman Kahn, "The Nature and Feasibility of War and Deterrence," lecture delivered at The Johns Hopkins University Applied Physics Laboratory, December, 1959.
[10] Bertrand Russell, *Common Sense and Nuclear Warfare;* New York, Simon and Schuster, 1959; p. 42.

cial structure relatively intact. Perhaps this would be true during the next few years, but as an able expositor of this position himself writes, "It is most unlikely that the world can live with an uncontrolled arms race lasting for several decades." [11]

A final point about nuclear explosions is that they permanently make the environment more hostile to man. The increase in radiation alone after a nuclear war would cause higher rates of genetic malformations for at least ten thousand years.

In short, it is extremely unlikely, even today, that any country could win a war fought with modern weapons, and the likelihood of it becomes smaller with each increase in the accumulation of destructive power. In the next war all humanity will be the loser. There may be a few survivors, but the way of life for which they fought would not survive. They would mainly be preoccupied with trying to stay alive.

As a psychiatrist, I am especially impressed with the dangers inherent in the steady diffusion of power to fire modern weapons. The diffusion among countries is bad enough; even worse is the spread within countries. As nuclear weapons multiply and the warning time for retaliation decreases, the power over these weapons filters further and further down the chain of command. At this point individual psychology is certainly relevant. Every population contains a certain number of psychotic or profoundly malicious persons, and it can only be a matter of time before one of them comes into position to order the firing of a weapon which in a flash will destroy a large city in another country. This danger is aggravated by the fact that a large proportion of the generation now coming to adulthood spent its formative years under conditions of unprecedented chaos in refugee camps and the like. Disorganized conditions of living and unstable human relationships in childhood may leave serious scars in the adult in the form of anxiety, bitterness, and emotional instability. The conditions following the last war were worse than those

[11] Herman Kahn, *The Nature and Feasibility of War and Deterrence;* Santa Monica, Calif., The Rand Corp., 1960; p. 43.

in Germany following World War I, which produced Hitler's followers. It is persons like these who will have the power to set the world on fire.

Americans have nominal command of the weapons in the bases in foreign countries, but they are enormously outnumbered and could not prevent local soldiers' seizing the weapons if at some future time they wished to become independent of us. The British have, in fact, pointed out that under the present system American control over the warheads is an illusion. The only answer to this is, as an American Air Force officer said, "You've gotta trust your allies." [12] Personally, I find it difficult to trust an ally like Germany, for example, which twice in my lifetime has been our mortal enemy.

The increasing diversity of modern weapons offers an ever-widening choice of means of delivering them, including the holds of freighters and suitcases. Coupled with their widening dissemination, this means that the margin of error between us and catastrophe is steadily decreasing. If this process continues, I can see no escape from the conclusion that the disaster will certainly occur.

In concluding this sketchy review of the dangers to mankind created by nuclear weapons, let me point out that if there is anything certain in this world, it is that accidents will happen. Even if atomic energy is confined to peaceful uses, disastrous accidents will occur. For example, on December 12, 1952, a nuclear reactor in Canada burst. A 10,000-acre area had to be evacuated temporarily, and the reactor had to be buried. The AEC found that a single major accident near a city the size of Detroit could, under adverse climatic conditions, cause 3,400 deaths, 43,000 injuries, and property damage of 7 billion dollars through radiation alone. It could require the evacuation of 460,000 people and restrict the use of 150,000 square miles of land.[13] A world at peace could cope with atomic accidents as it does with volcanic eruptions,

[12] Alfred Veysey, "British-U.S. Team Controls Thors," *Denver Post,* February 17, 1960; p. 10.
[13] Donald Robinson, "Can Your City Control 'Atomic Accident'?," *This Week,* May 11, 1958, pp. 10, 12, 13, 29.

earthquakes, and hurricanes. In a trigger-happy world, however, it is all too easy to envisage how such an accident could set an irretrievable chain of destruction in motion before its source was discovered.

The responses of individuals to the threats of modern weaponry include all the reactions that people customarily show to massive dangers which exceed their powers of adaptation. One of these is a kind of apathy or fatalism, often coupled with a melancholy pleasure in contemplating one's inevitable doom. This is illustrated by the following quotation, written in the spring of 1959, when many people believed that Khrushchev had set a deadline for our evacuation of Berlin in May:

> Last week I was invited to lunch with a tall, smiling young man, happily married, who has risen in a very short time to one of the highest executive posts in American journalism. . . . "My wife and children know what to expect, and they've accepted it," he said. "I've told them that there'll probably be an exchange of hydrogen bombs before the end of June and I've explained to them that it probably means the death of all of us." His voice was calm . . . he was not arguing a case but regretfully defining a position.
>
> I said that while I recognized his right as an individual to commit suicide rather than live under alien rule, I could not understand his equanimity at the thought that the whole of mankind would perish with him. At this he smiled a deep, forgiving, historian's smile. Other forms of life, he said, had been destroyed; what was so special about the human race, which was doomed to ultimate annihilation anyway, by the cooling of the earth? [14]

What is most disturbing about this anecdote is that the speaker had risen "to one of the highest executive posts in American journalism." If enough of our opinion leaders feel this way, we will go to our doom like cattle to the slaughter.

Somewhat similar in its effects on the person is habituation to the danger. Somehow we seem unable to sustain our feeling of fear in the presence of a constant, continual danger, and we lose our moral repugnance toward any evil which persists

[14] Kenneth Tynan, *The New Yorker*, April 4, 1959; pp. 114-115.

long enough. As Alexander Pope said of vice, ". . . seen too oft, familiar with her face,/We first endure, then pity, then embrace," [15] so David Cavers of the Harvard Law School says:

> Habituation to the thought of nuclear war has blinded us to the realization that what we are discussing is the end of our civilization. Like Samson, we now have the power to pull the temple down upon ourselves and our enemies, but Samson, eyeless in Gaza, knew what he was doing.[16]

We now talk of being able, through a massive civil defense program, to limit our casualties to "only five million dead" and show no qualms at all about exterminating all of Russia. Such statements would have been unthinkable before the Second World War, and probably even a decade ago.

A more common maladaptive response to an overwhelming threat is the denial of its existence. Denial is not always pathological. For example, the inability of most humans to contemplate their own deaths is a healthy form of denial under most circumstances, since constant awareness of one's own inevitable dissolution would produce nothing except depression. But denial, in the form of minimizing the dreadfulness of modern weapons, seriously impedes our efforts to solve the terrible threat they present. For example, we assume that somehow our weapons can wipe out Russia but theirs cannot wipe us out. Some time ago the *Wall Street Journal* devoted four and one-half columns to our capacity to destroy Russia "in several ways and several times over," but included just two references to what Russia can do to us:

> Even granting that Russia would have the advantage of surprise, U.S. officials reason that a first blow by the Soviets, although perhaps able to pierce this country's

[15] Alexander Pope, "Essay on Man, Epistle 2," in *The Complete Poetical Works of Alexander Pope,* Cambridge edition; Boston, Houghton Mifflin, 1931; p. 144.
[16] David F. Cavers, "Why Not Economic Sanctions?," unpublished manuscript.

defenses in part, would not cripple Western power to retaliate.

. . . either side certainly can inflict painful destruction on
the other.[17]

With nuclear weapons, piercing a country's defenses in part
or inflicting painful destruction on it would mean the destruction of that country's social organization.

A more subtle form of denial is a fallacious appeal to history: With the advent of each new weapon alarmists proph-
esied that it would destroy mankind, and they were wrong, so
those who say that nuclear, biological, and chemical weapons
threaten the existence of humanity are probably also wrong.
The fallacy lies in the proportionate increase in destructive
energy made available by the splitting of the atom. At the
dawn of history, when men killed each other with clubs and
stones, a blow could scarcely kill more than one person. By
1944 mankind had so improved the destructiveness of weapons that an average firebomb raid on Japan killed four thousand. Thus the killing power of weapons increased by a factor of four thousand over half a million years or so. Today
a moderate nuclear raid could kill fifty million people,[18] and
nuclear weapons could be made in sufficient quantity to wipe
out the entire human race. This represents an increase in destructive power over the most deadly nonatomic weapons by
a factor of somewhere between 12,500 and infinity in a scant
half-generation. Those who prophesy disaster, and their like-
minded forebears are in the position of the boy who cries
"Wolf" too often, so that when the wolf really comes no one
believes him.

Another form of denial is to believe that nuclear weapons
will not be used just because they are so terrible. Those holding this view point to the mutual restraint in the use of poison
gas in the last war. This comforting fallacy can be exposed in
a word. Our whole military policy commits us to the use of

[17] *Wall Street Journal*, March 25, 1959; pp. 1, 16.
[18] Joint Committee on Atomic Energy, Congress of the United States,
Biological and Environmental Effects of Nuclear War; Washington,
D.C., Government Printing Office, August, 1959.

nuclear weapons. If we got into a major war, we would have no other alternative, since we no longer have sufficient conventional weapons.

A very important obstacle to facing up to the dangers of a modern world has been termed the insensitivity to the remote. Nuclear weapons are not directly present to any of our senses. A few miles from me there is an accumulation of viruses, bacteria, and toxins more than sufficient to wipe out the human race several times over, yet it gives most of us not the slightest concern. The principle operating here is, I think, similar to the learning theory of the gradient of reinforcement. This is, in essence, that the effect of a reward or punishment on a response diminishes very rapidly as the time between the response and the reward or punishment increases. While symbolic thought may bring the anticipated consequences of an act into the present, so that they can have an effect on present behavior, this is not always effective. To return to the alcoholic, he takes a drink to gain immediate relief from anxiety, even though he knows through his memory and powers of anticipation that the following morning he will feel much worse.

Transferred to the international level, this principle operates in both space and time. Thus the mother who cannot bear to see her child's cut finger is unmoved by the extinction of eighty thousand people in Hiroshima or twelve thousand in Agadir. A good example of the soothing effect of temporal distance is the fixation of Russia and America on the immediate danger each poses to the other and their neglect of the greater long-term danger to both resulting from future dissemination of nuclear weapons. The immediate mutual threat will pale when China, Israel, Egypt, and many other countries have such weapons, for then it will be possible for any country to trigger a war in such a way as to conceal the source of the attack. Yet such is the soothing effect of temporal distance that this dire possibility carries practically no weight, compared with each country's supposed need to remain strong vis-à-vis the other.

A final, subtle form of denial is the universal tendency to use reassuring words to describe our predicament, even though they are rapidly losing their meaning in today's world. People talk of defense when it is clear that there is no defense. They speak of national security when it is clear that no nation will be able to maintain even a semblance of security for its citizens at the expense of the security of other nations. One need only remember that a good number of satellites are flying above the earth's atmosphere, quite oblivious of national boundaries; that America has launched one which can spy on any area in the world; and that it may soon be possible to melt the icecap at the North Pole, flooding the seaboard cities of the whole world.

To the extent that we do not succeed in denying the dangers of modern weaponry, we are made anxious by them. Anxiety in moderation facilitates thinking and motivates a search for new and better solutions to the threat. However, if it gets too severe, it tends to make thought rigid and to paralyze initiative. This may have something to do with the repetition compulsion in neurotics, when they keep trying to solve current problems with solutions which may once have worked, but no longer do. It may be that the neurotic is too anxious and demoralized to try something else; he finds it better to bear the ills he has than to risk new ones.

At the level of group dynamics, emotional tension is most seriously reflected in the formation of the stereotype of "the enemy." Whoever we are and whoever the enemy is, we gradually assume all the virtues and they become the incarnation of everything evil. It is frighteningly easy to create the stereotype, as Sherif and Sherif have shown. They set up two groups in a boys' camp whose members did not know each other and arranged competitive situations in which one or both groups felt frustrated. Within a few days, each group had become a cohesive whole, bragging about its own virtues and having only contempt for the other group.[19]

Many psychological factors go into creating the bogey-man concept of the enemy, such as the convenience of projecting the sources of one's own dissatisfactions and justifying one's

[19] See footnote 2.

own aggressive behavior by use of a scapegoat.[20] Here I am more specifically concerned with why a stereotype of the enemy is so hard to break down, and what some of its consequences are. It seems to be a manifestation of a fundamental law of the human mind—that one's perceptions are guided to a large extent by one's expectations or assumptions. This has been demonstrated very nicely by an experiment in which, by means of a stereopticon, different pictures are shown to the right and left eye simultaneously. When groups of Americans and Mexicans were shown by this device a bullfighter and a baseball player, the Americans tended to see the baseball player and the Mexicans, the bullfighter.[21]

Once we have cast another group in the role of the enemy, we know that they are to be distrusted—that they are evil incarnate. We then tend to twist all their communications to fit our belief.

> For Moscow to propose what we can accept seems to us even more sinister and dangerous than for it to propose what we cannot accept. Our instinct is to cast about for grounds on which to discredit the proposal instead of seizing it and making the most of it. Being distrustful of the Greeks bearing gifts, we are afraid of being tricked.[22]

If we meet individual members of the enemy group and find that they do not seem villainous, but appear to be ordinary, easy-going, fun-loving family men like ourselves, we preserve the stereotype by assuming either that they are diabolically clever at deceiving us or that it is their leaders who are villainous.[23] And all evidence indicates that the Russian view of the Americans is a mirror image of our view of them;

[20] These aspects have been well outlined by Arthur Gladstone in "The Conception of the Enemy," *J. Conflict Resolution* (1959) 3:132-137.

[21] Hadley Cantril, "Perception and Interpersonal Relations," *Amer. J. Psychiatry* (1957) 114:119-126.

[22] Louis J. Halle, "The Struggle Called 'Coexistence,'" *The New York Times Magazine,* November 15, 1959, pp. 14, 110, 118; p. 110.

[23] Charles E. Osgood, "Suggestions for Winning the Real War with Communism," *J. Conflict Resolution* (1959) 3:295-325.

that is, we—or our leaders—are war-mongering, untrustworthy, and dangerous, while they are peace-loving and honorable.[24]

The following quotation from a letter I received recently indicates how disruptive the stereotype of the enemy can be to rational thought. From his choice of words, this correspondent is obviously an intelligent man, and yet he is able to write the following:

> One cannot reason, bargain, or do business with a Khrushchev any more than with a Hitler, except possibly at the end of a long club. The intent of this maniac is to enslave forever, to "robotize," if you will, the *entire* human race. This fiend will consign humanity to an ant hill existence. Even the death of humanity is preferable to such an existence.

The mutual distrust of enemies has two dangerous consequences. First, it tends to disrupt communication between them. If a member of one group wishes to communicate with the other, this automatically subjects him to the suspicion of disloyalty. Even Senator Hubert Humphrey, who has maintained a steadfast anti-Communist position for many years, felt it necessary to reassure the public that his desire to talk with Khrushchev did not mean that he was favorable to Communists. Furthermore, since the enemy is viewed as so diabolically clever, each side fears that the other will be able to use improved communications to its advantage. Last November the Senate Internal Security Committee called the Soviet-American cultural exchanges part of a "poisonous propaganda offensive."[25] Soviet hoaxers are playing us individually and nationally for suckers, the Committee said. At virtually the same moment, the Russian counterpart of this Committee was warning that the Americans might use this program as a "Trojan horse." Thus leaders on each side fear that their people are so naive and innocent as to be easily misled;

[24] Urie Bronfenbrenner, "The Mirror Image in Soviet-American Relations: A Social Psychologist's Report," *Journal of Social Issues* (1961) 17:45-56.
[25] *Baltimore Sunday Sun*, November 8, 1959; p. 1.

that any favorable information about the enemy is bound to be false; and that their side could not use the contacts as effectively to further its own ends as the enemy could.

I am not suggesting that some enemies do not deserve to be mistrusted. But disruption of communication prevents gaining information which would help to rectify any incorrect perceptions of one's opponent. On the other hand, increased communication, however desirable, does not in itself remove the causes of war between groups. No peoples communicated more completely than Northerners and Southerners in the early days of our country. Yet because they were operating under systems of value which were incompatible on one crucial issue, that of slavery, they wound up fighting the most deadly war in history up to that time.

The second and greatest danger of the mutual stereotype of the enemy is that it tends to make itself come true by virtue of the mechanism of the "self-fulfilling prophecy," [26] which operates at both individual and group levels. We expect people to behave in a certain way and then behave in such a way toward them as to cause them to fulfill our prophecy. As an example at a group level, for many years psychiatrists expected patients at mental hospitals to be violent and unmanageable. They therefore put them in isolation rooms, locked them in chairs, and wrapped them in strait jackets. And, sure enough, the patients were violent and unmanageable. Recently psychiatrists have changed their prophecy and expected mental patients to be able to control themselves, and the patients have fulfilled these expectations.[27]

Unfortunately, with enemies the self-fulfilling prophecy tends to move in a malignant direction. Enemies may not be

[26] Robert K. Merton, Social Theory and Social Structure; Glencoe, Ill., Free Press, 1957.

[27] For example, the administrator of an admission ward in a naval hospital created strong group expectations that patients would not become violent and that restraint would never be necessary. Out of nearly 1,000 patients admitted over a 10-month period, he did not have to order restraint or isolation of a single one. Harry A. Wilmer, "Toward a Definition of the Therapeutic Community," Amer. J. Psychiatry (1958) 114:824-834.

untrustworthy to begin with, but if the mutual posture lasts long enough, they eventually become so, as each acts in such a way as to justify the other's suspicion.[28]

Since each believes the other to have aggressive intent, the same action is viewed as defensive by the side that makes it and provocative by the other. The crushing of the Hungarian revolution was for the Russians a defensive move to forestall the capitalist-imperialist powers from getting a foothold close to her borders. To us it was a step in the fulfillment of the Communist plan to dominate the world. The U-2 flight—a strictly defensive move in our eyes—was proof to the Russians that we were spying out her missile bases in order to attack her. Russian resumption of atmosphere nuclear tests is to us confirmatory evidence of their nefarious intentions. To them, it was a response to the need to reduce our advantage in nuclear weapons technology, which they feared they could no longer safely tolerate.

As this reciprocal process continues, the fear of each side that the other plans to strike first increases, and each therefore frantically builds up its own striking force so as to be able to forestall this by threat of retaliation. But this is not enough, because the side that strikes first has an enormous advantage. Therefore, each side must build up the capability of striking first if it sees that the other side is about to strike first. Thus each country's original policy, that under no condition would it strike first, begins to shift to the position that it must be prepared to strike first.[29]

[28] The House Appropriations Committee, in its report on the 1961 appropriations for the Department of Defense, stated, ". . . we should maintain our armed forces in such a way that . . . should it ever become obvious that an attack upon ourselves or our allies is imminent, we can launch an attack before the aggressor has hit either us or our allies. . . . No other form of deterrence can be fully relied upon" (House Report 1561; p. 8). There is evidence that Russian leaders are also considering similar plans. It is easy to imagine what will happen if either country concludes, erroneously or otherwise, that the other is about to attack. The first would at once attempt to strike, leading the other country to do the same. Obviously a policy of mutual preemptive attack enormously heightens the risk of nuclear war through an error of judgment.

[29] *The Morning Sun,* Baltimore, December 16, 1959; pp. 1, 8.

If one's efforts to cope with a problem are based on false assumptions, one arrives at absurd solutions. So far our attempts to resolve the threat of nuclear weapons are based on an assumption which used to be true but no longer is—that possession of superior destructive force assures victory. The proposed solutions which follow from this are self-contradictory. We support the UN resolutions calling for cessation of the spread of nuclear weapons and for general disarmament. In practically the same breath we talk of giving nuclear arms to West Germany and Turkey, and of having to build up our armed strength before we can disarm.

The argument for this "realistic" solution goes something like this: Disarmament is certainly necessary, but bitter experience shows that you can't trust the Russians. The only thing they respect is force. Therefore, only by being strong can we give the Russians an effective incentive to disarm. To quote Nelson Rockefeller, "Successful negotiation with Russia will be possible only if the United States is in a position of maximum military strength."

While this position has a superficial plausibility, just a little reflection shows that it is hopelessly self-contradictory. For a build-up of our armed strength practically compels our opponent to do the same, and both sides will have to reserve the right to accumulate those weapons which they believe to be the most effective. So they could negotiate only about relinquishing weapons that do not really matter, and negotiations would become merely a screen behind which the arms race would continue unabated. I think C. Wright Mills is correct in calling the policy of arming in order to disarm "crackpot realism." [30]

The military part of this argument has two interrelated aspects: the build-up of the capacity to wage limited wars, and the development of invulnerable or undetectable launching sites for deterrent weapons. The ability to wage limited wars requires an arsenal of conventional weapons and "small" atomic weapons, so that any aggression of the enemy could be

[30] C. Wright Mills, *The Causes of World War III;* New York, Simon and Schuster, 1958.

opposed by just enough threat of retaliatory destruction to make it not worth his while. This would be a good scheme, except that it requires retention of weapons of mass destruction as well, because an enemy facing defeat might use them if we did not have them. Furthermore, each country must have enough destructive power so that even if most of its bases were destroyed what remained would be enough to wipe out the other's population. Thus the threat to civilization would remain. Human judgment is notoriously fallible at best and becomes especially so under conditions of war. It may be possible to limit a few wars, but sooner or later one would trigger off the holocaust.[31]

The second plan stresses the development of invulnerable retaliatory bases to eliminate the advantage of surprise attack. We are doing this now through the Polaris submarine and Minute Man missiles. By assuring each side that the other cannot wipe out its retaliatory force by surprise, this approach allows more time for deciding whether to strike back and so diminishes the danger of an accidentally started war. However, this is the most it can accomplish, and even this is questionable. In view of the rapid advances in arms technology, a base that is invulnerable today may prove very vulnerable tomorrow. One thinks of the Maginot Line.

But the most serious flaw in the doctrine of invulnerable bases is that it would cause an enemy to conceal the source of its attack. This will become ridiculously easy when many countries have nuclear weapons and as they continue to shrink in size. Right now an atom bomb can fit into a typewriter case. A country could smuggle atom bombs into all our major cities and arrange for them to go off through a timing device

---

[31] Bernard Brodie, an able exponent of limited war, recognizes that to make this possible, ". . . the combatants would have to agree, without consultation, to hobble the tremendous destructive power they have already mobilized and would have to indicate their self-restraining intentions unmistakably. Nothing like this has ever happened in war's history, but Dr. Brodie thinks it can be done and that doing it is the hope of the world." Bruce Bliven, Jr., review of *Strategy in the Missile Age*, by Bernard Brodie, *The New Yorker*, March 12, 1960, pp. 186-195; p. 190.

six months later. Against whom would we retaliate? Or if a country chose to be more diabolical—and small countries would certainly have the incentive to be so—it might arrange to fire a weapon in such a way that it would appear to come from Russia, and we and Russia would then fall on each other.

All policies based on maintenance of military strength accelerate the diffusion of nuclear weapons, with its attendant dangers. Neither Russia nor America can be prepared to fight limited nuclear wars all over the world without entrusting control of at least tactical nuclear weapons—of about the destructive power of the Hiroshima bomb—to their allies. The major antagonists in a showdown will not risk their own annihilation to protect these allies, so they must be given the power to "defend" themselves. And the countries to whom we or the Russians do not give nuclear weapons will be strongly stimulated to devise their own for the same reason.

Finally, the effort to achieve a convincing nuclear deterrent forces the pace of weapons development. As Herman Kahn has pointed out, whereas in the pre-atomic age weapons revolutions never occurred more often than once in a generation, there have been three weapons revolutions in the 16 years since Hiroshima—the atom bomb, the hydrogen bomb, and the guided missile—and other equally drastic changes in weapons technology in the near future are predicted.[32] This runaway weapons development is in itself a major source of tension because it means that no one, including the military, knows what current weapons will do. Each crop becomes superseded before it is even tested. Moreover, weapons research creates the fear in all countries that one will achieve a technological "break-through" which will make present weapons temporarily obsolete. The country which accomplished this would be sorely tempted to destroy its opponents while it had the opportunity, and countries may be tempted to launch a preemptive strike out of fear that an enemy is about to exploit such a break-through. Thus arming in order to disarm can only increase the world's insecurity; and, in addition, it places

[32] Herman Kahn, "The Arms Race and its Hazards," *Daedalus* (1960) 744-780, Fall.

almost insuperable obstacles in the path of disarmament. As long as each side believes that it can negotiate only from a position of strength, the conditions for negotiations which are acceptable to one side are unacceptable to the other. And, since each country is convinced that it must maintain a superior military force, ". . . the true, if unavowed aim of every nation that goes into a disarmament conference is to increase its real or relative armament to the detriment of its rivals. Thus 'disarmament' turns out to be but one of the forms the armaments race can take." [33] As a result, all disarmament conferences have failed, with one or two minor exceptions.

There are two logical possibilities for disarmament—by agreement, or by unilateral action. Since we distrust the Russians and they distrust us, the fears of each create grave obstacles to disarmament by agreement. We demand an adequate inspection system to make sure that Russia is not cheating; but with the breakneck development of modern weapons, such inspection and control becomes ever less possible. An inspection system devised for today's weapons is obsolete for tomorrow's. Already it is impossible to inspect for stockpiles of atomic weapons, and we have been told that there can be no perfect inspection for underground explosions. But even if foolproof inspection could be achieved, the Russians would fear that they were being spied upon and we that we were being duped—both intolerable prospects to countries which view each other as enemies, because each contains the threat of the loss of national existence. Therefore, in a framework of reliance on superior force, disarmament by agreement seems almost impossible. Witness the fact that Russia and the United States have been unable to agree on something as simple as a ban on atmospheric tests of nuclear weapons, even though both countries stopped these tests for a considerable period.

Unilateral disarmament is even more difficult,[34] for any move of this kind would arouse initial suspicion by the other

[33] Salvador de Madariaga, "Disarmament? The Problem Lies Deeper," *The New York Times Magazine*, October 11, 1959; pp. 17, 72-75; see p. 74.
[34] See footnote 23.

side, such as we have shown toward the Russians' announced decrease in the size of their conventional armed forces. To be convincing and to produce the hoped-for reciprocal step, disarmament would have to involve obvious weakening and to be persisted in long enough to convince the other side that it was genuine. But in the context of reliance on superior force, it would undoubtedly be viewed as surrender by both the side that did it and the opponent, demoralizing the former and perhaps tempting the latter to attack while it had an advantage.

But even if the world achieved some degree of disarmament by agreement or by reciprocal unilateral action, it would be faced with another problem. With conventional weapons, the lower the general level of armament, the more secure the peoples of the world could feel. But with nuclear weapons, the lower the general level of armaments, the greater the instability, because of the greater advantages to the side which, secretly or otherwise, maintained a slight preponderance. If the rest of the world were totally disarmed, the country that had withheld a dozen nuclear weapons could blackmail all the rest. Therefore disarmament will get more and more difficult as it proceeds.

The knowledge of how to make weapons of mass destruction, like the knowledge of good and evil, will never pass from the mind of man. Even in a completely disarmed world, any nation that was so minded could reconstruct these weapons in a few months. To be sure, it might be difficult to construct nuclear weapons secretly, but there would be no difficulty at all in brewing deadly toxins, because this can be done in any basement. Therefore, the only ultimate solution lies in creating world conditions which would inhibit a country possessing superior force from using it. In brief, this means the abolition of war.

Let me reinforce this conclusion by an appeal to authority. At a Pugwash Conference in 1959, 26 scientists from eight nations, including some of the world's leading experts in atomic, biological, and chemical warfare, who were trusted advisors of governments on both sides of the Iron Curtain—

men who should know better than anyone else in the world the implications of modern weaponry—agreed unanimously on the following statement, which contains no qualifications or equivocation:

> In the end, only the absolute prevention of war will preserve human life and civilization in the face of chemical and bacteriological as well as nuclear weapons. No ban of a single weapon, no agreement that leaves the general threat of war in existence, can protect mankind sufficiently.[35]

In short, the drastically changed conditions of modern life produced by the shrinkage of the world and the advent of weapons of unlimited destructive powers mean that the two time-hallowed institutions—war and the nation state—have become threats to the continued existence of mankind and that new social inventions must replace them.

It is often argued that since war has been the constant companion of man, its elimination is impossible. Fortunately, there are many examples of equally widespread, deeply entrenched human institutions that vanished when they became incompatible with changing human conditions. Among these are human sacrifice in religious rites and slavery—the latter for millenia the foundation of civilization. Both took centuries to die out, but untouchability, a cornerstone of the Hindu way of life, was profoundly undermined by Gandhi in only a few decades.

The relinquishing of war would, to be sure, require very drastic changes in human value systems and behavior, analogous to those produced by a religious conversion. The psychological challenge is to find means of persuasion which are more effective than the threat of violence or its actual use, or to create conditions such that the possessor of superior military force will be inhibited from using it. This will require overcoming the thought barrier which has been constructed over the thousands of years in which conflict was always

[35] *Proceedings of Pugwash Conference of International Scientists on Biological and Chemical Warfare;* Pugwash, Nova Scotia, August 24-30, 1959; pp. 5-6.

settled in favor of the side with superior destructive power. It will require relinquishing a pattern of behavior as old as humanity and constantly reinforced by success, and adopting a new and essentially untried line of conduct.

Under these circumstances, it is not possible to prove that exclusive reliance on nonviolent means of resolving conflicts is feasible. If, however, one can show that it is not theoretically impossible, people may begin to take it seriously instead of dismissing it out of hand as a fine ideal but hopelessly impractical.[36] In beginning to think about this extremely difficult question, one must remember that the correct solution for an unprecedented problem is almost certain to appear ridiculous at first, for the habitual, and hence seemingly reasonable, solution almost by definition becomes maladaptive when conditions change drastically. Leo Szilard recently told how he and Enrico Fermi burst out laughing when they discovered the correct solution to a problem in atomic physics because it seemed so ridiculous.

It may help to clarify matters if I first discuss some common misunderstandings about nonviolence. Our language lacks a term to describe exclusive reliance on nonviolent means of persuasion. The usual terms, such as nonviolence, passive resistance, pacifism, and so on conjure up images of a person standing by with a holy look on his face while a soldier runs a bayonet through his sister. Actually, the aim of nonviolence is to prevent this situation from arising—to inhibit the use of destructive force by the person who possesses it. The achievement of this goal requires a very high degree of initiative, activity, and courage.

A second misunderstanding is that the reliance on nonviolence requires that conflict be eliminated from the world. On the contrary, it seems to me that conflict is not only a necessary but a desirable part of human existence. Life would

[36] For brief but comprehensive expositions of nonviolence, see: *Speak Truth to Power;* Philadelphia, American Friends Service Committee, 1955; and Cecil E. Hinshaw, *Nonviolent Resistance: A Nation's Way to Peace;* Wallingford, Pa., Pendle Hill, 1956.

be unbearably dull without it. The goal is rather to develop effective nonviolent means of resolving conflict.

A third common misconception is that nonviolence is offered as a simple, global solution to the dangers which threaten us. Actually it is an extraordinarily difficult one which incurs grave risks and demands the development of a wide variety of measures tailored to meet the specific requirements of different types of conflicts.

I shall not attempt to consider the religious and ethical arguments for the renunciation of violence. A psychological puzzle is why these arguments have motivated a small number of people so powerfully yet have left the great body of mankind untouched. Through the ages a few religiously inspired persons have kept the ideal of nonviolence alive, and in recent years two of them, Gandhi and Martin Luther King, have shown ways in which it might be practised on a mass scale. Yet the doctrine of nonviolence has been in existence for two thousand years in the form of Christianity and for longer than that in other religions, without having the slightest effect on war. In fact, differences between religious doctrines, both of which preach peace, have been used to justify extremely destructive wars.

One reason for the ineffectualness of pacifist preachments today is that we agree in principle, simultaneously dismissing them as hopelessly idealistic—an attitude which renders them impotent. Thereby we put our consciences at rest and avoid having to think further about the matter. To forestall this response from you, without denying the force or relevance of the moral arguments for nonviolence, I shall try to examine it in as hard-headed and realistic a manner as possible. Let me tackle the most difficult problem first—the nature of man.

Many hold that it is absurd to expect man ever to renounce war, because he is by nature aggressive and self-aggrandizing— the very qualities that have enabled him to conquer his environment and are responsible for the forward thrust of his development. On the other hand, humans also show strongly affiliate and altruistic behavior. Students of human nature, depending on their philosophies, tend to view man as basically aggressive but forced to tame his hostile impulses by the necessity to live in close relationships with his fellows, or basically affiliative, becoming hostile only when frightened or frustrated.

Freud was an influential exponent of the former view. It has been said of his daughter, Anna Freud, ". . . to hear [her] speak of the criminal tendencies of the one- and two-year old is to be reminded inevitably of the Calvinistic sermons on infant damnation," [37] and her father writes:

> Under primitive conditions it is superior force—brute violence . . . that lords it everywhere. . . . Brute force is overcome by union, the allied might of scattered units makes good its right against the isolated giant. Thus we may define 'right' (i.e. law) as the might of a community. Yet it, too, is nothing else than violence. . . .[38]

Freud holds that in each generation the child painfully learns to hold his self-aggrandizing, destructive impulses in check, under the pressures of his parents and his group, since social survival would otherwise be impossible. But they are always just beneath the surface, ready to break forth under the slightest encouragement. Moreover, says Freud, the more elaborate and complex civilization becomes, the more it necessitates damming up man's hostilities, which then eventually break forth with even greater fury. Human existence is thus a race between love and destructiveness, with the latter more than likely to win out.

This pessimistic view of human nature is hard to refute. In situations of extreme stress there is no doubt that the veneer of civilization drops off many people, and they become savage beasts. They trample each other to death in panics; they murder and eat each other under conditions of starvation. The more civilized societies become, the more destructive are their wars; and highly civilized societies, such as that of Germany under the Nazis, perpetrate the most fiendish atrocities. This

[37] David C. McClelland, *Psychoanalysis and Religious Mysticism;* Wallingford, Pa., Pendle Hill, 1959; p. 13.
[38] Albert Einstein and Sigmund Freud, *Why War?;* Geneva, League of Nations, Internat. Inst. of Intellectual Cooperation, 1933: pp. 28-29.

view of human nature may well be true; and if it is, mankind is doomed to become extinct, because there is a flaw in his make-up which is no longer compatible with survival.

Fortunately, there is evidence that man's affiliative drives may be at least as basic as his aggressive ones.[39] In infants loving as well as aggressive behavior appears spontaneously, and it gains a spontaneous loving response from the parent. Furthermore, for most people anger and hate are unpleasant emotions which they desire to terminate; whereas love is a highly pleasant one which they endeavor to prolong. Finally, just as aggressive drives can cause people to make heroic sacrifices, so can affiliative ones, which cannot be explained on the basis of self-interest, as when a person offers his life to save the life of a stranger. Gordon Allport, after an exhaustive study of the causes and forms of human prejudice, which is a gross manifestation of man's uglier side, is still able to write:

> Normal men everywhere reject in principle and by preference the path of war and destruction. They like to live in peace and friendship with their neighbors. They prefer to love and be loved rather than to hate and be hated. While wars rage yet our desire is for peace, and while animosity prevails the weight of mankind's approval is on the side of affiliation.[40]

The only reasonable conclusion concerning man's innate endowment is that he has both altruistic and self-aggrandizing trends, and that both are very strong. The elimination of war requires that the former be strengthened and the latter be inhibited or rechanneled.

The crucial point is that man is extraordinarily modifiable. His attitudes, feelings, and behavior are molded by the groups to which he belongs; his society transmits to him its values,

[39] D. O. Hebb and W. R. Thompson adduce interesting evidence that genuinely altruistic behavior increases as one ascends the phylogenetic scale, and is already prominent in the chimpanzee. "The Social Significance of Animal Studies," Ch. 15, pp. 532-561: in *Handbook of Social Psychology*, Vol. 1, edited by Gardner Lindzey; Cambridge, Addison Wesley, 1954.

[40] Gordon W. Allport, *The Nature of Prejudice*; Boston, Beacon Press, 1954; p. xiv.

standards, and ideals. Hunger may turn a man into a cannibal, but no purely personal drive will cause a Hindu mother to throw her infant under the wheels of a juggernaut or an SS man to roast little children alive on an open fire. It takes powerful group standards to cause such behavior. Mother love may lead a woman to give her life to save her child, but only dedication to a group ideal such as Christianity can cause a martyr to march singing to the stake.

In this fact lies the greatest hope for the renunciation of force. For war is a social institution, and the values and standards supporting it must be transmitted afresh to each new generation. It is conceivable that we can learn to adhere to a set of values which excludes the possibility of war. Anthropologists have described isolated societies which do not have the institution of war. For example:

> ... among the Hopi competition is the worst of bad taste and physical aggression is rigorously suppressed. Outwardly a Hopi learned to smile at his enemies, to use "sweet words with a low voice," to share his property, and to work selflessly with others for the good of the tribe ... but there remained another form of aggression open to him ... with a tongue as pointed as a poison arrow, he carries on a constant guerilla warfare with his fellows.[41]

This example is instructive in showing that aggression does not disappear, but can be rechanneled into socially less destructive forms. The Hopi are prone to nightmares, but I think any of us would be willing to settle for a few nightmares in exchange for the removal of the threat of extermination.

Even more instructive is the case of the Comanche. As plains tribes, war for them was the be-all and end-all of existence. But initially the same people, as plateau tribes, were "completely without war patterns; they did not fight each other even over trespass." [42] This tribe passed from the most peaceful

[41] Dorothy Eggan, "The General Problem of Hopi Adjustment," *Amer. Anthropologist* (1943) 45:357-373; pp. 372-373.

[42] Abram Kardiner, and others, *The Psychological Frontiers of Society;* New York, Columbia Univ. Press, 1945; p. 49.

type of existence to the most warlike in a few generations—a striking example of the power of group standards.

Within civilized societies there has been a steady reduction of the kinds of conflict for which personal violence is sanctioned. A little over 150 years ago Aaron Burr killed Alexander Hamilton in a duel over a matter of honor, which was at least tacitly condoned by their society, but today would be unthinkable. In our courts people are daily waging bitter conflicts; the man who loses a lawsuit may commit suicide, but it does not occur to him to shoot his opponent. Only two generations ago industrial conflicts regularly involved the use of violence by both sides. Yet the steel strike of 1959 was a prolonged and bitter conflict in which neither side entertained the possibility of resorting to force. Why not? Certainly today's steelworkers and plant owners are not less belligerent as individuals than their forebears, nor are the police stronger in 1960 than in 1910 when industrial warfare was common. The most plausible explanation is that the standards of today's society condemn the use of violence to settle industrial disputes, so that each party realizes that resort to force would cost more than it would gain.

These examples indicate at least the possibility that mankind may eventually subscribe to a set of values which exclude war. But what about the present, when violence is still sanctioned as a means of settling disputes between nations? The heart of the matter is whether it is possible to win by nonviolent means against an opponent whose group standards sanction the use of violence. Almost everyone unhesitatingly answers "No" to this question, but I believe that there may be some room for doubt. At the level of the individual, as I have mentioned, a very important aspect of behavior is that it is guided by the responses of the person to whom it is directed. A person's response to what I do influences how I respond to his response, and this, in turn, influences what he does next. Violent behavior, like all other behavior, is not self-sustaining. Whether it increases or decreases depends on how the victim responds. It seems to be stimulated by counter-violence or by fear and inhibited by a calm, friendly attitude which implies that the victim is concerned about the welfare of the attacker as well as himself. For example, a missionary's wife in China, whose husband was away, learned that the inhabitants of the village in which they lived were planning to come and massacre her and the children because they blamed a drought on the anger of the gods at the presence of foreigners. When the armed mob broke into the house, she walked calmly up to the tall, surly leader and offered him a cup of tea. Nonplussed, he accepted the tea, and the others uncertainly followed his example. After this there was nothing for them to do but to leave peacefully. Fortunately for the sake of the story, the drought was broken by a rainstorm the following day.[43] This example may be exceptional. If an attempt to meet violence with nonviolence fails, there is no survivor to tell the story.

Yet if a person can find the courage to meet aggression with calm friendliness, this may have a powerfully inhibiting effect.[44] Only a rare individual has such moral strength in the face of threatened death for himself or his loved ones; but when very strong group support is forthcoming, nonviolent campaigns may be surprisingly successful—as in the examples of Gandhi in India and King in Alabama. Certain features were unusually favorable in both cases; the group using non-violent methods was able to turn the values of the dominant group against them—that is, they could appeal in India to the British value of fair play and in America to the American values of the equality of all peoples and of individual freedom. In both instances the opposed groups were in close personal contact, so that the oppressors could not take emotional refuge in the insensitivity to the remote which I mentioned earlier. In each case, the oppressed group could use media of mass communication to sustain their own morale and to sway pub-

[43] Pearl Buck, quoted in *Victories Without Violence,* compiled by A. Ruth Fry; London, Edgar G. Dunstan, 1950; pp. 69-71.
[44] The successful renunciation of violence by the staff of a psychiatric admission ward illustrates both the reciprocal nature of human behavior and the power of group standards to control members of the group (see footnote 27). However, in that case the dominant group took the initiative, and the crucial problem is whether a similar initiative by the underdogs could also succeed.

lic opinion. But despite the favorable circumstances that can be seen in retrospect, no one would have predicted that the nonviolent campaigns could have succeeded, and one cannot exclude the feasibility of a nonviolent approach to some of the current conflicts in the world.

Scrutiny of these examples suggests certain conclusions which may have widespread applicability. First, the heart of nonviolent resistance is to fight the antagonism, not the antagonist. Gandhi makes a sharp distinction between the deed and the doer:

> Man and his deed are two distinct things. Whereas a good deed should call forth approbation and a wicked deed disapprobation, the doer of the deed, whether good or wicked, always deserves respect or pity as the case may be.[45]

That is, Gandhi rejects the stereotype of the enemy. He assumes that his opponents are acting righteously according to their own standards and tries to demonstrate how his position would achieve their aims better than their own approach. Second is his insistence that the conflict must be waged in a constructive way:

> In a group struggle you can keep . . . the ability to work effectively for the realization of the goal stronger than the destructive violent tendencies and the tendencies to passiveness and despondency only by . . . giving all phases of your struggle, as far as possible, a constructive character.[46]

Thus to oppose the salt tax he organized a march to the sea to make salt. Analogously, King named his organization of the bus boycott the Montgomery Improvement Association, implying that breaking down segregation in buses would be good for all citizens of Montgomery.

A third important point to be gained from the experiences of King and Gandhi is that waging a nonviolent battle is not

[45] Mohandas K. Gandhi, *An Autobiography: The Story of My Experiments with Truth;* Boston, Beacon Press, 1957; p. 276.
[46] Arne Naess, "A Systematization of Gandhian Ethics of Conflict Resolution," *J. Conflict Resolution* (1958) 2:140-155; p. 144.

a simple or easy way of fighting and requires the highest type of generalship, with an extraordinary level of flexibility, courage, and organizational ability. The leaders must be able to activate the strongest type of group ideals and controls in order to hold despair and violence in check, despite provocations. These controls will differ in different cultures. Gandhi fasted as a means of mobilizing guilt in his followers when they strayed from the path of nonviolence, and King held nightly prayer meetings with hymn singing to maintain the morale of the Negroes.

Because it rests on group controls, successful conduct of a nonviolent campaign does not require that the individual members be saints, or even believers in nonviolence. Gandhi, with less than 200 disciples, was able to free a nation of 350 million. King's followers, as individuals, are considered to be among the most prone to violence in our society, at least according to popular stereotype. But nonviolent methods of fighting, like violent ones, require a willingness to stake one's life on the outcome. The English killed many Indians, and many Negro citizens in Montgomery owe their lives only to the ineptitude of white bomb throwers. The psychological problem is to create group standards which impel people to offer their lives in a peaceful battle with the same dedication that they do in war.

In this connection, in the long run the most significant achievement psychologically of Gandhi and King may be that they broke the link between destructive force and courage. They were able to create group standards that made refusal to use violence a manifestation of strength and steadfastness, and resort to violence an admission of weakness. A main incentive for armaments races has always been the justified fear of tempting the enemy to attack by appearing weak or irresolute to him. The demonstration that one can convincingly prove one's steadiness of purpose by renouncing force may open up entirely new avenues to the achievement of a warless world.

To try to sum up the essence of nonviolent campaigns, I would say that they abjure all behavior which stimulates the enemy to continue being violent, and exploit all behavior which tends to inhibit his use of violence. They avoid fear or counter-attack or efforts to humiliate the enemy, while they treat him with respect and try to understand his viewpoint. They steadfastly look for a solution to the conflict which will satisfy his interest as well as their own.

While thus steadily inhibiting the aggressor's use of violence, they prove to him that he cannot gain his ends with it. In most battles destruction is not the primary end, but a means of coercing the adversary—except where the aggressive feelings have been very strongly fanned, or the group standards require the destruction of the enemy, as was the case with the Nazis and Jews. If the aggressor's violence continues to meet with no reinforcing response and if his destruction of members of the other group fails to coerce the survivors, then in time his violent behavior may grind to a halt as his own guilt feelings mount.

In trying to apply the lessons of Gandhi and King to present international conflicts, two cautions must be kept in mind. First, they are examples of the successful use of nonviolent means by one group against another within a single society, rather than between societies. Second, in each case the society was grounded on democratic values. One, therefore, has to ask whether nonviolent methods could work against a ruthless dictator, and whether they could solve international conflicts. Obviously I cannot give a completely satisfactory answer to either question, but I can at least suggest considerations to indicate that the answer might not be automatically negative.

The question of nonviolent conflict with a dictatorship arises in two forms. First, if a doctrine of nonviolence ever showed signs of winning the adherence of a majority of the American people, the remainder who still believed that force must be an instrument of policy would almost certainly attempt to seize power, to prevent the disaster that they feared. In this situation, as in India, most of the values of the ruling group and the opposition would be the same, and it would be possible to appeal to the ideals of the ruling group against itself.

The outcome would depend on whether the proponents of nonviolence had been sufficiently trained in the use of nonviolent methods and were able to be steadfast in their purpose. A dictatorship from within could not maintain itself against a persistent refusal of the masses of the population to cooperate.

If our renunciation of force tempted an enemy to impose a military occupation on us, the question would be: Can nonviolent methods prevail against a dictatorship by a group which does not highly value human life? First of all, it is an oversimplification to say that Gandhi's methods worked in India because of the British attitude toward human life. When the Mau Mau in Kenya used violent methods, they were met with extreme forms of violence by the very same British. But the most powerful argument, at least from an emotional standpoint, against the success of nonviolent methods opposing a dictator is the fate of the Jews in Germany. There are many flaws in this argument. First, there are some situations in which no method of fighting would work, and this was undoubtedly true of the plight of the Jews after World War II was under way. Incidentally, the murder camps were set up only after Germany was at war; whether even the Nazis could have perpetrated such atrocities in peacetime is problematical. The Jews had three choices, none of which could have saved their own lives: violent resistance, nonviolent resistance, and fatalistic acquiescence; and so all they could do was to die in the way most compatible with their own self-respect and most likely to win sympathy for them abroad. Most of them did not resist but simply acquiesced apathetically in their own destruction. There are many moving anecdotes of Jews who, having received a notice to report to the police station, would go to their non-Jewish friends and say farewell, without expressing any thought of attempting to escape. No one knows what might have happened had the Jews resorted to nonviolent methods of resistance early in the Nazi regime. Suppose, for example, in organized fashion they had refused to wear the stigmatizing arm bands and forced the police to publicly drag them off to prison. This would at least have made it more difficult for the German people to pretend they did not know what was going on. One cannot know what effect this might have had.

The question really comes down to whether the group standards of the rulers are sufficiently strong to sustain indefinitely a program of slaughter and torture against a trained, undefeated people who steadfastly maintain a pattern of behavior which tends to inhibit aggressiveness. It must be remembered that the maintenance of a dictatorship requires constant personal contact between the ruling group and the oppressed. As a clinical example of the difficulty of slaughtering a personalized enemy, an artillery observer in the last war found great satisfaction in the impersonal game of directing artillery fire until, one day, a German officer surrendered to him, and, a few minutes later, saved his life by directing him away from a heavily mined area. From that point on, directing artillery fire became in his mind a personal assault on the bodies and lives of fellow human beings. He rapidly developed incapacitating emotional symptoms and had to be hospitalized.[47] It might be added that some Russian soldiers were shot because they refused to fire on the East Germans in the nonviolent revolt which broke out in 1953. Thus, although it is clear that a nonviolent campaign against a dictatorship might be very costly in lives and difficult to maintain, it is not a foregone conclusion that it could not succeed.

Whether nonviolent methods of fighting can be used successfully in an international arena is unknown. Nations have resolved many disputes through peaceful negotiation, but these have always been held with the knowledge that violence could be resorted to if the negotiations failed. All I can hope to do, therefore, is again to indicate that nonviolent methods need not totally be excluded as a possibility.

One advantage that a nation would have, in comparison with an oppressed group under a dictatorship, is its greater command of the instruments of mass communication. It could wage a massive propaganda campaign in favor of its view,

[47] John C. Whitehorn, "Stress and Mental Health," *Northwest Medicine* (1959) 58:822-830.

and of a form which would tend to inhibit the enemy's use of violence, such as, for example, Russia is doing fairly successfully today.

The fragmentary experimental data on the resolution of conflicts between groups suggest that the most successful way to resolve an intergroup conflict is through the creation of goals of overriding importance to both groups, which can be attained only by their cooperation. For example, in the experiment in a boys' camp, which I mentioned earlier, the experimenters eventually tried to resolve the mutual antagonism between the two groups. Merely bringing them together in social and other activities had no effect. Antagonism was markedly diminished, however, by confronting both groups with urgent threats which could be overcome only by cooperation. For example, the counselors interrupted the camp water supply, creating an emergency situation which required the efforts of the entire camp to overcome. After a few such experiences, the boys began to choose friends from the other group as well as their own.[48]

On the international scene, there are many potential goals which are analogous—for example, the exploration of the undersea world, the conquest of outer space, and cooperative efforts to speed the economic advance of the undeveloped countries. Moreover, these activities would offer substitute goals for the satisfaction of drives which in the past have been satisfied by war. Many years ago William James pointed out that one of the major attractions of war lay in the opportunity it afforded for heroism, adventure, self-sacrifice, group solidarity, and so on. He called for the development of "moral equivalents for war" [49] which would meet similar needs. Modern technology has made such moral equivalents potentially available on a scale never before possible. This imaginative exploitation could lead to the redirection of much human energy now expended in warlike pursuits.

Let me in conclusion try to make this discussion of non-

[48] See footnote 2.
[49] William James, *The Varieties of Religious Experience;* New York, Longmans, Green, 1902; p. 367.

violence more concrete. Suppose that America has committed itself to exclusive reliance on means other than military force for pursuing its aims and defending its values. It then would welcome the Russian proposal for complete disarmament in a given number of years—not out of fear but from the conviction that it would be to our advantage, because our goals can be achieved only through peaceful means.

In this connection, it should be stressed that commitment to nonviolent means does not require instantaneous total disarmament, any more than belief in the decisive power of superior violence requires the immediate launching of nuclear war. Actually, drastic disarmament by the United States without considerable advance preparation might plunge the world into chaos.

Ultimate values, however, guide day-to-day behavior, so renunciation of violence would be promptly reflected by a change in attitude at the conference table. If, instead of being trapped in the absurd position of having to rearm in order to disarm, we committed ourselves to the long-term goal of the nonviolent solution of disputes, at each choice point of negotiations we would select that line of action which would most foster the development of a peaceful world. We would be prepared to run risks in order to achieve this end, knowing that at worst they would be less than those entailed by the continual build-up of weapons of unlimited destructive power. We would, of course, try to establish such controls and inspection as the Russians would permit, but we would not make our disarmament contingent on having precisely the controls we desire. As we disarmed in accordance with a prearranged schedule, assuming that Russia was doing likewise, we would be taking certain other very important steps. That is, disarmament as a means of carrying out a program of nonviolence could not occur in a vacuum.

To abolish armies as well as war colleges and general staffs, as the Russian proposal requires, each country would have to wage a peaceful propaganda offensive within its borders as well as outside them; failure to do so would in itself be an evidence of bad faith. Therefore, a major task would be to change certain of our values. Today, although we give lip service to peace, we glorify violence, as our TV programs bear witness.[50] We would have to learn to venerate heroes of peace as we now do gangsters and desperados. This would require extensive changes in educational curricula as well as in programs of entertainment.

We would have to be prepared to make the necessary economic readjustment required by disarmament—remembering, as we did so, that arms contribute nothing to the national wealth and that if we hurled them into the sea as fast as we made them, we would be no whit poorer. The only problem would be to overcome the psychological barrier against making the necessary plans for conversion of the armaments industries to other types of production.[51]

Believers in nonviolence would have to learn the methods of nonviolence, for the most pessimistic possibility is that they might have to resist seizure of power by internal as well as external groups, or even that an internal group might try to foment a war in a desperate effort to keep control. The optimistic possibility is that the growth of a movement for nonviolence in any one country would encourage the like-minded in other countries, leading to increasing pressures on all governments to negotiate their differences peaceably.

Externally we would make every effort to expand peaceful communication, not only with Russia but with the rest of the world. We would especially emphasize cooperative activities toward the attainment of superordinate goals, such as the highly successful International Geophysical Year. The stronger habits of cooperation became, the more effectively they would inhibit a subsequent resort to violence. Along the same lines, we would work toward peaceful resolution of outstanding

[50] "Today there are 27 Westerns and 20 whodunits on the weekly programs of the major networks. . . . All the . . . damned and doomed dregs of humanity, giving an advanced course . . . in all the techniques of crime and the modes of violence." Clare Boothe Luce, "Without Portfolio," *McCall's*, March, 1960, pp. 18, 176, 178; p. 176.

[51] Byron L. Johnson, "If Peace Were to Break Out," *Christian Century*, December 9, 1959; reprinted in *Congressional Record*, January 7, 1960; p. A-25.

tension spots in the world, such as Berlin and those in Asia. We could not expect to resolve all the disputes in our favor. We have gotten ourselves into certain positions which are untenable with or without war, and we would have to recognize this fact. We would in each case seek the solution which most furthers the cause of universal peace, rather than the one which seems to promote an illusory national interest.

We would launch an all-out effort to win over the uncommitted countries to allegiance to our way of life. This would involve measures to raise their economic level by self-aid, expansion of medical help, and so on. We would endeavor wherever possible to conduct these programs in cooperation with the Russians, rather than in competition with them.

Finally, we would work toward bringing about world-wide disarmament and building up institutional machinery for the peaceful solution of international disputes. This would, of course, require surrender of some aspects of national sovereignty. This may not be so difficult as we come to realize that the advent of modern weaponry has doomed unlimited sovereignty, in any case.

The most favorable outcome of this program would be that each successive disarmament step would become easier as its advantages to all countries became increasingly obvious, culminating in an increasingly prosperous world which contained strong inhibitions against resort to violence and increasingly effective institutional means for peaceful resolution of disputes.

In such a world, any government that contemplated taking advantage of the general disarmament to blackmail another country through threat of force would face extremely unpleasant consequences. First of all, such a move would have a profoundly demoralizing effect within the country that made it. Even an absolutely ruthless dictatorship cannot make major changes in policy overnight without consideration of the feelings of the population. It can change its tactics, as the Hitler-Stalin Pact shows, but it cannot swing instantly from a peacetime to a wartime psychology. Even Hitler, who probably conducted the most vigorous internal campaign to glorify war in the world's history, required several years to rouse Germany's martial fervor sufficiently to enable him to start the last war. Russian leaders would have a considerably more difficult time, especially if the liberalizing process in Russia had been accelerated by increasing prosperity, rise in educational level, and removal of the threat of war.

An even more serious consequence would be that every country of the world would rearm as rapidly as possible, and the aggressor would be the enemy of them all. Since the countries would still know how to make weapons of limitless destructive power and since some of these weapons—notably bacteriological ones—are very cheap and easy to produce, the government which threatened violence would have to be prepared to police the entire world. Finally, she would know that she would meet stubborn nonviolet resistance in the countries she occupied.

But what if one country did announce, after the world was disarmed, that she had retained enough nuclear weapons to destroy America, and therefore attempted to coerce us? To keep the discussion concrete, I shall assume that this country is Russia, although it could be any other country. America, if we continued to follow the policy of nonviolent resistance, would refuse to submit, pointing out that although Russia could destroy us, she could not coerce us. Three choices would be left to Russia—to exterminate us with a nuclear raid; to occupy us; or to use her superior force to weaken our influence internationally by threatening our allies and the uncommitted nations.

The first choice—a nuclear raid—would be unlikely, for the main incentive for such a raid—the fear that we would strike first—would be gone. Moreover, her aim would be coercion, not destruction, and she would much prefer to take over an intact country and make it work for her than to have to deal with a radioactive desert. Thus the risk of nuclear attack under these conditions seems worth taking in view of the infinitely greater risk of destruction through involvement in a nuclear war.

An attempt to occupy us would be more probable, but this

would be difficult, for she would have to reassemble an invasion force. Meanwhile, we would use all possible means of mobilizing world opinion against her and of strengthening the will to resist of our own people by propaganda and refresher courses in nonviolent resistance. She would then know that if she did succeed in occupying us, she would be in for a long and difficult fight, while world opinion would become more antagonistic and the danger of other countries' arming would be steadily increasing. These considerations might prove to be powerful deterrents, especially if living conditions were rapidly improving at home, through the freeing of intellectual and economic resources for peacetime pursuits. Under such conditions it might be difficult to persuade one's citizens to leave the homeland and invade a highly organized country publicly committed to making life unpleasant for the invader.

If the occupation were attempted anyway our nonviolent methods would probably be costly in lives, and they might not succeed. But even if they failed, it would be better to die in a course of action which held out some hope for the future than as part of a general holocaust. The cause of freedom might be set back for a time, but I am convinced that eventually it would prevail, for the only sure way of extinguishing the spark of liberty is through the destruction of the human race.

More likely than outright occupation would be the effort by Russia to use her superior force to overcome our influence in doubtful areas of the world and to gradually encroach upon us in this way. But she would have to be prepared to cope with the disillusionment of her own people and to face the reinstatement of international anarchy and resort to arms all over the world. If, nevertheless, she persisted, we would have to rely on the determinations of the peoples involved to resist because they had been convinced of the superiority of our way of life. Obviously, we would lose in some areas, as we will if we rely on force. But again in the long run the future for humanity would be much brighter.

It therefore seems possible that, having considered nuclear blackmail, Russia would decide that the game was not worth the candle, and would commit herself to the peaceful competition she already professes to want.

This analysis of the renunciation of violence does not mean failure to appreciate the evils of communism, or underestimation of the Communist drive for world domination. It does imply recognition of the fact that the values we believe in can be promulgated only by peaceful means. Commitment to winning through possession of superior destructive power leads further and further along the road to a garrison state at home and tyranny abroad. At home we are witnessing a steady erosion of freedom. Dissent becomes ever more dangerous. Recently in Baltimore some high school students mobbed a young man who was merely trying to peddle a Socialist newspaper. We are told that technology has become so complicated that decisions concerning the life and death of mankind can be made only by experts, unharassed by the pressures of public opinion. A few years ago our President rebuked no less a person than the Chairman of the Senate Foreign Relations Committee for daring publicly to question our China policy on the ground that this endangered our will to resist. Abroad, by compelling countries to assume large, uneconomic arms burdens we hinder their development and heighten international fear.

I believe it is safe to assert that all human beings aspire to freedom. The common denominator of all psychiatric illnesses is that they impose limits on the patient's freedom, and his longing to be free of the tyranny of his symptoms is a very strong motive for accepting the work and suffering often entailed by psychotherapy. At the level of societies, men have always striven for freedom, even though poverty, ignorance, and fear have sometimes made them willing to accept tyranny as the price of food and safety. As Gandhi said: "For the starving men and women, liberty and God are merely letters put together without the slightest meaning; the deliverer of these unfortunate people would be the one who brought them a crust of bread." A rising level of education and prosperity in a world at peace is regularly accompanied by a growth of freedom. In this connection, evidence of the growth of individual freedom in Russia is overwhelming; only those completely blinded by the stereotype of the enemy can fail to see this. And our commitment to the renunciation of force, far from being a surrender to communism, might be the most effective way of fighting its tyrannical aspects and fostering a growth within Communist societies of the values in which we believe.

What are the chances that conversion to abandonment of force as an arbiter of international conflicts could come about? As I have already suggested, this would involve a change in attitudes of the magnitude of the religious conversion of an individual or a major revolution inside a country, such as took place in Russia with the overthrow of czarism. Not much is known about the conditions fostering either individual or group conversions, but it must be confessed that the little that is known is not encouraging. Individual conversions may be the result of a long, gradual process of education and indoctrination, or they may be precipitated suddenly by a catastrophic psychic experience. Sudden religious conversions occur typically in persons who have undergone a long period of desperation, hopelessness, or panic. To use a phrase of which alcoholics are fond, they have "hit bottom."

But sometimes the alcoholic "sees bottom" before he hits it; the disastrous ultimate effects of the course on which he is embarked become very vivid to him before they actually transpire, and he is converted to abstinence. Perhaps it may be possible for the peoples of the world to renounce violence if they see the "bottom" to which modern weapons are leading them before it actually comes to pass.

While even less is known about the conversion of groups than of individuals, there are some hints that it may be easier to change group standards than to change those of individuals. Witness the fact that Germany and Japan have changed in our eyes from diabolical enemies to trusted allies in about a decade.

In all honesty, the most likely source of conversion of mankind to renunciation of mass violence would be a nuclear accident which would bring home the horrors of modern war.

We must, however, bend every effort to develop group standards of nonviolence through intensive educational methods. It may be hopeful that America, in contrast to many European countries, has glorified nonmilitary figures, such as Benjamin Franklin, Thomas Jefferson, and Thomas Edison. Even Abraham Lincoln and Woodrow Wilson, although they became war leaders, might be included in this category. Perhaps we can exploit the potent TV image of the heroic cowboy who throws away his gun and faces down the villain by sheer will power. To be sure, this scene usually culminates in a glorious fist fight, but basically it is a situation in which the person who possesses superior destructive power is inhibited from using it.

In view of the present grave and entirely unprecedented threat to survival, it is important to examine all our patterns of behavior to discover which are still useful and which must be modified. Then we must fully exploit those which still work and endeavor to change the others. Among patterns of human interaction which undoubtedly still are valid are certain features of internal organization of societies, such as relations of larger to smaller units of governments and of governments to individual citizens, the role of the legal system in a society, and so on. Certain patterns of negotiation and diplomacy at the international level are probably also appropriate to present conditions. But the time-hallowed institution of war must eventually be abandoned if the human adventure is to continue.

As an eminent German scientist, C. F. von Weizsacker, said at a conference recently: "The renunciation of war is no longer a pious hope but a necessity. The only question is whether mankind will arrive at it before or after a catastrophe." [52] It seems to me that the necessary first step toward achieving this goal without a catastrophe is to combat the world-wide hypnotic fixation on superior violence as the ultimate arbiter of conflict. This would release the imaginations of the world's intellectual, moral, and political leaders to devise constructive alternatives for war. If this can be accomplished, it would liberate man's energies to create a world of unimaginable

[52] Personal communication.

plenty in which humanity, freed at last from poverty and war, could develop its full potentialities. One may hope that the human mind, which has proved capable of splitting the atom and putting satellites in space, will also prove equal to this supreme challenge.

Notes on Contributors

HERBERT BUTTERFIELD Born 1900. Professor of Modern History, Master of Peterhouse College and Vice-Chancellor of Cambridge University, England. Among his books published in this country are: *Christianity and History, History and Human Relations, Man on His Past, Napoleon, The Origins of Modern Science, The Statecraft of Machiavelli* and *International Conflict in the Twentieth Century*, from which this essay is taken.

NORMAN COUSINS Born 1912. Editor of *The Saturday Review* since 1939. On the day Hiroshima was bombed, he wrote an editorial called "Modern Man Is Obsolete" which was reprinted throughout the world. In it he foresaw present world tensions, called for a United Nations, and urged a policy of disarmament. Since then he has pursued these ideas in many editorials and a number of books: *In Place of Folly, Who Speaks for Man, Talks with Nehru*, and others. He is honorary president of United World Federalists and co-chairman of the National Committee for a Sane Nuclear Policy.

ALLAN FORBES, JR. Born 1919. Producer and director of documentary films. He and his wife conduct a film company in Cambridge, Mass., and have produced, among other films, *March to Aldermaston* (on the first CND peace walk in 1958); *No Governors* (on the street entertainers of London's West End); and *The Anonymous* (a study of slum children in Naples). He has written a number of magazine articles and is now at work on a novel about an armored division in Germany during World War II.

JEROME D. FRANK Psychiatrist, university professor, Director of Clinical Services, Henry Phipps Psychiatric Clinic of Johns Hopkins Hospital, Baltimore. He has published about seventy-five scientific papers, many of them dealing with aspects of group psychotherapy, and two books: *Persuasion and Healing* and *Group Psychotherapy* (with Florence Powdermaker).

ERICH FROMM   Born in Germany, 1900; came to the U.S. in 1932. Psychoanalyst and author; since 1951 professor at the National University of Mexico. He has published a number of books (several of them bestsellers), dealing with both the technical aspects of psychiatry and the application of psychiatric principles to the problems of world society. Among them are: *The Art of Loving, Civilization's Last Chance, Escape from Freedom, Man for Himself, Marx's Concept of Man, Psychoanalysis and Religion, The Sane Society* and *Sigmund Freud's Mission.*

HOWARD E. GRUBER   Born 1922. Associate Professor of Psychology at the University of Colorado. An experimental psychologist, his work lies chiefly in the fields of visual perception, the psychology of the mind, and the history of science. He is a member of the steering committee of the Rocky Mountain Peace Research Conference. He has written a number of scholarly articles and has helped to edit two symposia: *Contemporary Approaches to Cognition* and *Contemporary Approaches to Creative Thinking.*

MICHAEL MACCOBY   Social psychologist. Has taught at Chicago, Harvard and University of Mexico. Has published articles in *The New Republic, Commentary* and "The Social Psychology of Deterrence" in *The Bulletin of the Atomic Scientists.* Now working with Erich Fromm on a study of a Mexican village.

JOOST A. M. MEERLOO   Born 1903 at The Hague, Holland. M.D. from Leyden. Ph.D. from Utrecht. Professor and psychoanalyst. Escaped from the Nazis to London and served with the Dutch government-in-exile. Now an American citizen, practicing in New York. Among his books are: *Conversation and Communication, Patterns of Panic, The Rape of the Mind, That Difficult Peace, Total War and the Human Mind* and *Two Faces of Man.*

THOMAS MERTON   Born 1915. Graduated from Columbia, was converted to Catholicism, entered the Trappist Monastery of Our Lady of Gethsemani in Kentucky in 1946, ordained to the priesthood in 1950. Among his many books are: *The Seven Storey Mountain, Selected Poems, The Ascent to Truth, The Wisdom of the Desert, New Seeds of Contemplation, The New Man* and *Original Child Bomb,* a commentary on Hiroshima and atomic war.

LEWIS MUMFORD Born 1895. Author, lecturer, university professor. Although his main concern has been social criticism as applied to architecture and urban planning, his broadly cultural and humanistic bias has led him to write about many other aspects of modern life. His twenty published books include: *Art and Techniques, The City in History, The Condition of Man, The Conduct of Life, The Culture of Cities, The Human Prospect, In the Name of Sanity, Technics and Civilization, The Transformation of Man* and *Values for Survival.*

WALTER STEIN Born 1924 in Graz, Austria. Lecturer in Philosophy and Literature, University of Leeds, England. Helped found and edit *Humanitas,* a national British review devoted to criticism and moral issues, especially the morality of atomic militarism. Recently edited the anthology *Nuclear Weapons: A Catholic Response* and is now at work on an analysis of the principles of Tragedy.

TOM STONIER Born 1927 in Hamburg, Germany. Ph.D. in biology from Yale. Has worked at Brookhaven National Laboratory and is now on the staff of Rockefeller Institute, New York, as a Research Associate. A charter member of the Scientists' Committee for Radiation Information, a voluntary organization based in New York.

GORDON C. ZAHN Born 1918. Professor of Sociology at Loyola University of Chicago. A conscientious objector during World War II, he chose to study the social backgrounds of other objectors for his doctoral research program. Grants under the Fulbright program and from the American Philosophical Society enabled him to study in Germany and Austria, and his work resulted in the recent book entitled *German Catholics and Hitler's Wars.* He also contributed a chapter to the symposium *Morality and Modern Warfare.*

NEW DIRECTIONS PAPERBOOKS

Send for free catalogue describing all Paperbooks
NEW DIRECTIONS   333 Sixth Avenue   New York 14